Opposing Poetries

VOLUME 2

Readings

Opposing Poetries

VOLUME 2

Readings

HANK LAZER

Northwestern

University Press

Evanston

Illinois

Northwestern University Press
Evanston, Illinois 60208

Library of Congress Cataloging-in-Publication Data

Lazer, Hank.
Opposing poetries / Hank Lazer.
p.   cm. — (Avant-garde and modernism studies)
Includes bibliographical references (p.   ).
Contents: v. 1. Issues and institutions.   v. 2. Readings.
ISBN 0-8101-1264-7 (cloth : alk. paper : v. 1). —ISBN
0-8101-1265-5 (paper : alk. paper : v. 1). — ISBN 0-8101-1413-5 (cloth :
alk. paper : v. 2). — ISBN 0-8101-1414-3 (paper: alk. paper : v. 2).
1. American poetry—20th century—History and criticism—Theory,
etc.   2. Experimental poetry, American—History and criticism—
Theory, etc.   3. Modernism (Literature)—United States.   I. Title.
II. Series.
PS325.L39   1996
811'.5409—dc20
                                                              96-12315
                                                              CIP

The paper used in this publication meets the minimum requirements
of the American National Standard for Information Sciences—
Permanence of Paper for Printed Library Materials, ANSI Z39.48-1984.

FOR MARJORIE PERLOFF

Contents

Acknowledgments, ix

Introduction, 1

1   Outlaw to Classic:

    The Poetry of Charles Bernstein and Ron Silliman, 6

2   Language Writing; or, Literary History and the

    Strange Case of the Two Dr. Williamses, 19

3   A Reading of Lyn Hejinian's *My Life*, 29

4   "Travelling many direction'd crossings":

    The Poetry of Rachel Blau DuPlessis, 34

5   "Singing into the draft": Susan Howe's Textual Frontiers, 60

6   Partial to Error: Joan Retallack's *Errata 5uite*, 70

7   "To make equality less drab": The Writing of Bruce Andrews, 77

8   Thinking About It: David Antin's *Selected Poems, 1963–1973*, 95

9   Mouth to Mouth: Douglas Messerli's *Maxims from My Mother's*

    Milk/Hymns to Him: A Dialogue, 110

10 Charles Bernstein's *Dark City*:

    Polis, Policy, and the Policing of Poetry, 123

11 Atomic Epistemology and Constituent Knowledge:

    James Sherry's *Our Nuclear Heritage*, 147

12 Reading and Writing Ron Silliman's *Demo to Ink*, 168

    Conclusion, 177

    Works Cited, 195

    Index, 203

Acknowledgments

My thanks to many friends and students who, over the past ten years, listened to my ideas and shared with me their questions, perspectives, and observations on contemporary American poetry. Thanks also to James D. Yarbrough, dean of the College of Arts and Sciences at the University of Alabama, who supported my work on this book, and to Debbie St. John and William Martin for their dedicated work in preparing the final manuscript. And, finally, special thanks to Marjorie Perloff, an articulate and energetic enthusiast on behalf of new poetries; *Opposing Poetries* is dedicated to this inspiring friend, colleague, and exemplar.

Many of the chapters in this volume of *Opposing Poetries* originally appeared, often in different form, in the following journals. I thank each of the editors of these journals for their encouragement and assistance.

"Outlaw to Classic: The Poetry of Charles Bernstein and Ron Silliman" appeared in a slightly different form (under the title "Radical Collages") in *The Nation* 247 (July 2–9, 1988).

"Language Writing, Or Literary History and the Strange Case of the Two Dr. Williamses" was delivered at the 1989 University of Louisville Twentieth Century Literature conference.

"A Reading of Lyn Hejinian's *My Life*" appeared in *The UCSD Archive Newsletter*, Winter 1988.

" 'Travelling many direction'd crossings': On the Poetry of Rachel Blau DuPlessis" appeared in *Temblor* 8 (1988).

" 'Singing into the Draft': Susan Howe's Textual Frontiers" appeared in the *American Book Review* 13, no. 4 (October–November 1991).

"Partial to Error: Joan Retallack's *Errata suite*" appeared in *RIF/T* (SUNY-Buffalo), an electronic journal, 1994.

" 'To make equality less drab': The Writings of Bruce Andrews" will appear in a special issue of *Aerial* in 1996.

"Thinking About It: David Antin's *Selected Poems 1963–1973*" appeared in a shorter version in the *Virginia Quarterly Review* 69, no. 2 (spring 1993).

"Mouth to Mouth: Douglas Messerli's *Maxims from My Mother's Milk / Hymns to Him: A Dialogue*" appeared in a much shorter version in the *Washington Review* 15, no. 6 (April–May 1990) and in a complete version in *Screens and Tasted Parallels* 2 (1990).

"Charles Bernstein's *Dark City*: Polis, Policy, and the Policing of Poetry" appeared in the *American Poetry Review* 24, no. 5 (September–October 1995).

"Reading & Writing Ron Silliman's *Demo to Ink*" appeared in *lower limit speech* 7 (1993).

I am grateful to the authors and publishers listed below for the permission to reprint material quoted in *Opposing Poetries*. The list that follows is for material in both volumes of *Opposing Poetries*.

Reprinted with permission of the author and the publisher passages from *Getting Ready to Have Been Frightened* by Bruce Andrews, New York: Roof Books, Copyright 1988.

Reprinted with permission of the author and the publisher phrases from "Swaps Ego," by Bruce Andrews in *Give Em Enough Rope* (Los Angeles: Sun & Moon Press, 1987), pages 84 & 114. Copyright 1987 by Bruce Andrews.

Passages from *Code of Flag Behavior* and *Meditations* by David Antin in *Selected Poems 1963–1973* (Los Angeles: Sun & Moon Press, 1991), pages 35–36, 39, and 143, Copyright 1991, 1971, 1968 by David Antin. Reprinted by permission of the publisher and the author.

Reprinted with permission of the author and publisher passages from *Talking at the Boundaries* by David Antin, New York: New Directions, Copyright 1976.

Reprinted with permission of the author and publisher passages from *Tuning* by David Antin, New York: New Directions, Copyright 1984.

Reprinted with permission of the author and publisher passages from *What It Means to be Avant-Garde* by David Antin, New York: New Directions, Copyright 1993.

Reprinted with permission of the publisher and the author passages from *A Poetics* by Charles Bernstein, Cambridge: Harvard University Press, Copyright 1992 by Charles Bernstein.

Reprinted with permission of the publisher and the author passages from *Controlling Interests* by Charles Bernstein, New York: Roof Books, Copyright 1980, 1986.

Passages from *Dark City* by Charles Bernstein, Los Angeles: Sun & Moon Press, 1994, pages 22–23, 51, 64, 81, 85, 105–106, 114, 139, 145–146. Copyright 1994 by Charles Bernstein. Reprinted by permission of the publisher and the author.

Passages from "You" in *Resistance* by Charles Bernstein, Windsor, Vt.:

Awede Press, 1983, Copyright 1983 by Charles Bernstein. Reprinted by
permission of Sun & Moon Press and the author.

Reprinted with permission of the author and the publisher passages from
Striking Resemblance by Tina Darragh, Providence, Rhode Island:
Burning Deck, Copyright 1989.

Reprinted with permission of the publisher passages from *Tabula Rosa* by
Rachel Blau DuPlessis, Elmwood, Conn.: Potes & Poets Press,
Copyright 1987.

Reprinted with permission of the author and the publisher, phrases from
My Life by Lyn Hejinian, Los Angeles, California: Sun & Moon Press,
pages 25–26, Copyright 1980, 1987 by Lyn Hejinian.

Reprinted by permission of the author and the publisher passages from
Writing Is an Aid to Memory by Lyn Hejinian, The Figures, copyright
1978.

Susan Howe, excerpt from *Singularities*, pp. 49, Copyright 1990 by Susan
Howe, Wesleyan University Press, reprinted by permission of the
author and of University Press of New England.

Reprinted with permission of the author and the publisher, "The Wrong
Can of Words" by Stuart Klawans, letter to the editor, October 3, 1988,
in *The Nation*.

Passages from *Maxims from My Mother's Milk / Hymns to Him: A Dialogue*
by Douglas Messerli, Los Angeles: Sun & Moon Press, 1988, pages 13,
17, 18, 43, Copyright 1988 by Douglas Messerli. Reprinted by
permission of the publisher.

Reprinted with permission of the author, excerpt from *To the Reader* by
Bob Perelman, Berkeley, Calif.: Tuumba Press, Copyright 1984.

Reprinted with permission of the author and the publisher passages from
Errata 5uite by Joan Retallack, Washington D.C.: Edge Books,
Copyright 1993.

Reprinted with permission of the author and the publisher passages from
Lit by Ron Silliman, Elmwood, Conn.: Potes & Poets Press, Copyright
1987.

"The House Was Quiet and the World Was Calm," from *Collected Poems*
by Wallace Stevens, Copyright 1947 by Wallace Stevens. Reprinted by
permission of Alfred A. Knopf Inc.

Introduction

Readings is the second volume of *Opposing Poetries: The Cultural Politics of Avant-Garde American Poetry*. In the first volume, *Issues and Institutions*, I consider various cultural, material, and institutional perspectives. In this second volume, I focus more steadily on readings of specific texts and the poetics at work in the writings of a range of innovative poets. The two volumes offer mutually supplementary and reinforcing modes of critical scrutiny.

As is the case in Volume 1, the essays in *Readings* represent a selection of nine years of writing on innovative poetries. The chapters in this volume are not monological: I do not trace a single argument from beginning to end. I have deliberately left in the occasional nature of many of these essays and addresses, rather than manufacture expository transitions in the name of chapters pretending to belong to a unified book. There are, of course, disadvantages to retaining the original format of these essays and addresses. There are overlaps and repetitions. Certain key quotations and key claims get repeated, though I hope in different enough contexts to be worth the shifting reconsiderations. If I were to write today on these same subjects, I would have different things to say. Of course, we all tend to imagine that with time we get wiser, more insightful, more intelligent, and less inclined to naive enthusiasms. But that naive enthusiasm, especially in the case of readings of individual books of poems, also is energizing and revelatory, and should not be erased. In the case of a number of these essays, I have restored previously deleted material and have attempted throughout to update references and publication information.

While the Language poets are the principal group of poets I analyze, they constitute only a part of what I call "opposing poetries," that is, poetries that critique and contest assumptions and practices of more mainstream poetries. The term Language poetry itself is, in the course of this collection of essays, gradually questioned and understood to be a label or metonym that enables certain conversations and discussions, but the term itself (as I use it) actually comes to refer to a broader range of experimental poetries—including varieties of ethnopoetics, oral and performance poetries, and feminist poetries—many of which have at most a tangential relationship to the group of poets actually associated with $L=A=N=G=U=A=G=E$ magazine in the late 1970s and early 1980s.

Readings is less general than *Issues and Institutions*; rather than explore key issues and concepts, it offers principally readings of important experimental texts. *Readings* begins with "Outlaw to Classic: The Poetry of Charles Bernstein and Ron Silliman," which—after an introduction to key premises of Language writing, an examination of Language writing's relationship to modernism, and a consideration of Language writing's institutional setting—offers a reading of work by Charles Bernstein and Ron Silliman. In "Language Writing; or, Literary History and the Strange Case of the Two Dr. Williamses" (Chapter 2), I present a detailed reading—principally by way of William Carlos Williams's major works of the 1920s, *Kora in Hell, Spring and All,* and *The Embodiment of Knowledge*—of ways in which Language writing necessitates a rereading of modernist texts. I do so by contrasting the version of Williams's poetics constructed by Louis Simpson (and others of his generation, such as Denise Levertov and David Ignatow) with the version of Williams's poetics emphasized by Bernstein and Silliman.

"A Reading of Lyn Hejinian's *My Life*" (Chapter 3) introduces the concept of a new realism and offers an instance of an alternative version of selfhood by means of a self constructed in language. " 'Travelling many direction'd crossings': On the Poetry of Rachel Blau DuPlessis" (Chapter 4) serves as a corrective to a (my?) tendency to overformulate, specify, and stabilize the term Language poetry. This essay also extends topics briefly raised in Chapter 3: the place of lyricism in experimental poetry, the challenges to lyricism posed by experimental poetry, and the recontextualizing of beauty and the lyrical in experimental writing. In Chapter 4 I also put forward an extended analysis of avant-garde writing practices in relation to feminism, particularly by way of the writing of Julia Kristeva. It is DuPlessis's question, What is realism / made of? that becomes a recurring concern in *Readings*.

" 'Singing into the Draft': Susan Howe's Textual Frontiers" (Chapter 5) studies Howe's enactment of fractured narratives of exploration, her reinhabitation of early American writing, and her critique of normative historical accounts. I suggest that "Howe's poetic exploration belongs . . . to an American literary tradition of frontier writing—the frontier being understood as both a physical and textual place. She weds a contemporary linguistic frontier to the wilderness of early Puritan writings." This chapter on Howe's writing and the next chapter, "Partial to Error: Joan Retallack's *Errata 5uite*" (Chapter 6), establish and explore a critical development in avant-garde poetry: a textually innovative feminism. In addition, Chapter 6 delves into the productive domain of error and play: I consider the ways in which errors, mistakes, and collage-compositions raise fundamental issues about how we read (and "master"?) poetry.

In Chapter 7, on Bruce Andrews's writing, I extend my efforts to pluralize and diversify the term Language writing and to avoid the tokenization of recurring attention to a selected few writers. This essay also involves a more skeptical and sustained investigation into the somewhat platitudinous (or utopian) concept of the reader as a collaborator in the production of meaning. Andrews's writing raises the possibility of a subject's dissolution in language and offers a sharp critique of the concept of a writer's work as an act of personal, individual expressivity. Andrews's avowed goal—"to interrupt comprehension-as-consumption"—returns us to the thorny issue of poetry's ambiguous status as a commodity, and Language writing's more general project (though also an ambivalent one) of producing a writing that is resistant to commodification. Andrews's work calls into question preconceptions of literariness. His writing also leads me to study and question the formal conservatism of most Marxist critics' readings of poetry.

"Thinking About It: David Antin's *Selected Poems, 1963–1973*" (Chapter 8) continues Andrews's critique of literariness and returns *Opposing Poetries* once again to the issue of reconceiving modernism (and questioning the necessity or value of designating a postmodernism). Antin's early work provides an essential theorizing and enacting of the possibilities for collage-composition and relates to the work of artists such as Marcel Duchamp, Robert Rauschenberg, and John Cage. Antin's early work leads toward a redefinition of poetry as "the language art" and toward a reconsideration of poetry's vocabulary.

"Mouth to Mouth: Douglas Messerli's *Maxims from My Mother's Milk/Hymns to Him: A Dialogue*" (Chapter 9) offers a reading, by way of Roland Barthes, of the import of pun, wit, and wordplay in Messerli's poetry. I offer suggestions about the possible social and political dimensions of such disruptive wordplay. This chapter also marks my growing discomfort with the confining protocols of professionalized essaying. Thus this chapter (as will Chapters 11 and 12) takes a more tropical and formally playful relationship to their respective texts.

In "Charles Bernstein's *Dark City*: Polis, Policy, and the Policing of Poetry" (Chapter 10), I present an extended reading of Bernstein's twentieth book of poetry. While I do consider the cultural politics of the reception of and resistance to Bernstein's work, I devote more attention to the formal properties and stylistic signatures of Bernstein's poetry, as well as to certain recurring thematic issues. The chapter on *Dark City* delves into a poetics of awkwardness, Bernstein's ambivalent inhabitation of earlier English metrics, and his organization of large books of poetry based on a compositional principle of difference.

In "Atomic Epistemology and Constituent Knowledge: James Sherry's *Our Nuclear Heritage*" (Chapter 11), I offer a reading of Sherry's book in relation to the writings of Jürgen Habermas, especially as Sherry's book proposes a sociology of knowledge and investigates the ways in which knowledge is organized. Sherry's multigenre thinking enacts most fully poetry as (in Charles Bernstein's words) "epistemological inquiry." Sherry's book seeks to restore seriousness to literature—a seriousness that, as much of *Opposing Poetries* argues, has been severely undercut by poetry's narrow professionalization and institutionalization—as well as by many poets' own complicity in the ghettoization of poetry as a merely decorative mode of knowledge (subordinated to the project of individual bourgeois sensitivity and personal development).

Sherry, like Habermas, is skeptical of postmodernist or theory-based claims for "revolution" or "emancipation"; thus this essay forms an important counterweight to some of the more unreflective enthusiasms found in earlier essays in *Opposing Poetries*. Sherry directs (sympathetically) a critique at contemporary innovative poetic practices. Perhaps because he takes seriously the question of how poetry fits into a quest for truthfulness, Sherry reins in poetry's self-serving claims for its own comprehensiveness and greatness. He values poetry's specialized function as a critique and exploration of meaning-making, but he also wishes to end poetry's sequestration by engaging, as a poet, in serious relationships and mappings with other modes of knowing. Sherry lessens Poetry's claims so that poetry can participate, as a citizen, in a broadened version of the constituting of human knowledge.

Finally, "Reading and Writing Ron Silliman's *Demo to Ink*" (Chapter 12) is an exercise in tropical criticism. It is writing both about and in the style of Silliman's *Demo to Ink*. By lessening the more customarily appropriate critical distance, I enact a questioning of the boundaries among essay, poem, criticism, imitation, and quotation. Of course, such "unprofessional" behavior arises out of issues raised throughout *Opposing Poetries*.

Thus, the xenophobic regulation of form by institutions (explored in *Issues and Institutions*) is also pertinent to the writing of criticism on poetry. The range of allowable styles, particularly in academically sanctioned journals and in more widely circulated reviews and quarterlies, is, as one might expect, quite narrow. While the concluding chapters in *Readings* begin to explore some formal alternatives for critical writing, my more recurrent concern in developing the essays in *Opposing Poetries* has been to intervene in a traditionally expository manner, often in academic journals and more widely read magazines, in ongoing discussions and conceptualizations of contemporary American poetry. Some of the essays in this volume first appeared in *The Nation*, the *American Poetry Review*, the *Virginia Quarterly Review*, and the *American Book Review*, while some material in the first volume was published in the *Missouri Review*, *Contemporary Literature*, *American Literary History*, and *Collection Management* (an important journal for university libraries). Of course, both style and location (of publication) constitute political and cultural acts. As with these prior attempts at right-wrong placement, through a conscious effort to publish in venues that might alter the flow of traffic, it is my hope that *Opposing Poetries* will inform and stimulate an ongoing conversation about the nature and value of contemporary American poetry.

1. Outlaw to Classic

The Poetry of Charles Bernstein
and Ron Silliman

You will not find the poems of Language poets in the *American Poetry Review*, *New Yorker*, and *Poetry*, nor will you find their work reviewed there or in the *New York Times*. Nor will you find these writers receiving many offers of teaching positions or readings through the MFA industry and the Associated Writing programs. But over a period of nearly twenty years—beginning with poetry magazines such as *Jogglars* (edited by Clark Coolidge and Michael Palmer, 1964–65), *Tottel's* (edited by Ron Silliman, started in 1970), and *This* (edited by Barrett Watten and Robert Grenier, 1971–73, and continued by Watten through 1982), and brought to a focus in a magazine devoted to poetics, reviews, and experimental essays, $L=A=N=G=U=A=G=E$ (edited by Charles Bernstein and Bruce Andrews, 1978–81)—the Language poets have been building a network for the writing, publication, reading, distribution, and criticism of poetry outside the interlocking network of the universities and official verse culture. By now, this movement (based principally in New York City and in the San Francisco Bay Area) presents us with a body of writing and thought that could prove to be the most significant in American poetry since the modernists. The greatest virtue of Language Writing is its reintegration of poetry into a fuller cultural and intellectual context, providing us with a poetry and poetics once again immersed in politics, history, and the broad range of debates in the human sciences.

There is a commonly accepted platitude that poetry in our time has no audience, few readers, no "major" poets, and is thus irrelevant and marginal, particularly when viewed through the lens of conglomerate-owned, profit-driven "major" presses. This so-called crisis in poetry is actually a reflection of the difficulty of knowing what is out there. The writings of the Language Poets in particular may go a long way toward restoring an appreciation of the ambition and excitement to be found in contemporary American poetry. Silliman (1987b) declares that "the history of poetry since the Allen anthology [*The New American Poetry*, 1960] has been one of decentralization," due in large part to the low-cost technology of the small press revolution (134). Such decentralization makes knowledge of the whole virtually impossible; when academically based poets and critics, as well as the chief reviewers for the most widely disseminated literary reviews, book review sections, and poetry reviews ignore a significant body of work, the more casual reader/consumer of poetry has little or no opportunity of ever being introduced to much of the vitality and excellence to be found in American poetry today.

Affirming the most adventurous work of Gertrude Stein, Louis Zukofsky, William Carlos Williams, and Jack Spicer, Language Writing can be seen as an oppositional literary practice. Rather than consider poetry as a staging ground for the creation and expression of an "authentic" voice and personality, Language poetry affirms the radical formal experimentation of modernism, arises out of an "exploded self," blurs genre boundaries (not only the boundary between poetry and prose, but also the functional boundary between poet and critic, between poetry and criticism), and seeks actively collaborative relationships between reader and writer, thus foregrounding the political dimension of literary activity. Language Writing assumes that language is experience-engendering, rather than that the writer's task is to find language to represent experiences that somehow exist outside of or prior to language.

A challenge exists for American poets today to be something other than "an ornament to the national culture" and to resist once again what Laura Riding called (in 1926) "the forced professionalization of poetry" (quoted in Silliman 1987b, 21). As Silliman (1987b) and the Language poets remind us, "poetry is part of a larger, oppositional strategy and cannot be viewed as an end in itself" (183). Silliman's (1987b) contribution to Language Writing and to our particular moment in literary history is to fuse the aesthetic and the political: "The problem of poetry at the end of the 20th century is who shall write it, not in the sense of which persons, but rather persons *of what order?* How will they be constituted, understand their own 'individuality,' and relate this to such audiences as each attempts to construct? Such questions are both literary and social" (171). Silliman (1987b), who worked for a number of years in the California prison movement and subsequently served as the executive editor of the *Socialist Review*, argues that

> the primary ideological message of poetry lies not in its explicit content, political though that may be, but in the *attitude toward reception* it demands of the reader. It is this "attitude toward information," which is carried forward by the recipient. It is this attitude which forms the basis for a response to other information, not necessarily literary, in the text. And, beyond the poem, in the world. (31)

For Silliman (1987b) "poetics must be concerned with the process by which writing is organized politically into literature" (4), and "there can be no such thing as a formal problem in poetry which is not a social one as well" (173–74).

Silliman, who, as of 1988, had published thirteen books of poetry, has advanced the interrelationship between poetry and prose, using the sentence as a measure for poetic composition in important writings such as *Ketjak* (1978), *Tjanting* (1981), and *Paradise* (1985), and his essay "The New Sentence" (in Silliman 1987b) offers an essential poetics for a poetry of the sentence. Since 1980, Silliman has been working on a massive project called The Alphabet. He has (as of 1994) completed seventeen of The Alphabet's twenty-six books, of which *Lit* (for the letter *L*) is the twelfth (Silliman 1987a). *Lit* typifies Silliman's structuralist work: the book consists of twelve sections, each with a particular formal relationship to the number twelve. The guiding structural concept for *Lit* is stated in section 8, from Thoreau's journal (12 November 1851): "Let there be as many distinct plants as the soil and the light can sustain" (44).

In spite of Silliman's (1987a) careful constructions, *Lit*'s overall effect is not one of rigidity and constraint. Silliman's writing is fun to read, and one source of pleasure lies in a reader's gradual detection of intricate forms. His poetry builds on puns, declarations, parataxis, sounds and sights from our daily environment, and a range of references from philosophy to baseball. In the course of *Lit*, we encounter an outrageous range of sentences: "History leads to the t-shirt" (32), "Between language and thought / stands a cop" (40), "A minor leaguer to be named Later" (41), "I don't intend to homogenize my meaning for the sake of an enemy" (24), "The shadow of Stein crosses the text" (56). Silliman's humor partakes of the exuberant, deflating coolness of the postmodern, whether he is parodying the proverbial—"Nature abhors a dachshund" (27)—or parodying the great moderns: "I know a house of mud and wattles made (no I don't)" (69), "Tamed by Milton, I lie on Mother's head" (28), "make it noise" (67), and "The antennae of the race have been snapped off by idle youth" (49). Part of the attraction of Silliman's humor lies in the collision of vocabularies: "fee fi / phoneme, name it, sit straight / sing, 'Hail to the Chief, / he's a dirty little thief'" (50).

Silliman, who never graduated from college but who, by the time he was twenty-one, had had poems accepted by *Poetry, Chicago Review, Southern Review, TriQuarterly*, and others, can employ a conventionally lyrical style: "India my Indiana, say that particulars do not fade nor rust consumed in their own dust, or that memory's fair, an old funeral barely the scene of thought's return" (63). But the display of a lyrical bauble is not Silliman's goal. Instead, he immerses us in a welter of details, dictions, awarenesses, and perspectives, as in the fifth paragraph of the final section of *Lit* (1987a):

The yard understood as a mixture of motives, porch paint spotting sage and spider, sawdust and old boards killing the lawn, strange bird half yodels in the plum tree against the sound of a garden hose inside a trash can or another bird's higher trill, ears absorb while the eye scans, skin senses the fog's damp, butt upon the step, sound of a broom in which driveway, wind felt in eyebrow's hair, here in the little things (who I am), three flies articulate the sky between porch & tree, poetry is that this thought thus, body but a metaphor (who I was) for a medical model of that thing lit. Of late much work, little light, leads humor stuttering home, get the lead out (of the pencil, the penis), the point scratching paper's skin seen to signify mind means the made marks the maker's mask (meet science), ear stitched to side of head, hard wood weds floor to foot (I am not that), float from word to word as if there were a reason, as if there were reason, beyond *as* and *es*. "Ease awes," guffaws the talking mule, eyes as corrective to ear's reduction of kitten's seductive vocabulary turned to "mews" is snot enough to lose amid typos the essence of our text beckoning assent. Anxiety of response conducts meaning to lowest denominator, prefaces foreplay plying tongue to punctuation, a setup. "My reputation is in your mouth" is in your mind (read aloud) allows no reading. Speak up or forever hold your piece: this is the place. Word bytes man, and the apple drops. Submit to reading. Now read this. And this. This. This. (64–65)

This paragraph exemplifies Silliman's ongoing attempt to make the moment of composition part of the text (here, "point scratching paper's skin," midway in the book: "A / young Asian man wearing thick glasses watches me write this through the window of the laundromat where / two small boys circle the washers, playing tag" [40], or near the book's end: "activity grounded in its own proceeding, bleeding store-bought ink onto spongy page" [66]), as well as some of the ways in which his text engages our own reading of it.

This running commentary on reading and poetry forms a major subtext in much of Silliman's work. In *Lit*, one such thread might be constructed out of the following remarks: "What are you going to do with all those connections?" (21), "an assault on habit" (66), "seeming clarity inhibits thought as it ought not" (66)," "anxiety of response conducts meaning to lowest denominator" (65), "no ideas but in context" (66), "poetry is that this thought thus" (64), "These sentences occur in this order. I hate what narrative does to time" (49), and "partial truths are all we get, letters home, honed, the bone of thought rings in the head, a sort of bell within a spire, what is higher than sight is heard, hurt, herds these small black beasts of graphics forth" (67). Yet, such thematic readings fly in the face of an antithematic approach to writing and transgress Silliman's own resistance to a content-centered writing. As the full paragraph I quoted earlier indicates, the collision of various kinds of remarks constitutes the primary reading experience of the work. Nonetheless, two of the more engaging paradoxes of Silliman's writing are that he is loyal to the immediacy of composition, while at the same time honoring a preconceived structure; and that he invites the reader to become the writer's collaborator in the construction of meaning, while simultaneously conditioning that collaboration by writing in his own reading of his text-in-progress.

There is a distinctly utopian strain to Silliman's writing, perhaps because "the writer cannot organize her desires for writing without some vision of the world toward which one hopes to work, and without having some concept of how literature might participate in such a future" (1987b, 59). That utopian vision energizes *Lit*, so that this book leaves "a trail that sought only to lay a track which, sounded, marked a possible present (this), activity grounded in its own proceeding" (1987a, 65–66). Silliman's writing inspires us precisely because of its kind of labor: "Among the several social functions of poetry is that of posing a model of unalienated work: it stands in relation to the rest of society both as utopian possibility and constant reminder of just how bad things are" (1987b, 61).

In contrast to Silliman's poetry of the declarative sentence, Charles Bernstein's writing presents greater initial stylistic difficulties and may be considered overall as an intensified blurring of the boundaries between poetry and philosophy. He titles his eleventh collection of poetry *The Sophist* (1987b) and attempts to undo the damage that has accumulated since Western culture absorbed Plato's fear of poetry. Silliman (1987b) describes Bernstein's stance as one that enables Bernstein "to 'liberate' philosophy from its context of professional pedantry by preferring the decentralized, economic marginality of poetry as the discourse through which to proceed" (175). In *Artifice of Absorption* (1987a), a book-length essay on poetics written in the form of a poem, Bernstein, who nearly twenty years ago studied philosophy at Harvard with Stanley Cavell, declares his "insistence / that poetry be understood as epistemological / inquiry" (12). Like Silliman, Bernstein attacks the narrowness of official verse culture, which Bernstein (1987a) claims has for the past twenty-five years "engaged in militant / (that is to say ungenerously uniformitarian) / campaigns to 're-strict the subversive, / independent-of-things nature of language' / in the name of the common voice, clarity, sincerity, / or directness of the poem" (33). Through an oppositional and transgressive poetic practice, Bernstein (1987a) wishes to end the "monotonizing of experience" (61) that comes from a plot-centered insistence on the sole legitimacy of "clear" writing.

Seeking to "wake / us from the hypnosis of absorption" (1987a, 39), Bernstein does not destroy meaning, but he does attack the hegemony of "various utilitarian & / essentialist ideas about meaning" (1987a, 13). Bernstein's argument fuses stylistic and political concerns:

> This century has seen an explosion
> of nonabsorptive forms, which together comprise
> a significant investigation
> of the possibilities for poetry
> —both absorptive and impermeable.
> It would be difficult to map even a
> small portion of these traditions,
> which spread out over many languages
> &, importantly, into the
> translation practices within & among
> many languages. The range
> of writing made available in English
> in the past hundred years, from the

poetries collected in *Technicians of the Sacred*
to *The Greek Magical Papyri*
to "lost" diaries of women from every walk of life,
    to hundreds of specialized-language publications (from
surfing to genetics to computers)
has sharpened an awareness of the interrelation
of cultural distance & opacity as played out in language.
To be absorbed in one's own immediate language practices
& specialized lingo
is to be confronted with the foreignness
& unabsorbability of this plethora of
other "available" material;
the ideological strategy of mass entertainment,
from bestsellers to TV to "common voice" poetry
is to contradict this everpresent "other" reality through
insulation into a fabricated "lowest" common
denominator that, among its many guises, goes under
the Romantic formula "irreducible human values."

                                (1987a, 39–40)

The Sophist, a 177-page collection of thirty-six poems written over a ten-year period, is Bernstein's most important book of poetry to date. As the title suggests, the book affirms poetry as a form of philosophical inquiry and acknowledges the place of rhetoric (or the medium of thought, that is, language) as primary in producing thought and meaning. Paradoxically, the book is unified by a principle of difference: each poem differs radically (in style and layout) from the previous poem. Throughout his career, Bernstein has worked scrupulously to achieve a poetry that resists, and thus calls into question, the staple of the MFA industry's version of poetic craft: the achievement of a distinct voice. This is not to say that Bernstein is incapable of writing beautifully lyrical lines of poetry, as in the concluding lines to "The Voyage of Life":

                                 We
Carve and so are carved in twofold swiftness
Of manifold: the simple act of speak-
Ing, having heard, of crossing, having creased.
Sow not, lest reap, and choke on blooming things:
Innovation is Satan's toy, a train

That rails to semblance, place of memory's
Loss. Or tossed in tune, emboss with gloss in-
Signias of air.

(1987b, 14)

Bernstein can sound the register of late nineteenth century impressionism, as in "From Lines of Swinburne": "As a voice in a vision that's vanished / Perjured dark and barer accusation / Song of a pole congealed / Whose soul a mark lost in the whirling snow" (1987b, 37)," but he serves up lines that, while they have the sound and rhythm of familiar form, withdraw a fixed content or subject. Unlike Ashbery, who finally does settle upon a recognizable, laconic, bemused voice, Bernstein gives enough space to so many vocabularies and rhetorics that no one style or position can possibly emerge as comprehensive. Thus his poetry enacts and affirms principles scattered throughout *The Sophist*: "The world deals with negation and / contradiction and does not assert any single / scheme" (11); "By objectifying, that is to say / neutralizing one's regard, allowing the integrity / of the other and all that it cedes by its dominion" (11); "no teleology holds here" (124); "every instance an embarkation" (54).

His forte as a poet may prove to be a form of radical collage, with a new rapidity and elusiveness, what Bernstein, drawing on his many years as a writer of medical research abstracts, calls *dysraphism*: "a word used by specialists to mean a dysfunctional fusion of embryonic parts. . . . *Raph* literally means 'seam', so dysraphism means misseaming—a prosodic device! But it has the punch of being the same root as rhapsody (*rhaph*)— or in Skeat's—'one who strings (lit. stitches) songs together' " (1987b, 44). Often, as in Silliman's poetry in prose, Bernstein stitches fabric together at the level of the sentence. Consider here "Surface Reflectance":

Debby

had just about tied the bow of her pink
taffeta dress when she heard the porch
door creak open. "At least when I close
my eyes nobody can see me." Early
warning sighs. Buttressing broncho-
dilation, arcadian
microseconds jostling pansynchronic obsidian vases in the
collation of infrequent mention.

(1987b, 166)

In "Amblyopia" various typefaces reenforce the multiple planes of discourse:

> *Blessed are the grieved* for
> they at least have seen their
> inheritance; the rest wait in maxivans
> to collect as available. THE BITTER COKE
> OF JIMMY CARTER; the greased palm, the
> adored swan; all are crepuscular,
> dilated, dogged, dictated.
>
> (1987b, 114)

Bernstein states quite clearly the kind of writing and thinking that does not interest him: "Each limb flows gracefully into / the next, with the effortlessness of good thinking" (1987b, 29). No dysraphism there; in such smooth transparent writing, the writer covers his tracks, closes up all the seams.

In spite of its at times almost forbidding difficulty, Bernstein's poetry does have its humorous moments. He mocks the posturing that goes with specialized vocabularies: "Emergence of mush: the hermeneutic ovoid crashes in / on the Pesto Principle; or, he's hooked up / with a poststructuralist woman who's changed / his pew. *Don't speak so loudly, people/ will hear what you think*" (1987b, 170). More often, Bernstein's forms of humor are extended, instructive, and function within a specifically developed context. In "The Value of Depression" (the eighth section of "A Person Is Not an Entity Symbolic but the Divine Incarnate"), Bernstein reports on sales and promotions of drugs for the "fifteen to twenty million Americans two-thirds of them / women — [who] are medically diagnosed as 'depressed' " (1987b, 148). Especially in the context of a poem that explores the construction, manipulation, and narrowing of versions of "a person," a section reporting the ways in which high profit potentials lead to huge promotional spending ("Two new drugs were backed up by promotional spending of / eight million dollars and thirteen million dollars each") and attempts to convince physicians to prescribe full doses ("Underdosing is seen as a major problem for the dollar / return of the product") becomes a politically charged passage.

Bernstein's recent work (1987a and b) makes it clear that, while a master ironist (in Kierkegaard's sense of irony as a withdrawal of content), he is, like Silliman, a poet given to affirmation and to a distinctly utopian vision. Bernstein's affirmative vision stems from his critique of the supposed opposition between thought and emotion. In "The Only Utopia Is in a Now," Bernstein (1987b) ridicules the assumptions of much mainstream poetry, particularly the aversion to so-called abstract thinking:

> "On this block," the voice was steady now and almost seemed to sing, "what is called 'thinking' is absolutely forbidden in the name of what is called 'emotion.' You're only supposed to write and say what everyone else knows, and to write and say it in the way everyone else has already heard it. In fact, they issue a manual, *Acceptable Words and Word Combinations* and everyone talks and writes only in permutations derived from this book." (35)

But Bernstein's (1987b) guiding premise is that "emotion doesn't express itself only in words we already know" (35). He reverses polarities on his mainstream opponents: "the people here are so ideologically pro-emotion they make it into an abstract concept that is more theoretical than the intellectuality they renounce" (1987b, 35). For Bernstein new forms of written expression enact an oppositional politics and affirm our common birthright as language users, able to question and make the meanings and truths by which we situate and construct ourselves in this world.

The writings of the Language poets, and especially recent work by Silliman and Bernstein, offer us an accomplished poetry as a revived medium for thought and pleasure. Yet the dismissal and suppression of Language Writing make pertinent Gertrude Stein's (1962) observations in her 1926 lecture "Composition as Explanation":

> Those who are creating the modern composition authentically are naturally of importance when they are dead because by that time the modern composition having become past is classified and description of it is classical. That is the reason why the creator of the new composition in the arts is an outlaw until he is a classic, there is hardly a moment in between and it is really too bad very much too bad naturally for the creator but also very much too bad for the enjoyer, they all really would enjoy the created so much better just after it has been made than when it is already a classic, . . . and it is very much too bad, it is so very much more exciting and satisfactory for everybody if one can have contemporaries, if all one's contemporaries could be one's contemporaries. (514–15)

While still the art of outlaws, the writing of the Language poets represents some of the finest and most important expressions of our most worthy contemporaries.

Postscript. I append the following letter and reply, both of which appeared in *The Nation* in the weeks following the publication of "Outlaw to Classic" (published as "Radical Collages"). The letter by Klawans typifies the kinds of misrepresentations to which language poetry is often subjected.

The Wrong Can of Worms

Hank Lazer's article on the language poets ["Radical Collages," July 2/9] served admirably as a down-to-earth introduction to this somewhat up-in-the-air school. I'm glad the first extended discussion in *The Nation* was sympathetic. Perhaps a more critical analysis might follow.

For example, one could examine the philosophical theories that, for the language poets, take the place that is occupied for other writers by emotion, sensuous pleasure and the love of literature. Must these theories be taken seriously? If so, must they result in writings with the texture and allure of drying asphalt?

The answer to the first question is yes. The language poets borrow their theories from highly respectable thinkers, all of whom are agony to read. The answer to the second question is no. Just because reading Derrida is like dragging your naked body through a bed of hot coals and broken glass doesn't mean that poets have to copy the effect.

The language poets argue that the discontinuous, self-contradictory yet ideological nature of writing must be emphasized. Yet if their theories are valid (as I believe they are), then all writing is *already* full of discontinuities, etc. Why build what's already been constructed? The language poets also seek to overcome the ideology that dominates writing (and dominates through writing). Fine. But since they believe that the unity of any given piece of writing is fictitious, how can they think that a large body of writings (and the criticism written about them) is somehow unified as an ideology? Why tear down what's already in ruins?

The final questionable theory is that of non-referentiality. It is now a commonplace that in any sign (that is, any combination of signifier and signified), the signifier does not refer to a single, solid thing but rather to a network of other signifiers. The logic of this argument is too complex to summarize in a letter; for the moment, let the reader accept or deny it at will. My point is that the language poets expand this analysis of the sign into a new version of Zeno's Paradox. By taking the individual word, rather than the sentence, as the unit of meaning, they prove the language never arrives at a reference to shared experience (or what us common folk call the real world). Sure—and Achilles never overtakes the tortoise.

I would suggest that the language poets are barking down the wrong can of worms. Their philosophical theories are more useful in the texts from which they were borrowed. Their political goals would be attained more easily by aspiring to the clarity and wit that the *New York Post* demands of its sports writers. As for poetry, try thinking of it this way: The substance of literature is not language. It's words.

Stuart Klawans
—October 3, 1988

Lazer on Klawans

While I appreciate Stuart Klawans's praise in his letter "The Wrong Can of Worms" [Oct. 3] for the clarity of my introduction to the language poets ["Radical Collages," July 2/9], I do wish that I had been given the opportunity to respond directly to his characterization and critique of the premises of language writing. I am in complete agreement with Klawans's desire for critical debate and analysis of language poetry. However, it would be nice if such a discussion could be an informed one. In each of the five concluding paragraphs of Klawans's letter, he makes erroneous remarks about the nature of language writing.

First, in language writing philosophical theory does not "take the place that is occupied for other writers by emotion, sensuous pleasure and the love of literature." Nor is only one texture—that of "drying asphalt"—to be found in language poetry. Nor is language poetry somehow "borrowed" from Derrida. It would be much more accurate to locate the premises of language poetry in the American modernist tradition of the 1920s, especially the writings of Gertrude Stein and William Carlos Williams. Nor are the theories of language writing borrowed; nor are the effects of language poetry copied. It would be accurate to assert that language poetry operates in a text milieu that is not hostile to a broad range of theoretical writings, and that language poetry does not (unlike much mainstream poetry) attempt to prevent commerce between poetry and philosophy. Furthermore, all theory is not an "agony to read." In fact, much theory can be and is being read with "emotion, sensuous pleasure and the love of literature."

One of Klawans's oddest assumptions is that language poets "seek to overcome the ideology that dominates writing." Just the opposite: They wish to make ideology more obvious and more visible. As for Klawan's assertion that language poets are partisans of a theory of nonreferentiality, that too is erroneous, a position that has been refuted in numerous essays and books. (See, for example, Charles Bernstein's *Content's Dream*, or his *Artifice of Absorption*, one of the books that I reviewed in "Radical Collages.")

But it is Klawans's next-to-last paragraph that leads me to write this response. A writer should at least read the books he pretends to refute. Klawans asserts that language poets make the mistake of "taking the individual word, rather than the sentence, as the unit of meaning," an especially odd position to take in response to a review of Ron Silliman's *The New Sentence*, a book whose title essay discusses nothing but the use of the sentence as a unit of meaning and composition. In fact, almost all of Silliman's writing, especially longer works such as *Ketjak, Paradise* and *Tjanting*, develop possibilities of using the sentence as the essential unit for poetry.

I am not arguing that language poetry is the only true poetry of our time, nor that attention to it should supplant attention to all other forms of poetry. I am claiming that language poetry is of great vitality and importance, and thus that it merits careful reading, scrutiny and discussion. But as Klawans's response all too clearly demonstrates, many responses to language writing consist of an ill-formed, convenient dismissal. If he had read the four books I reviewed, he would not have been able to put forward any of the generalizations by which he characterizes the language poets. But more important, what readers of language writing will find out is that there is not a monolithic thing called "language writing." There is a great range of thoughts, textures, styles and assumptions—even some of the kind of wit and clarity to be found in the *New York Post* sports pages, which Klawans so admires—in language writing. I once again suggest Berstein's *Artifice of Absorption* and *The Sophist* and Ron Silliman's *Lit* and *The New Sentence* as excellent introductions to language writing. As Gertrude Stein lamented, in 1926, "It is so very much more exciting and satisfactory for everybody if one can have contemporaries, if all one's contemporaries could be one's contemporaries."

Hank Lazer
November 7, 1988

2. Language Writing; or,
Literary History and the Strange
Case of the Two Dr. Williamses

One thus far neglected form of attention to Language poetry is the way in which that project involves a rereading and rewriting of American modernism. As is often the case with responses to avant-garde writing, initial readings of Language poetry tend to emphasize what seems new and different about it. Language poetry, like nearly every avant-garde writing practice, has its particular traditions. Some affinities and influences for Language writing have been noted and listed: Stein, Zukofsky, Oppen, Riding, Spicer, and so on. But only a more detailed and specific study, indeed an examination of a deliberate act of rewriting literary history, can begin to illuminate both the basis of Language Writing in American poetic experiments of the 1920s and the traditions behind current Language Writing practices. Such an examination also puts to rest the mistaken dismissal of Language Writing as a mere subset of Jacques Derrida's theorizings. Such a mistake (as seen, for example, in Stuart Klawans's letter in *The Nation*, "The Wrong Can of Worms"; see postscript to Chapter 1), stems from the inference that because Language Writing is not hostile to a broad range of theory and philosophy, that it must therefore be derived or borrowed exclusively from these sources.

To understand the particular version of American modernist poetry that gives direction to Language Writing, I study the particular reading and emphasis given to the work of William Carlos Williams by several

Language poets. And I do so in a contrastive manner to illustrate precisely how Language poets are offering a (re)new(ed) paradigm for the poet, one that overturns the prevailing mainstream model for the poet. I shall therefore contrast the version of Williams put forth by several Language poets (particularly Charles Bernstein and Ron Silliman) with the Williams espoused and created by poets of the previous generation (particularly Louis Simpson). It is in this previous generation's (partial) reading of Williams that much of the basis for today's dominant academic poetics—direct presentation of the thing itself; show, don't tell; immediacy of presentation; plainspoken directness, clarity, lucidity; speech-based writing; free verse based on recognizable syntactical units with a subtle but recognizable vowel and consonant music—can be found.

In "Z-Sited Path" Ron Silliman (1987b) argues that

> No poet in the 20th century has come to be seen as more "All American" than this Rutherford pediatrician. . . . Williams' verse is also taken to be the apotheosis of clarity. . . . For every poet who has felt the impact of Pound's innovations, there are a score who operate under the far-more-readable spell of Williams. That virtually every American poet can now be called "Williamsesque" has rendered the term meaningless. (130)

While the term "Williamsesque" may have become, through its multiplication of meanings, meaningless, I do believe that two distinct readings of Williams can be discerned. Silliman is correct to refocus our understanding (of the appropriation and re-creation) of Williams by asking, "Which is the Williams you think you read?" (1987b, 130). Surprisingly, in achieving two rather violently opposed versions of Williams and his poetics, the two generations of poets I examine were in fact often reading the *same* texts by Williams, principally his writings of the 1920s, and especially *Spring and All* (1923; in Williams 1970).

If we take remarks by Louis Simpson as typifying the making of the first Dr. Williams, the contrast with the second Dr. Williams put forward by Silliman and Bernstein will help us to understand the oppositional nature of Language Writing. There is no dispute between either generation about Williams's importance to American poetry, nor about his importance to the contemporary mainstream and the writing workshop. In a lecture given in 1986, Simpson (1988) concludes that "this side of Williams has had considerable influence on the poets who came after. I don't think it is an exaggeration to say that Williams's theory of poetry is the basic text of most poetry-writing workshops" (115). But which "side" is Simpson referring to?

> Williams's own poems are located in "real events," or at least a recognizable scene. In many a poem by Williams his curiosity about people is enough to carry the day. But poems that have no human characters, that seem to be simply describing a landscape or some common object, hold our interest for another reason. Williams is obsessed with the need to make poetry out of the most seemingly antipoetic materials; it is a challenge he has set himself. He said, "the thing that stands eternally in the way of good writing is always one: the initial impossibility of lifting to the imagination those things which lie under the scrutiny of the senses, close to the nose. It is this difficulty that sets a value upon all works of art and makes them a necessity." (1988, 115)

But in making this version of Williams—the poet of common objects, immediate description, and common life—Simpson both selects from the poetics of Williams's work of the 1920s and represses or denies other elements. (These repressed qualities will, of course, be affirmed by the Language poets.)

In the passage I have quoted above, Simpson cites with approval Williams's remark about writing of "things which lie under the scrutiny of the senses," a principle put forward in Williams's prologue to *Kora in Hell: Improvisations* (in Williams 1970). As presented by Simpson, Williams seems to be calling for a new kind of realism, an immediacy through careful attention to the materials of our daily life. But *Kora in Hell* is not such a work, mixing as it does improvisational prose and italicized commentary, nor is the prologue. In fact, the entire prologue advances the opposite argument: realistic description is a tired form of writing and only that writing which sweeps aside the habitual is of value. Here are the sentences that immediately follow the ones cited by Simpson:

> The senses witnessing what is immediately before them in detail see a finality which they cling to in despair, not knowing which way to turn. Thus the so-called natural or scientific array becomes fixed, the walking devil of modern life. He who even nicks the solidity of this apparition does a piece of work superior to that of Hercules when he cleaned the Augean stables. (Williams 1970, 14)

What Williams has in mind is not a careful, photographic description of a red wheelbarrow. (And "The Red Wheelbarrow" is a poem we repeatedly misappraise when we remove it from the context of the radical formal experimentation of *Spring and All*.) To sweep away the crap of tired description, we would need the kind of new attention to objects that Stein gives in *Tender Buttons*, or any other poetry that affirms the violent energy of the new. In the prologue, Williams (1970) argues (by way of his artist-friend Charles Demuth) that "the poet should be forever at the ship's prow" (28). It is not in the plainspoken, clear, insightful, personalized description—the version of Williams made by Simpson and his generation—that Williams locates excellence. Williams sought poetry's chief quality in the violent overturning that comes with new modes of writing: "It is in the continual and violent refreshing of the idea that love and good writing have their security. . . . Nothing is good save the new. If a thing have novelty it stands intrinsically beside every other work of artistic excellence" (1970, 22–23). Throughout the prologue, Williams defends and praises "the brokenness of composition" and the "instability of these improvisations" (1970, 16). For Williams, or at least for the Williams of *Kora* and *Spring and All*, what matters most is "the energy of the imagination" (1970, 18), a quality that makes itself most manifest in formal experimentation. Williams revels in the excitement of such a revolutionary position, knowing full well its disruptive force: "There is nothing in literature but change and change is mockery. I'll write whatever I damn please, whenever I damn please and as I damn please and it'll be good if the authentic spirit of change is on it" (1970, 13).

Simpson and poets of his generation construct a Williams made in part from poems extracted from *Spring and All* (an extraction that denies the juxtapositional energy of the overall book) and from a prose poetics made in part from *Kora* and *Spring and All* (and here the extracts are used to sanction an argument that is nearly the opposite of the one that Williams was advancing). In order to create the "no ideas but in things" version of Williams, Simpson and others must tame or dismiss the violent energy of renovation that is equally essential to Williams. So Simpson (1975) dismisses *Kora*, for example, as misguided: "In *Kora* Williams tried to show that though he lived in New Jersey he could be as sophisticated as writers who lived in Greenwich Village" (265). The theoretical basis for this dismissal becomes clearer when Simpson (1982) offers a more general pronouncement about innovative writing:

Insistence on originality is symptomatic of a decline in the importance of poetry. The wish to write a poem that in its form and style is unlike any other poem, to express an idea that no one has ever thought of, leads to writing poetry no one wants to read. And the wish of poets to be original is complemented by the wish of readers not to appear unfashionable. So they honor the writing they do not understand. (132)

Simpson must, in order to create a Williams in his own likeness, blunt the far-reaching nature of a fundamental Williams pronouncement, one which Simpson (1975) acknowledges when he cites Williams's statement " 'IT IS THE FORM . . . I have tried so hard to make this clear: it is the form which is the meaning' " (273; the remark comes from Williams's "The Poem as a Field of Action"). But for Williams, and the Language poets, form *is* meaning, and for the Language poets the affirmation of that position, in theory and poetry (with the two often occurring simultaneously), becomes crucial.

For Simpson, as for other poets of his generation such as David Ignatow and Denise Levertov, Williams is a figure returned to again and again for clarification, self-confirmation, and espousal (via Williams's own statements) of a poetics for contemporary American poetry. Simpson (1975) writes about Williams (and Pound and Eliot) in *Three on the Tower*, a book noteworthy because it is one of the first to argue that Williams is of greater importance to contemporary poetry than his (until then) more highly esteemed peers Eliot and Pound. Simpson also wrote several key essays on Williams, including "William Carlos Williams's Idea of Poetry" (1978), "William Carlos Williams" (1979), "To Celebrate Williams" (1983), and the Dancy Lectures of 1986 (published in 1988 as "The Poet's Theme"). In the first of these essays, Simpson (1981) saves Williams from being reduced to a formless poet of common speech. He argues that "the point is important because nowadays, especially among younger poets, there is a belief that Williams stood for writing out your thoughts just as they arise, in the language of conversation, and that this is enough to make poetry" (345). But even as he rescues Williams from this form of reduction, Simpson already creates his own narrowed version of Williams, where poetry stays neatly separated from prose and from theory.

In "William Carlos Williams," again Simpson (1986) makes sure that the insistently innovative Williams is seen as an aberrant, unimportant version of the poet: "Williams's devotees have said that the very lack of structure is what is great about *Paterson*. They would like to make Williams one of the artists of chance, being to poetry what John Cage is to music. But Williams disliked chance; his whole life as man and artist was an attempt to give structure to experience. Beginning with particulars does not mean surrendering to them but transforming them into a significant shape" (103). Simpson is exactly right to suggest that there are different Williamses to be made. But Simpson's version of Williams, and the version of Williams that has dominated until the advent of Language Writing, begins with particulars and subordinates language and form to those particulars. It is a Williams of subjects (which Simpson and his generation label "common life") and a Williams of a narrow range of particular styles — the crafted short lines of the early poems (but taken out of context) and the personal, generalizing voice of the final phase of the triadic foot.

Thus Simpson's particular affirmation of Williams consists of an unusual compound: the poetics of Williams's radicalized 1920s, used to support and affirm (for the most part) the poetry of his final phase of writing. In "William Carlos Williams," Simpson again cites with approval the sentences from the prologue to *Kora in Hell* about "lifting to the imagination those things which lie under the direct scrutiny of the senses." While Simpson (1986) praises the material — that is, the subject matter of Williams's poetry — he also claims that "it is not the material that makes it poetry, rather the method" (107). And then Simpson proceeds to quote extensively from "Asphodel," a poem written nearly forty years after *Kora*. My point is not to quibble over chronology, but to trace the way in which a version of Williams is constructed and to examine precisely what gets affirmed and what gets denied. Specifically, Simpson and his generation of poets deny the full range and force of Williams's focus on method and innovation.

As Simpson (1986) shows clearly in "To Celebrate Williams," any time Williams becomes associated with radical innovation, Simpson will say that that is the wrong Williams: "In the first place Williams tells us to look around and make poetry out of the things we see and hear every day, in language that can be understood. This is radically different from what some conceive to be the aim of poetry — that it should take us away from the familiar into a fantastic situation, and that it must be written in an affected style" (110). This tyranny of the "natural," a version of poetry that could not read Williams's own *Kora* or *Spring and All* sympathetically, constitutes its own theory of poetry and is essential to creating this first version of Williams. While Simpson thinks that the biggest threat to his version of Williams comes from critics who prefer complexity and ambiguity, it is a new generation of poets who offer a powerfully different reading of Williams. In "To Celebrate Williams," Simpson argues that critics are losing the battle for Williams's kind of writing, or at least the version of it that

Simpson is putting forward, because "they [critics] have very little under-standing of the kind of poetry that addresses itself to our common life. For them poetry consists of words alone, and the best poet is the one who can contort a subject until it is no longer recognizable" (1986, 110–11).

The hegemony of this version of Williams can be seen in two ways. First, in its dominance, as put forward by Simpson and others, as the main aesthetic of the contemporary poetry workshop: close attention to particu-lars; show, don't tell; use a natural, personal voice; and so forth. Second, in the dominant anthology version of Williams that gets presented. For example, the 1985 edition of *The Norton Anthology of American Literature* offers this description: "Williams also opposed making general statements or expressing abstract ideas about poetry, either overtly or by implication, as both Pound and Eliot did in their works about the decline of West-ern civilization. His poetry stayed at the surface of life, presenting details of the urban, ordinary scene around him without comment" (1083). The poems presented in the Norton anthology bear out Charles Bernstein's (1986) fear that "as Williams passes through the narrow and well-guarded gates of official verse culture, it likely will be at the expense of so decon-textualizing and neutralizing his work that it will be unrecognizable in his own terms" (246). Bernstein voices these complaints in "The Academy in Peril: William Carlos Williams Meets the MLA," an address given on the same day as Simpson's "To Celebrate Williams." The Norton anthology, for example, presents poems such as "The Red Wheelbarrow" and "To Elsie" completely apart from their context in *Spring and All*. The only in-dication the Norton's editors give as to what has happened to Williams's poems is a footnote: "In *Spring and All* (as originally published, 1923), prose statements were interspersed through the poems and the poems were identified by roman numerals. Williams added titles later and used the vol-ume's title for the opening poem" (1087). But of course for anyone who has read *Spring and All* that is only part of the story: What about the inno-vative typographical layout and design, the odd chapter orderings, the free movement between "poetry" and "prose"? Not to mention the argument found throughout the book (an argument that is the exact opposite of the one put forward by Simpson) that "to understand the words as so liberated is to understand poetry. That they move independently when set free is the mark of their value" (Williams 1970, 149).

Bernstein and other Language poets, especially Ron Silliman, affirm (and make) a Williams who enacts form as meaning and expresses a revo-lutionary poetics and an ethic of perpetual renewed (and self-renewing) discovery, as found in *Kora in Hell* (1920), *Spring and All* (1923), *In the American Grain* (1925), and *The Embodiment of Knowledge* (essays and lectures written in 1928–30, but only first published in 1974). Bernstein (1986) argues that "Williams may be a token inclusion in a canon that excludes what he stands for" (246). What Williams stands for, according to Bernstein and several other Language poets, is the position "that poetry's function 'is to re-enkindle language, to break it away from its enforcements, its prostitutions under all other categories. . . . Thus Jefferson said, Liberty to be preserved requires a revolution every twenty years'" (Bernstein 1986, 246). Here, Bernstein is quoting from Williams's *The Embodiment of Knowledge* (1974). (Perhaps we should modify Silliman's question and ask "Which Williams do you quote?") In so doing, Bernstein (1986) begins to shape a new version of Williams, one that honors his predecessor as a significant theoretician and innovator, one whose principal value lies in his ability to disturb literary convention and to inspire others to perpetuate that process of revolution: "Williams, more than almost any other American poet of his time, took an activist position in respect to the place of poetry—his work is an intervention within the culture against static forms of knowledge, against schooled conceptions and traditional formulation" (244). This rereading and redescription of Williams is part of a broader project by the Language poets to reread American modernism, elevating and rediscovering the work of Gertrude Stein, Louis Zukofsky, George Oppen, Laura Riding, and H.D., as well as making a new version of William Carlos Williams.

This new Williams stands in precise opposition to the one put forward by Simpson. Rather than finding words and forms to fit the objects and experiences of the "common world," Bernstein's Williams insists that "'writing to be of value to the intelligence is not made up of ideas, emotions, data, but of words in configurations fresh to our senses'" (Bernstein 1986, 245). Again, drawing on *The Embodiment of Knowledge* (and by his method of presentation, Bernstein fuses Williams's remarks with Bernstein's own lecture in a seamless presentation), Bernstein/Williams asks, "'Does it not occur to someone to stress the reality of the word—as distinguished from the things which the word engages and which kill it finally?'" (Bernstein 1986, 247). Obviously, this version of Williams overturns Simpson's separation of poet and theorist. Thus, by reading and considering Bernstein's version of Williams, as well as Ron Silliman's, we can begin to specify the precise ways in which Language poetry is oppositional. As Bernstein's (1986) version of Williams illustrates, that opposition is to official verse culture and the dominant poetics of "a restricted vocabulary, neutral and univocal tone in the guise of voice or persona, grammarbook syntax, received conceits, static and unitary form" (245). Through our examination of this second version of Williams, we can also discern the manner in which Language poets advance a new paradigm for the poet, one that does not respect the mainstream's dualisms of poet and thinker, poet and theoretician, or poet and philosopher. As Bernstein (1987a) argues, poetry is thus insisted upon as "epistemological inquiry" (12).

Silliman (1987b) too wishes to rescue Williams from the kind of partial reading that has "rendered 'no ideas but in things' the battle cry of anti-intellectualism in verse" (59). Like Bernstein, Silliman (1987b) too finds

> a critical element of oppositionality in the work of William Carlos Williams, as indeed there is in Stein, Zukofsky, Olson or Creeley. In each instance it lies in the identification of method with content. Opposition to the horrors of daily life in the twentieth century, whether or not these are equated with any given social and economic system, is expressed through opposition to the normative or inherited practices of that literature which embodies the status quo. (132)

As his chief example, Silliman too points to Williams's *Spring and All*. What Silliman wishes to undo is a bland neutralizing of Williams's innovative force, a neutralization that has occurred as Williams's writing has been used to sanction "a new poetics of the 'middle ground,' a neo-academic verse" (Silliman 1987b, 135) that has become well-entrenched and institutionalized. Silliman (1987b) argues that "what remains are the surface features of Williams' poetry. What is profoundly absent is the identification of method with content, and any recognition of a linkage between this and a broader social vision. In dramatically extending the message of Williams over a period of three decades, what has been lost is the essential oppositionality of his work. What is missing is precisely its challenge to the perceptual limits of the reader" (135–36). But the vigor and disturbance of Williams's oppositionality are what Bernstein and Silliman, and by extension the movement of Language Writing, wish to affirm and emulate.

In presenting these contrasting versions of Williams, I am not attempting to position myself for a seemingly objective adjudication. The point is hardly which version is "right"; this issue is thoroughly muddied by Williams's own shifting of views, recastings of his earlier writing, and the many different editions (many sanctioned by Williams himself) that alter the context of his experiments of the 1920s. The case of the two Dr. Williamses serves as a paradigm for the writing of literary history. Either version—that of Simpson's generation (currently entrenched in the academy), as well as that of the Language poets (who exist, at present, primarily outside of the academy)—is partial. Each version of Williams, in a manner that typifies the writing of literary history, is partial in both senses of the word: incomplete and highly subjective (through an advocacy linked closely to self-affirmation). The case of the two Dr. Williamses illustrates, through a highly specific instance, the nature of Language poetry's challenge to the mainstream. The differences over which Williams we affirm are political and ideological, as well as aesthetic, in nature. The most crucial point to keep in mind is that literary history, especially descriptions and evaluations of particular poets's writing, is a *made* thing, a construction that has its own specific historical and social circumstances. At the heart of this instance of making literary history is a dispute over a particular conception or paradigm of the poet. Silliman (1987b) reminds us,

> Whether carried out under the guise of criticism or as a contest of bards, what is hidden is the fact of the struggle between different groups (not, in this instance, necessarily classes) within the larger social ensemble of the nation. The question is not, as [Harold] Bloom formulates it, "Which poet shall live?" but which community shall dominate the other, whose set of values will prevail. (133–34)

3. A Reading of Lyn Hejinian's *My Life*

One of the most exciting, enjoyable pieces of writing to appear in the 1980s, and in a supplemented second edition to reappear, is Lyn Hejinian's (1987) *My Life*. First published by Burning Deck in 1980, written in 1978 when Hejinian was thirty-seven years old, the first edition of this book contained thirty-seven unnumbered sections, each composed of thirty-seven sentences. The second edition, published by Sun & Moon in 1987, "updates" the earlier version by adding eight new sections and eight sentences to each earlier section. This second edition, the work of a forty-five-year-old, is thus now in forty-five unnumbered sections, each composed of forty-five sentences. As in the talk-poems of David Antin and the sentence-compositions of Ron Silliman (particularly *Ketjak* and *Tjanting*), Hejinian manages to retain elements of personal narrative within an avant-garde writing practice, the personal no longer fetishized nor constricted to tight theatricalized settings and habits of presentation. While the title *My Life* has the ring of fact and contemporary confession about it, it evades and deconstructs such a limited view of autobiography in favor of a life, our life, as emerging from acts of composition, perception, and construction. It is a life lived within and of language that becomes the subject for *My Life*. It is "my life" as a user of language, a composer in language, a subject within the terrain of language. Or, as Hejinian observed in an earlier essay ("If Written Is Writing"): "In such are we obsessed with our own lives, which lives being now language, the emphasis has moved" (Andrews and Bernstein 1984, 30).

In one of the new sections of *My Life*, Hejinian offers a paradigm for oppositional views of literary history: "So from age to age a new realism repeats its reaction against the reality that the previous age admired" (104). Discussions of Language Writing have often overemphasized the assault on varieties of representation and mimesis, failing to note as well the projection of a new realism. Pair Hejinian's observation with Rachel Blau DuPlessis's (1987) question "What is realism / made of" (73) or with Hejinian's (1986) own extensive considerations of Stein's work, and this attempt to achieve a new realism becomes evident. An important principle for the realism of Stein and Hejinian is, as Hejinian (1986) argues, "the discovery that language is an order of reality itself and not a mere mediating medium—that it is possible and even likely that one can have a confrontation with a phrase that is as significant as a confrontation with a tree, chair, cone, dog, bishop, piano, vineyard, door, or penny" (129).

In *My Life* Hejinian, like Stein, is "possessed by the intellectual passion for exactitude in the description of inner and outer reality" (a passage cited by Hejinian (1987, 129) from Stein's *The Autobiography of Alice B. Toklas*). Hejinian's sentencing covers great range. Some sentences are, in the more traditional senses, narratively based, suggesting the entire aroma and context of a novel. Some are conventionally autobiographical and personal. But one major source of joy in reading *My Life* comes from the collision of various sentences and subjects. In that very collision—vaguely cubist or collagist—lies the humor and pleasure of this text, which is a kind of supercollider, a site for high-energy linguistic experimentation. Rather than accelerating our reading, however (as in the hypnotic blur of popular, "communicative," "natural" prose), these particles—"Things are real separately" (111), "the rapture of units" (112)—by virtue of their differences and discontinuities, slow us down and focus our attention on their own materiality. In quoting a substantial passage from *My Life*, I become acutely aware that such a miniaturization, my extraction, arrests the diffusiveness that is basic to the realism of this particular form of autobiography. I do so merely to give some sense of the kinds of sentences placed in collision, this example from the eighth section (sentences 18 through 38):

> I wanted to be a brave child, a girl with guts. And how one goes about educating that would-be audience may very likely determine the history of that moment, its direction, the qualities that become emphatic and characteristic of its later influence. As if by scratching at the paper one could dig out the names. Things bound in their cases plunge and erupt. Now when I build something, for example, the job does not

seem beautifully done until all the tools have been properly put away. Sadness and thirst, and hence sadness and water, have ever been associated in my imagination. She lay in bed pretending to be a baby or a wounded soldier. The fellow in the dark would be the good guy with a harmonica. He was talking about oil paints, the body of the pigments, and the ground, with its distortions as they're actual, really seen. This is my portrait-bowl. But of any material, the first thing to make is an ashtray. When I wake up in the morning and it's raining, I feel like rolling in the mud. I was eventually to become one person, gathered up maybe, during a pause, at a comma. Roller skating, I could jump lines, hop cracks. What was the meaning hung from that depend but lupine in the pastures, mustard in the vineyards. How was Yosemite. I missed the flavor that chilling had stolen from the peach and the apricot, and the cold of the apple hurt my teeth. The pedal was squeaking on the piano. Can one "feel" that it is an instrument of discontinuity, of consciousness. When the child in my class whom I thought of as my "boy-friend," though we were then only nine years old, was sick and absent from school, I felt concerned, protective, both vulnerable and responsible by virtue of that relationship which was not friendship but love, and I gathered up the homework assignments and his books each day and took them to his house after school. Something is similar. (25–26)

Hejinian's overall poem or book itself becomes a field for thinking: "Of course this is a poem, that model of inquiry" (105), willingly reflecting upon its own occurrence and its methods of composition. It is a Heideggerian thinking in its lack of closure—the book ends with "Reluctance such that it can't be filled" (115)—and in its primary identification of thinking with questioning and listening. A hearkening. Unto what? The emergence of meanings, a life, a self, a person, a reality, plurals of each of these by means of composition. Thus, if *My Life* runs counter to expectation raised by its title, it does so to decry "the reduction of expression to experience" (114). As Hejinian asks earlier in the book, "Isn't the avant garde always pedagogical?" (92).

My Life denies a reductively Freudian version of selfhood. Instead of a psychosexual history staged within the matrix of a nuclear (bourgeois) family, Hejinian's self is the sum of its textuality: "My life is as permeable constructedness" (93). As Hejinian reminds us, "one is growing up repeatedly" (24), and "a person is a bit of space that has gotten itself in moments" (114). But for Hejinian, these moments and instances of growing up are primarily textual: sentences. Appropriately, Hejinian's book shuttles back and forth between then and now: "Now where on our long walks my grandfather had gone with his walking stick I go with my mace" (110). As it goes, Hejinian's composition meditates upon dependency: "What was the meaning hung from that depend" (21). The latter example is one of the kernel sentences that keep reappearing and modulating throughout the book, with the same blurring of events and repetitions that occurs in a life: echoes, suggestions, modifications, with a dim sense of having heard that and been there before, embodying "the rhythm of cognition" (96). Hejinian's "depend" suggests too William Carlos Williams's "so much depends upon," and in Hejinian's "life" much depends on memory, but even more depends upon the present moment of construction: "It was there that she met the astonishing figure of herself when young" (22). Marjorie Perloff (1985) is exactly right when she refers to *My Life* as conveying "the archetypal life of a young American girl" (225). It is at once a specific and a generic life: the emergence of a life in the process of its textual (re-)construction. For Hejinian's act of self-composition, humor too gets mobilized. Puns and wordplays interrupt any tendency to rely too heavily on narrative: "The obvious analogy is with music. Did you mean gutter or guitar. Like cabbage or collage" (1987, 22–23). Such disturbances are necessary because "we had to wash the windows in order to see them" (23). In calling attention to the frames and means of seeing (rather than to what is seen through the windows), Hejinian (1986) aligns her writing with Stein's: "for Stein, it was not truth but understanding that was of value—a shift of emphasis from perceived to perceiving, and thus to writing, in which acts of observation, as complex perception, take place" (129–30).

Each section of *My Life* begins with a floating (upper-lefthand corner) superscription or caption written in italics. This caption, another means of emphasizing the materiality of the signifier, causes us to ask: What do I do with this italicized phrase? What is its relationship to the body of the text? Is it a title, an abstract, a commentary, a distillation, a decoration? The first such caption is "*A pause, a rose, / something on paper.*" Just as Hejinian deconstructs traditional versions of autobiography, so too do her captions, in their humor and deliberate inadequacy, undercut the attempt to make a life into a lyrical moment of concentration. The caption-phrases subsequently appear in the text, usually subject to modification. Each opening page of each section thus presents the lyrical—conceived as brevity and image—set in opposition to a more meandering writing, a more inclusive form of realism (which is the larger text). The text's loyalty is to the accumulative compositional process that becomes a life.

What impresses me as nearly miraculous about the new edition of *My Life* is Hejinian's ability to reenter her earlier text and add to it so effectively. She has suggested that perhaps twenty years from now she might like to return to *My Life* to make a new edition. For now, we can enjoy her recent publications (1992; 1994) and look forward to her completion of a collaborative work with Carla Harryman (on sex and sexuality). In returning to *My Life*, no doubt Hejinian rediscovered the exactness of Gertrude Stein's (1962) observation made in "Composition as Explanation": "The time in the composition is a thing that is very troublesome. If the time in the composition is very troublesome it is because there must even if there is no time at all in the composition there must be time in the composition which is in its quality of distribution and equilibrium" (522). What imitations of *My Life* will not be able to achieve is the peculiar distribution and equilibrium—of sentences, experiences, varieties of perception—that Hejinian manages. She has built on Stein's awareness that "beginning again and again and again explaining composition and time is a natural thing. It is understood by this time that everything is the same except composition and time, composition and the time of the composition and the time in the composition" (Stein 1962, 516). Out of this intersection of time and composition comes a life, *My Life*, for which I am grateful. I conclude with an example of Hejinian's (1987) delightful distribution and equilibrium:

> The intellect lingers, this too is erotic—the anticipation of the pleasure of making sense. It's true, there are too many pieces to my idea, and I like to move them around (but continuity craves time). We all were learning Russian letters, which looked like twigs, upper limit trees. I became obsessed with patience, its patterns, the amount of time it took, the containment of the requisite recurrence and ultimate disconnection. (104–5)

4. "Travelling many direction'd crossings"

The Poetry of Rachel Blau DuPlessis

With the publication of *Tabula Rosa* Rachel Blau DuPlessis (1987b) achieves a complex and satisfying level of writing that commands and holds our full attention. Her earlier books of poetry, *Wells* (1980) and *Gypsy/Moth* (1984), did not prepare us fully for the extraordinary accomplishment of *Tabula Rosa*. Perhaps her critical writing— *Writing Beyond the Ending: Narrative Strategies of Twentieth-Century Women Writers* (1985b), *H. D.: The Career of That Struggle* (1986b), essays such as "For the Etruscans" (1985a) and her essays on poets such as George Oppen, Susan Howe (1987c), and Beverly Dahlen (1986a)—should have alerted us to the kind of intelligence that was being formed.

I begin with such summary and praise because DuPlessis is emblematic of an emerging new paradigm for a poet. The poet/critic or poet/thinker split, which has been fostered and reinforced by the intuitive emotionalism, unified subjectivity, and "naturalness" of the MFA-sponsored mainstream, is decisively overturned in DuPlessis's work. The poet/scholar again becomes an exciting possibility, but tied this time to political/ideological realms that are neither elitist nor authoritarian.

While DuPlessis's writing manifests certain tendencies in Language Writing, her writing also helps us to understand the fictitious or reductive nature of such a term—Language poetry—as that term seems to imply a fixed or narrowly specified thing. Her at times thematized version of feminism, her myth-orientation (as with many of the writers who publish in the journal *Sulfur*), and her particular variety of lyricism are somewhat atypical of Language Writing. Her disturbance of syntax, her assimilation of a broad range of theoretical writing, the distribution or multiplication of subjectivity, and the variety of her uses of the page (as a field for innovative layout)—especially overwriting and double-writing—situate her work within an experimentalism for which the term Language poetry, like the term postmodernism, is becoming a fuzzy but well-entrenched metonym.

To understand the social or communal context of DuPlessis's poetry, the group effort involved in the feminist journal *HOW(ever)* provides a helpful touchstone. So too do DuPlessis's (1986b) remarks in her preface to her book on H.D., where a vision of a woman writer's career is garnered from the critical writings of Myra Jehlen:

> How a woman writer creates and re-creates the possibility of her creativity is a central site for investigation. These acts [of creating and re-creating a site for literary activity] are not a purely psychological manoeuvre which might be relegated only to a biography; they are 'conceptual' and 'linguistic': a matter of situating the self in relation to conventions of representation and then of constructing various 'enabling relationships' with, and in, language. (xiv)

Thus the first of *Tabula Rosa*'s (1987b) two sections is part of DuPlessis's ongoing "History of Poetry," an act necessitated by the situation declared in the section's epigraph: "She cannot forget the history of poetry / because it is not hers." Section 1 consists primarily of lyric poems, often in clipped, "traditionally" musical lines (via Oppen, H.D., and others); these poems are essential to DuPlessis's revisionist history of poetry and remaking of the terms of myth. Section 2 of *Tabula Rosa* marks DuPlessis's maturity as a poet. In these longer poems, she makes full use of her arsenal of skills, placing at risk the accomplished though sometimes tidy skills of a lyric poet. Of the three long poems that constitute section 2 of this book, I call attention to "Writing," a provocative poem of considerable genius. Along with the poem "Crowbar," "Writing" constitutes the major accomplishment of *Tabula Rosa*. Her more recent poems, particularly the series of poems called "Drafts" (the first two of which appear in *Tabula Rosa*), consolidate and extend the work of "Writing."

Before I enter into a sustained reading of "Writing" and several other of DuPlessis's poems, I shall consider, by means of perspectives developed in Elizabeth Meese's *Crossing the Double-Cross: The Practice of Feminist Criticism* (1986), DuPlessis's position as a feminist writer and as a poetic innovator. Meese, in analyzing feminist writing and the versions of authority which it must undo or question, cites Mary Jacobus's description of how women's language works:

> The transgression of literary boundaries—moments when structures are shaken, when language refuses to lie down meekly, or the marginal is brought into sudden focus, or intelligibility itself refused—reveal not only the conditions of possibility within which women's writing exists, but what it would be like to revolutionize them. In the same way, the moment of desire (the moment when the writer most clearly installs herself in her writing) becomes a refusal of mastery, an opting for openness and possibility, which can in itself make women's writing a challenge to the literary structures it must necessarily inhabit. (Meese 1986, 120)

For DuPlessis, it is precisely this refusal of mastery—reflected in the title "Drafts" and in the recurring "smudge" of "Writing"—that allows her writing its most exciting developments. In part, that refusal takes the form of a resistance to lyricism (but not its elimination).

In "For the Etruscans," DuPlessis (1985a) asserts that "the 'female aesthetic' will produce artworks that incorporate contradiction and nonlinear movement into the heart of the text" (278). DuPlessis concurs with Deena Metzger's understanding of the word "new" as signaling an antithesis to dominant values (1985a, 279). Thus the act of stylistic innovation fuses the realms of politics and aesthetics. DuPlessis's writing affirms assertions made by Julia Kristeva (1984) in *Revolution in Poetic Language*: "This shattering of discourse reveals that linguistic changes constitute changes in the *status of the subject*. . . . The text is a practice that could be compared to political revolution: the one brings about in the subject what the other introduces into society" (15, 17). For DuPlessis, that newness, the innovation and renovation of her own writing, especially as seen in "Writing," partakes of a mixture of expanded inclusiveness and a rigorous self-questioning:

> The holistic sense of life without the exclusionary wholeness of art. These holistic forms: inclusion, apparent nonselection, because selection is censorship of the unknown, the between, the data, the germ, the interstitial, the bit of sighting that the writer cannot place. Holistic work: great tonal shifts, from polemic to essay to lyric. A self-questioning, the writer built into the center of the work, the questions

at the center of the writer, the discourses doubling, retelling the same, differently. (1985a, 279)

While I definitely do wish to situate DuPlessis's writing within a feminist literary practice, this principle of subversion, particularly by means of the question, is obviously not confined to feminist writing. That process of self-questioning applies equally well to the work of Ron Silliman (most obviously in "Sunset Debris"), or David Antin, whose talk-poems are often structured around and by recurring questions, or Edmond Jabès, whose *Book of Questions* (1976) most fully sustains the top priority of questioning as a work's primary questing. DuPlessis herself acknowledges that "what we here have been calling (the) female aesthetic turns out to be a specialized name for any practices available to those groups—nations, genders, sexualities, races, classes—all social practices which wish to criticize, to differentiate from, to overturn the dominant forms of knowing and understanding with which they are saturated" (1985a 285). Herein lies much of the force of Language Writing: in its overturning of dominant forms of knowing and understanding, such writing returns subversion and fundamental epistemological inquiry to the domain of poetry, making of poetry an enriched field for the activity of cultural critique.

While DuPlessis, I think, would agree with Meese's (1986) assertion that "feminist writing is a movement toward remembered or re-bodied writing that materializes woman's specificity" (131), each also argues for a multiple notion of feminist writing and aesthetics. DuPlessis concludes, "therefore there is female aesthetic, but not *a* female aethetic, not one single constellation of strategies" (1985a, 273). In her book on H.D. (1986b) DuPlessis (by way of Julia Kristeva and Carolyn Burke) wonders whether the "I" in women's poetry is not "plausibly a self-conscious producer of and commentator upon discourse and her positions within it. In short, is the speaker a 'self' (whole, homogeneous, or seeking wholeness/identity, transcendence), or may a speaker be a 'subject' (naming her place in and absences from registers of language and culture)" (111). In Meese's (1986) brilliant analysis of the relationship of feminist criticism and deconstruction, the two are seen to share "the displacement of hierarchization as an ordering principle" (85), a remark that echoes DuPlessis's own textual practice in the palimpsestic overwriting of "Writing." Feminism thus continues to develop from its proximity to deconstruction by resisting a tendency to become essentialist or univocal: "to further its own project, feminism needs to struggle to become more like deconstruction by sharpening its own critique and, while articulating its method, resist the monolithic specification of its own ideology to the extent that it requires a simplification of the difference within in order to represent itself to the world outside" (Meese 1986, 84). Conversely, Meese (1986) argues that "deconstruction needs to struggle to become more like feminism in terms of specifying its political goals" (84).

For DuPlessis, as for much of the entire Language Writing community, acts of resistance (to authority and monolithic specification) are enacted through style, through poetics and through form. Politics and aesthetics overlap in a revisioning of writer, reader, and their relationship to one another:

> Not positing onself as the only, sol(e) authority. Sheep of the sun. Meaning, a statement that is open to the reader, not better than the reader, not set apart from; not seeking the authority of the writer. Not even seeking the authority of the writing. (Reader could be writer, writer reader. Listener could be teacher.) (1985a, 275)

Such a refusal of mastery brings DuPlessis (1985a) to a doubling of vision:

> A both/and vision born of shifts, contraries, negations, contradictions; linked to personal vulnerability and need. Essay and sermon. A both/and vision that embraces movement, situational. (I don't mean: opportunistic, slidy.) Structurally, such a writing might say different things, not settle on one, which is final. (276)

It is precisely such a both/and vision that I see at work, for example, in DuPlessis's doubled relation to lyricism.

While Meese (1986) argues that "by virtue of the masculinist claims to objectify, literary critics have created the need for a criticism of advocacy, espousing special perspectives based on gender, sexual preference, race, and class" (13), I would extend that list of positions of advocacy to include aesthetic preference, particularly the advocacy of innovative writing practices. As I have argued here and elsewhere (see volume 1, *Issues and Institutions*, chapter 1, "Criticism and the Crisis in American Poetry"), such aesthetic innovation is fundamentally political in nature. Meese (1986) is quick to grant that "interpretive communities, like tribal communities, possess the power to ostracize or to embrace, to restrict or to extend membership and participation, and to impose norms—hence their authority" (9). For DuPlessis, the most actively beneficial version of community to nourish her own writing (and to which *Tabula Rosa* is dedicated) is the community of innovative feminist writers that constitutes the magazine *HOW(ever)*, a group that Eliot Weinberger (1988), in an otherwise highly critical appraisal of Language Writing, calls "the most exciting group activity occuring in American poetry today" (201).

And if to such a writing community, with DuPlessis as a principal representative (for an admittedly group activity), we pose what Meese (1986) calls "the feminist's most pressing axiological concern—what is valued and why?" (63), we see (both in the form of the writing and in its content) an answer taking shape in the construction of DuPlessis's "Writing" and "Drafts," as well as in her remarks in "For the Etruscans" (1985a):

> If it's really the forms, the language, which dominate us, then disrupting them as radically as possible can give us hope and possibilities. What I'd like to try to understand and explain to other people *(you yourselves are the riddle)* is how the form of women's writing is, if ambiguously *(of double, sometimes duplicitous needs)* nonetheless profoundly revolutionary (as are, in their confusing ways, modernism and postmodernism, also written from positions of marginality to the dominant culture). (287)

Such disruptions of dominant habits of order-making are fused linguistic and political acts; Kristeva (1984) argues that such changes "disturb the transparency of the signifying chain and open it up to the material crucible of its production" (101). To understand DuPlessis's gradual achievement of a position of poetic innovation, an achievement that occurs as a part of a dialectic of mastery and disturbance, I first call attention to her more traditional or conventional lyrical skills before examining her more heterodox textual practices. Typical of the cadence and conciseness of DuPlessis's (1987b) version of the lyrical is this passage from "Praxilla's Silliness":

> Wood white
> large white little white
> littler fritillaries
>
> wayward
>
> "lords" of air.
>
> (5)

But such compact vowel and consonant music today is only of limited appeal and, for the most part, represents an inherited and overused form of craft. In *Tabula Rosa*, DuPlessis (1987b) offers two other directions of movement within a lyrical method of composition. One is, in the manner of Oppen or H.D., to push conciseness to a maximized efficiency, a point at which that conciseness seems to implode, denying the very fixity and focus of the lyric in the act of attaining its ideal of concentration:

> Snow on o-
> pen
> yellow for-
> sythia.
>
> 'Sno
> won
> open force
> scythe
>
> ya.
>
> (11)

Here, multiplicity speaks from the very heart of focus, multiple sense is seen and heard to inhabit lyricism's very act of paring down; puns and multiple sayings of the words' sounds subvert unified attention.

DuPlessis's (1987b) other strategy is to resist the lyrical impulse. She commands herself, "no postcard poetry" (89); she cautions herself, "to reinvent 'attention' is narrow tho tempting" (89). That is precisely why part 2 of *Tabula Rosa* represents such an important development for Du-Plessis, especially given her affinities with Oppen and H.D. The desire for an only slightly renovated lyricism—which comes down to focused attention—*is* there. But DuPlessis's longer works open up onto "folding," a multiplicity of thought, voice, and rhetoric that is less possible within a lyric of attention. As I shall also be claiming, the residue of that lyric-apprenticeship *enhances* the longer poems, giving them pith and beauty, a tension that calls for attention. Thus her longer poems, by virtue of their proximity to a lyrical desire, have a dialectical force, their openness and multiplicity existing proximate to an impulse to narrow and to pare.

While phrases in DuPlessis's poems suggest somewhat familiar terrain, at least within the realm of current Language Writing, I find too a double-ness, an ambivalence that undercuts and multiplies what might otherwise remain thematically fixed. Based on a phrase such as "whose feet slog sullen / over the gnarly ground of gnosis" (23) I suggest a kinship for DuPlessis's writing with Charles Bernstein's view of poetry as a variety of epistemological inquiry. Or the phrase "the stretched pulse of number /

singing in my heart" (23) links her work to the Fibonacci variations found in Ron Silliman's *Tjanting* and *Lit*. (Indeed DuPlessis's phrase pinpoints the exact emotional exuberance of Silliman's mathematics). But in each case DuPlessis's full statement is more ambivalent (or polyvalent) than what I have extracted:

> Lay dee
> dear hood ship sheathe
> in the wild wift wood
> whose feet slog sullen
> over the gnarly ground of gnosis,
>
> if ever
>
> .   .
>
> Rupture
> the reverberating lyric cell by cell
> edge of the tree-green strips'
> deciduous space
>
> the stretched pulse of number
> singing in my heart.
>
> (1987b, 23)

Between these two, with their qualifying "if ever" and their rupture of the lyric, we encounter "Precious poetry? ha! / Rage of being / the impossible self." The more heroic or essential task of DuPlessis's poetry is, to borrow from Oppen, the task of being numerous, even while being in the proximity of thematic coherence.

In the excellent poem "Crowbar" (from which I have been quoting), DuPlessis's (1987b) double question and double gesture gets stated as "woman like what? poem like what? / complicit with the repetoire / ambivalent to the repetoire" (23). It is an ambivalence later described as a kind of decentering: "below, above, below, above; / in sum there is no 'where' " (from "Selvedge" 51), an ambivalence on the verge of further fracturing: "plural seed-filled thought" (51). To return to "Crowbar," it is an ambivalence of "rivulets that rush into the body of / argument, / double crossing streams / brightheaded arrows / engorged with this ancient targeted song" (24–25).

If in relation to the "repetoire" a double crossing stream of subversion and incorporation is called for, such a doubleness of "tradition" and "individual talent" is not so arresting as DuPlessis's double crossing of the page in "Megaliths" and "Writing." "Megaliths," arranged in two vertical columns side by side on the same page, seems prelude to the more adventurous doublings of "Writing." In "Megaliths" DuPlessis begins to explore more fully a writing by means of otherness: "the way of the poem / is the way / of this / border," a destabilized place where writing "moves mark to mark and makes a crossing" (32), traversing the space between and across the double columns. If DuPlessis makes a strategic error it is in her note at the back of the book, over authoritative and monological: "Read down each column, then across both." An error because (as in John Ashbery's two-columned "Litany") one of the great virtues of such a poem is that— if presented without guidance—it forces a reader, before any reading becomes possible, to reflect upon the act of reading and the ways in which a reader will choose to make order out of a text. There is no "natural" or merely unreflective reading possible for such an array. DuPlessis ought to stand aside and let each reader decipher and recipher the poem as she will. The composition of "Megaliths" is exciting, but its specific language still verges on a sentimentality, a romanticized strained lyricism, a mere thematizing of disorder by means of a forced vocabulary of "standing beyond the threshold of silence," of beckoning, of the "boundless," of the "vast before, vast after," of "no path" and "the abyss" and the "empty dark."

But there are no such problems with "Writing," a truly remarkable poem, one I have been enjoying since it first appeared in the first issue of *Ottotole* (1985). It is a poem that staggered me then (but in bits and pieces—the first bit to stick being the remark "what is realism made of") and that now takes me aback whole. At this juncture in the reading of Language poetry and in the writing about it, we had best begin to move beyond an espousal of interesting principles, a proselytizing, to a sharper reading of poems (and even to an elucidation of differences within and among poets). Of course the danger of such readings is that they become close readings only, a re-isolating of the reading and writing, a subduing of the poem to a monologic of theme. But "Writing," which I shall dwell on, with, beside, and within, begins with a proper ending; it begins with a period (as nearly each of the poem's twenty-eight sections begins), foreclosing its own closure by mocking it and inverting it from the start, calling its own beginning ".Smudge, ballpoint," invoking an awareness of its own graphicity, its own materiality of signification, and its participation in a somewhat imperfect, haphazard process. Within the first section, the word "underpainting" hints at the palimpsestic version of writing that will soon emerge from "Writing," the first section of which ends with a kind of petition or invocation:

What paths inside
other
territory of utterance
hear me

smudge and hear me

whiteness

(55)

But even now as I return merely to the poem's first section, I realize that I have overlooked these lines: "Black lines / dot nylon rope about, / tie scout knots," lines that casually drop us into the domain of dots and period, lines and knots, intersections and intentions that will be very much to the point of this poem: a kind of figural prefiguration.

The second section alerts us to time itself—"One year after, like a punctuation; one month together"—as a governing form of punctuation under investigation, these loose prose lines coming right after their lyrical, tight opposite:

Plumb line, pul-
sing, eye to eye, drinks
dusks of light.

(1987b, 56)

So the terms of "Writing"'s thoughts of form begin to take shape, a balancing plumb line, the opposing desires of pulse or eye or dot, stretching out into "sing." But this is still a bit formulaic, still not yet (though beginning to find "an arbitrary path cut through possibly a mistaken hole in the floor") a risky accommodation of otherness.

With the third section, with the introduction of the two-columned writing and the overwriting in a different script, "Writing" begins to achieve that "travelling many direction'd crossings" that makes it such an impressive poem (see p. 44). It is the tension between condensation and expansiveness that, paradoxically, holds together "Writing." One test is whether "condenses" (the art of much of DuPlessis's lyric orientation), the "spots" and "fine tip flairs" and "nipples," the writing that is "canalized" (later: "swollen vivaporous rivers / flooding silences that never / get

```
.A wri-
ting marks the
patch of void
foggy reflecting
mist catches wet carlight

that everything tests          film
condenses                      fine tip flairs
refracted silence              baby wipes
The cold rush up               khaki thread
the dark dark trees            nipples
Somnulent spots of travel

Letters are canal-
ized as white foams
zagging, a fissure on the
sheet,
        *tangle of branches unorganized without the leaves*
cock-eyed underbelly of
plenitude of

mark. *outtakes, can imagine conversations?*
      *conversions?*
      *Long passages of satisfaction swallowed up*
      *in darkness.*
                                        (1987b, 57)
```

drained") can break out, can acknowledge its own other. Hence a double-
writing and an overwriting, a kind of double-crossing of unity (of meaning, of layout and design). Even the script itself looks spontaneous, added
on, but has also its own other authority. Called "outtakes," it takes us out
(and her too) somewhere else. These scripted words, called a "tangle of
branches unorganized," a branching out, surrounding the assertion of a
"cock-eyed underbelly of / plenitude." (And I have just begun to think of
the doubleness of "cock-eyed," a word DuPlessis resorts to more than once
in *Tabula Rosa*. A seeing slant, a seeing skewed, but also a patriarchal seeing that DuPlessis will contradict and subvert.) These scripted words are
the "underbelly" of the other more organized writing.

DuPlessis offers notes after "Writing," and here her fragmented ex-
plainings do not (as in the note to "Megaliths" that I criticized earlier)
undercut or narrow the effect of the poem. These notes merely reconfirm
the multiplicity—truly the politics and ideology—of "Writing"'s work:

Writing from the center of, the centers of, otherness.
Making otherness central. . . .
Sections contained by other sections, over writing, writing over, or simultaneous with. So that one section does not have hegemony. So the reader does not know which to read first, or how to inter-read . . . the reader is at large, as the poet is. We are strained companions. . . . Making alternative poetries be in the same page-space. (1987b, 84)

In the next section the overwriting gets bolder, is capitalized, begins to gain the upper hand. DuPlessis's vigor in exploring "imbeddings" and "the canvas" of the page as a site for "overlayering" makes for invigorating reading. This kind of page catches more, picks up some of what the carlights cannot on a wet dark night among "the dark dark trees," a script that carries the impression of "long passages of satisfaction swallowed up / in darkness."

Still, "Writing" (1987b) tries to find a way to honor expansiveness and precision:

> .Voracious swelling ocean all
> smallest possible words of all
> To a
> time thickened initial
> the tee
>
>   have so many little tasks
>
> which oscillation
> speeding, seems to fix.
>
>   picking this and tending that
>   my back hurts
>
>   (59)

Thus the dialectical tension of "swelling ocean" and "little tasks" can be survived, even made into the "buntings of stories," a "precious bundle." The poem as it is made, as it is deployed upon the page, its very multiplicity (a Silliman-like enactment of the political, of contestation) a "'Utopian' living in the deep," but also too a willed dividing, a parceling, "maybe political cynicism with odd / borders gerrymandered." "Writing" thus comes to exist in a space nearly torn apart by conflicting desires, a drive toward randomness and a drive toward an erotic focused attention:

> And, in the space between entropy
> and arousal,

Philomel,
or, longing for liquid
song.
(60)

Then, with the eighth section, "Writing" takes a crucial turn, unfolding
and exposing its own procedures and concerns:

Imbedding some   extruding some   the interplay between selection.
imbedding, and loss. Some few words, chosen, and why; but are also
chosen from, once the day was awash in pinpricks, a pull in the back
muscle, overlay and no experience. No experience because all. Say. Saw.
Operations. Addictions. And no shadow and it was dark within this
icy **one knows** brightness all disappearing all intense writing **what;**
does it save it? "diaristic" in impulse, but unbargained, imponderable.
Over written. Written then over written. over ridden, the selection is
one thing, this (the globule, clot) another. Different plans and different
pictures.

	uneven picture patterns,
Most poetry something—	irregular blocks, a rebus
imagery, structure.	trued, held in a rose-pink
	border.

Dreaming I'm crying
it's she's crying.

(1987b, 62)

I have felt for some time now that part of Language Writing's significance comes from such a rethinking of poetry as "Writing" enacts; in one
of my own poems ("Compositions," in Lazer 1992, 139) I suggested that to
be thematized is to be demonized. DuPlessis: "Most poetry something— /
imagery, structure." In our time, Language Writing offers a poetry of
otherness, the entropic, the aleatory, "uneven picture patterns," a poetry
of Georges Bataille's irrecupurable heterogeneous matter. A multiple writing that as I argue for DuPlessis's poetry, can and does include aspects
of the lyric and the lyrical, but set in new tensions and attentions. Such
a questioning of poetry's nature is far from the much tidier lament of a
last-gasp Robert Lowell, a unified subject's bittersweet retrospect, stock
theatricality, and fine Puritan meiosis:

Those blessèd structures, plot and rhyme—
why are they no help to me now

I want to make
something imagined, not recalled?
    (Opening lines of "Epilogue,"
    the final poem in *Day by Day*,
    Lowell's final book of poetry)

DuPlessis risks more than that. What Lowell, even as he acknowledges the deficiencies of an overordered crafting of words, cannot do is risk a fundamental disturbance of syntax and the most ingrained traditional gestures of poetry (including layout and the presence of a unified speaker). DuPlessis engages in a more disturbing and genuinely risky self-consciousness.

But it is the self-commentary of section 8 that I think about (for, to be candid, it is essential to my own writing and much of the writing I like, such as Ron Silliman's or Lyn Hejinian's). This self-commentary, alternately describable as a self-reading of the poem-in-progress or as an aspect of self-consciousness, constitutes a kind of fulcrum. I have received a couple of letters (one that specifically invoked the notion of post–Language Writing) wherein younger Language Writers criticize this habit of self-commentary as a form of sentimentality or self-indulgence. And herein may lie a slight shift, perhaps in part along generational lines (for indeed there is and must be a "next" poetry). If indeed a post–Language Writing is already being formed, it may, in part, be based on a preference for a poetry of (more "purified") enactment rather than a mixture of enactment and substantial self-commentary.

For DuPlessis, such self-commentary unfolds what has begun to gather within the poem's "underbelly," so that as the next section of the poem suggests, she and we can "keep it in mind." As section 9 begins to make explicit, such poem-making parallels, is consonant with, self-making. As with the contradictory pulls toward entropy and toward focus, DuPlessis's double-columned writing displays and enacts its own struggle for subordination and insubordination. One lament is that for the poem to proceed, for it to go along, *"I can't keep it [the poem] in mind if I / don't connect // repress, it // (as it) // goes along."*

In part, DuPlessis's quest is for a new version of dailiness, a task that, for example, leads a writer like Lyn Hejinian (in *My Life*) in a substantially different direction. But in "Writing" this quest for a new dailiness, a making new of the diaristic impulse, is not fulfilled:

Impossible maybe to write
the techne of dailiness the hand reaching onto the shelf the dust

collected in a particular corner the objects also a little dusty with
the spring light through the back door objects directly in the sunlight
the coupon torn or cut, saved
as a lacy proof of thriftiness
the unmendable crack this,
attempt at exactness, is readable the intersecting rhythms of
muscles small muscles when cutting when sorting how
to assimilate how to discuss to represent
the pulse of pleasure and heartlessness

(65)

Instead, DuPlessis's attention returns to the "cracks" and intersections, the winnowing and sorting of surface, "Writing" as a process of coming to consciousness of the process of writing, a writing that entails its own undoing (rather than specificity and fixity of "the techne of dailiness"). As in section 13 of the poem, DuPlessis opts to pay attention in a painterly manner to the materials of writing, to the letters as "staining / inked jelly" that "floats loosely" on "paper: thick rags, even sometimes / flowers leaf bits." It is the process of coming to be of words—"A rose weathers out of the page / o death"—until the previously limited conception of the lyric as a point, a narrowing down, becomes transformed, through attention to the materials of the graphic, into "a finger, a bud who / curls there, comma, / period, sky-reading / marks / creating marks for 'others' (ellipses) . . ."

Each time DuPlessis's "Writing" threatens to achieve a focus, a fixity, it immediately exceeds itself, contradicts itself; completion or focus is not what must be accomplished, but an ever broader accommodation, in the manner announced in section 14: "*Borderline takes many forms.*" For DuPlessis, critic of the novel:

> People worry the ends of novels,
> marry. Sonnets like novels.
> Still lives encode bounty.
> Still,
> smudging these discourse cross-
> hatches terminii
>   the end (ends up) every
> where.

(1987b, 68)

Nowhere is this cross-hatching, this dispersing of terminii, better enacted than in the section that follows (no. 15):

birds	.cumulus color of red sandstone, coal shale	resume
they	and close tabulated bunching	resume
re they	unfirm unpleasant undulent	re who
tcho	unconscious	tcho

pattern up	crests, its opposite	pitter pity
hole in the	touching hard and fast	they poke a
house	disperse	little nest
	thick places	
	bound to violent narratives.	

(69)

Section 15 offers a way of keeping tabs on arrangements of writing. Here, layers of discourse criss-cross. The array itself testifies to contrary tendencies: one to tabulate, to order, to build crests and patterns and little nests and holes, "close tabulated bunching," repetition and the tight columns of the vertical; the other a process of undoings, from within and at the center of the tabulations something "unfirm unpleasant undulent / unconscious," a dispersal, so that "thick places" are forever wed to "violent narratives." Such a moment in DuPlessis's "Writing" allies itself with Julia Kristeva's (1984) description of the double nature of the functioning of the semiotic:

> The text signifies the unsignifying: it assumes within a signifying practice this functioning (the semiotic), which ignores meaning and operates before meaning or despite it. Therefore it cannot be said that everything signifies, nor that everything is "mechanistic." In opposition to such dichotomies, whether "materialist" or "metaphysical," the text offers itself as the dialectic of two heterogeneous operations that are, reciprocally and inseparably, preconditions for each other. (65–66)

Just when DuPlessis's self-conscious reflection on graphic process begins to fix itself as a theme and a method (one that my own reading tends to overemphasize), DuPlessis (à la Stein) disturbs her own writing by descending into the cauldron of sound: "a mewling into maybe milky dark. // mirror of dream milk smile mirror of actual noticing" (70). Such a disturbance of thematization by way of sound confirms Kristeva's (1984) description of such a space as "indifferent to language, enigmatic and feminine, this space [which Kristeva calls the semiotic rhythm within language] underlying the written is rhythmic, unfettered, irreducible to its intelligible verbal translation; it is musical, anterior to judgment, but restrained by a single guarantee: syntax" (29).

As I continue through DuPlessis's "Writing," I begin to suspect that it is a poem that can be endlessly read. As Robert Frost, the epitome of the anti-avant-gardist, wrote in "The Figure a Poem Makes," "Read it a hundred times: it will forever keep its freshness as a metal keeps its fragrance." I puzzled over Frost's sentence for many years until the correctness of a metal's fragrance came to me (and came to me seeing Dave Smith's sculpture works; *there* is an artist who worked with his materials closely enough to know each metal's fragrance). In "Writing" the two sections that best support and repay the investment of rereading are 18 and 19, the former concluding with a Beverly Dahlen–like statement of the quest for otherness so critical to Language Writing's current communal writing project:

> How to be that which is unspoken   how to speak that which is
> "repressed"   elusive anyway   tangential   different
> impending space   different enough   how to write that which
> is / is
>
> unwritten.

(72)

How to respect and speak for/from otherness without reducing that otherness to a limited/limiting version of definiteness? It is, of course, a political question: via representation the rights of "others" get enacted in the elaboration of style and aesthetics. A writer's acts of representation are the primary political acts of writing. How to give voice/space/imprint to what exceeds us without "capturing" or colonizing that otherness in our representation of it? It is one thing to valorize the "other," to turn it into a stylistic signature, a personal style, as in the silence-absence-disappearance poems of the 1960s and 1970s of W. S. Merwin. But that is merely a stylized rendering, a bourgeois capturing (and producing of the effect of) otherness. Not a satisfactory answer to these questions.

For DuPlessis, an answer (and by no means a definitive one) involves a calculated (and incalculable) besideness as seen in section 19:

> .Some words much
> syntax or   *Narrative as betrayal?*
> allusions thereto   keep going
> some invention, but
> if *the laws*
> *of language are*
> *socio-*

logical laws then poetry
is provisionally
complicit resistance.

The poet's wife, old woman,
hunched in the kitchen drying
dishes, the whole
interview. Such things
happening on the side.
What is realism
made of?

The bitterness of already
unspoken bitterness?

your soul—
out!
—among the little

spaces
before entropy
(foreground, bulbous foyer)
becomes arousal
sparrows?

Verification (Docu-
mentation): What
types to verify
my evidence?
Statistics?
Expert testimony—
quoted, paraphrased,
or summarized?
Personal experience
or eyewitness accounts?
Opinion polls
or surveys?

Language as betrayal?

betrayal of "what?"

keep going

(73)

Here, statement, question, self-interrogation, and format enact a multiple (though primarily doubled) inquiry into the nature of poesis. To her credit, and in our interest, DuPlessis acknowledges a doubleness in poetry's being: at once a gesture of resistance, yet an act that is also (by at least minimal laws of language) only complicitly resistant. Narrative itself is both a giving in to sequence, to a narrowing order, hence possibly a betrayal (a betrayal of *what* is a more difficult question). But narrative, as it is a going on, also allows for dispersal, for motion, and thus for the breaking up of constriction. DuPlessis's own poem is a poem honoring (truly, bodying forth) "things / happening on the side." Beside the "expert testimony," the inevitable anthologizings of shards from the dead in the overwritten palimpsest of the poem, DuPlessis makes space for the "old woman," "the poet's wife," her unspoken words coequal with the husband's words given in the interview. Here we have an instance of what DuPlessis (1988a) calls "words in secret twin" (54).

But the question for "Writing," and I believe for much of Language Writing, is "What is realism / made of?" This question is momentary self-interrogation for "Writing"; it also (along with section 18's "how to write that which is") makes clear DuPlessis's affinity with Gertrude Stein, as well as with a contemporary such as Lyn Hejinian. To write without betrayal, to write what will inevitably be partial but with as great a fullness as possible, to write that which is along with what is unspoken/unwritten, while acknowledging and evading the rehearsed and theatricalized forms of poesis—such demands (and others) take us into the restlessness and bravery that is "Writing" and that tracks its way through DuPlessis's more recent "Drafts" as well.

In my own betrayal, my somewhat persistent narrative for "Writing," a narrative I know to be incomplete, I nevertheless wish to make it to the end, suggesting a few of the routes that open and close, cross and cross over as the poem moves toward completion. Many of the debates, arguments, and irruptions that take place in the latter sections of "Writing" are ones already familiar to us in our proceeding through the poem. DuPlessis continues to make and assert "the open square / between letters a piazza / of unlikeness" (74), spaces and disturbances between the fixities of black letters and definite assertions. Thus the poem struggles with its own tendencies to bead and to encapsulate (see section 23), versions of resistance (and complicity) to lyricism. The poem and poet continue to swerve away from too narrow constitutions: "Not a question of / making images. Making / what?," so that

> the word passes phatic or elegant
> passes bounded passes through
> grammar to get past syntax's single-borders
> to funny half-seens, stumbles;
> all routes, all specks, all
> snarled in matted eager acts.
>
> (78)

In the final section of "Writing," a poem where each section begins with a period—an endstop that is immediately overcome, a reversal of the essential dot's authority, a reversal of its habitual signification—the attempt to end the poem becomes congruent with the poet's own physiology, the mark of the period, in pun and figure, in sound and shape, being a blooddrop marking the end of a twenty-eight-phase making:

> Invisible staining
> a bubble one two or three arcs
>   flake of clotting or something
>
> It's all part of being
> part of me
> beet red drops at the bottom
> of pee
>
> of me making this
> this end and of
>
> just happening.
>
> period.
>
> (82)

But the period, as an insertion to stanch the flow (of language, to keep it "clean"), is here, at the end, replaced by its "secret twin," the question (and the question mark):

> But in writing?
>
> Just one event among flux,
> the many yet so
> foregrounded
> as fourth, maybe the sixth
> tampax in writing?
>
> (83)

And thus "Writing," even with its cyclical but unobtrusive twenty-eight-section shape, sides with the irruptive force of questioning, with flux, even as it makes its "one event" present.

I now turn back to issues raised earlier in this essay: the nature and importance of palimpsest and overwriting for DuPlessis; her position of difference within Language Writing; and her double relation to the lyric. In "An Essay on Beverly Dahlen's *A Reading*," DuPlessis (1986a) discusses the peculiar nature of overwriting. She understands overwriting as a version of palimpsest, a writing simultaneously whole and multiple: "Such a text, made of at least two kinds of scribble at different times yet on the same parchment, is split between its wholeness as object or ground and its veering multiplicity as figure" (160). Here is one point where deconstructive critical practice and Language Writing share a common project: a paradoxical act of writing that acknowledges (and even thrives upon) its own incompleteness, its foreordained fragmentation and diffusion. For DuPlessis, palimpsest suggests a means of representing consciousness; here the affinity of her work (with that of many other Language Writers, such as Hejinian, Howe, Messerli, and Silliman) to Gertrude Stein, becomes apparent: "Palimpsest indicates the desire to manifest, by some verbal or textural gesture, the sense of presence, simultaneity, multiple pressures of one moment, yet at the same time the disjunct, absolutely parallel and different, the obverse sensations of consciousness in reality" (1986a, 160).

To distinguish DuPlessis's thinking—and writing on Language poetry to date has tended to articulate generic descriptions and generic principles—we must note her openly psychoanalytic slant. Such an openness to psychoanalytic premises is not a universal quality of Language Writing. Charles Bernstein's poetry, for example, presents a rigorous challenge to any supposition of a unified subjectivity as understood via psychoanalytic models (unless one begins to consider the most radical psychoanalytic models offered by Deleuze and Guattari). DuPlessis, marking her own difference within Language Writing, suggests that palimpsest and overwriting take "a different tack (tact) towards time, suggesting a psychoanalytic sense of the persistence of earlier configurations, and residues which are volcanic, irruptive" (1986a, 160). This view makes her work part of the (admittedly varied, but decidedly mythic and psychoanalytic) writing project found in Clayton Eshleman's *Sulfur* magazine.

DuPlessis's writing on Dahlen's *A Reading* is also helpful for understanding DuPlessis's own doubled relationship to the lyric as well as her understanding of the term "writing." DuPlessis believes that *A Reading* articulates a place between "lyric (the force moving) and documentary (record without judgment)" (1986a, 160). DuPlessis's own poetry, especially as seen in "Writing," contends between lyric (as the force moving and as a concentrated point or focus) and diffusion (as multiplicity and openness). DuPlessis cites with approval Dahlen's remark in *A Reading* that "I am preparing in the most banal way to say everything possible"; such a remark applies to DuPlessis's own writing project. Indeed, such a wish may animate the writing of many American poets of the late twentieth century. DuPlessis absorbs from Dahlen the reciprocity of writing and reading: "reading precedes writing, inflects writing, saturates writing, is writing. . . . The writing can be 'a reading' because of the enormous quantity of these allusions. No 'writing' exists that is not in fact a reading of former writing, an anthology in part, an appropriation of prior texts" (1986a, 164, 166).

As DuPlessis realizes, and again in this respect she represents a new paradigm for that thing called a poet, the efforts of Language poets to assimilate critical theory and philosophy to poetry have had the salutary effect of revitalizing "Poetry as an institution made sloppy by its unquestioned reliance on banalized romanticism" (1988b, 188). That is, DuPlessis and others seek a writing "not depending on conventionalized 'pleasures'" (1988b, 190). (Please note: this is not the same as doing away with either pleasures or beauty!) But as I have been asserting, part of DuPlessis's difference within the community of Language writers stems from her attachment to premises of lyric beauty. In a letter of 18 January 1988, DuPlessis's contribution to the Weinberger/Davidson exchange of letters in *Sulfur*, vol. 22, DuPlessis asks about many of the innovative poems of our time, "What do they do with pleasure? what do they do about transcendence? what do they do with understanding community? How do they negotiate specific rises of passionate feeling passionate nodules of feeling and agglomerated psycho-political force in language   how do they negotiate feeling   without romantic   transcendence?" (1988b, 190). In her own writing, and particularly in "Writing" and the subsequent "Drafts," DuPlessis again and again works out responses to her own questions. Her attachment to lyric force requires her to include (or at least to attempt to include) moments of passionate intensity. Her task, and perhaps the generic task of "making it new," is to "negotiate feeling without romantic transcendence." Not that transcendence itself is the villain here, but a banalized romanticism (discussed at length, for example, by Altieri 1994), a lyric of personal epiphany that has become formulaic, rhetorically predictable, and theatricalized.

While DuPlessis acknowledges that "idealizing poetry is a useless gesture" (1988b, 191), she does not wish to do away with poetry's "loftiest" or most transcendental impulses. Instead, her writing moves toward "resituating the upper limits of poetic diction, yearning, transcendence among a number of other discourses, rather than as the culmination or crown of language" (1988b, 191). It is the recontextualizing of transcendence that is crucial to her work and to the overall enterprise of Language Writing. I certainly know that such an act matters in my own poetry, and it is crucial to the work of many Language Writers, Silliman, Hejinian, Pearson, Ott, Howe, Bernstein, and Armantrout among them. The struggle of DuPlessis and other poets with the place of transcendence should also put to rest the misconception that Language poetry is somehow emotionally cool or hostile to feeling. More difficult, however, is the complex issue of values: "The question is how to find and to figure or represent value when certain conventional forms/forces of value—the epiphany, the appeal to transcendence, myth, Poetry as an Ideal, the Poet as a Figure, not to say Poetic Diction—are sidelined or equalized with a blast" (1988b, 191). (For a provocative analysis of this very issue, though from within the discipline of critical theory and deconstructive practice, see Jay 1987–88.) For DuPlessis and others, this projection of value comes, in part, from a renovated relationship of reader and writer, of reading and writing.

To return, though, to DuPlessis's double reaction to a lyric mode of thought and composition, her essay "For the Etruscans" (1985a) both displays the attractiveness of the narrowly focused lyric and departs from that singular focus. DuPlessis begins by quoting a passage from Dickinson that could summarize the essential concentration at the heart of the lyric impulse, especially as DuPlessis herself practices that act of concentration (in the recurring figure of the period) in "Writing": " 'This is a Blossom of the Brain— / A small—italic Seed' (Dickinson, no. 942)" (1985a, 271). But the great step taken (a step taken *without* abandoning the lyric) in "Writing" and the more recent "Drafts" is a move away from the at times constraining form of mastery that goes with the lyric impulse.

In the "Drafts," the first two of which are included in *Tabula Rosa*, the (de)liberative force of "Writing" finds other manifestations, but ones less focused on layout as a principle of enactment. Of the first group of "Drafts," the finest is #6, an elegiac fusion of lyrical (nearly archaic) phrasing with the more entropic workings of "Writing." In the "Drafts" too, part of DuPlessis's project is a disturbance of the lyric:

> Words come just like that, vision.
> beak black bleak
> cut back through arced site protocol,
> member the day. Each micro-face splice gutted
> that
> brekkkl they brekk the lyric ruck.
>
> (1987a, 23)

In "Draft #6: Midrush," lines such as "Wraithes of poets, Oppen and oddly / Zukofsky / renew their open engagement with me / wreathing smoke-veils" (1988a, 51), with their intricate music of *o* and *a* sounds, present us with moments of an exquisite (but familiar) lyricism. More typically, such vowel-music occurs within a context of deliberately juxtaposed flatter tones:

> Some flatten the paper
> for next year.
> Ark opened, the paired
> zoo aired and marched.
> The colors had been beautiful.
> And we have gained more objects
> whose provenance is tombs: lavish
> pristine colors of the acrid lock.
>
> (1988a, 51)

Where "Draft #6" proves most engaging is in its development of double- and overwriting, extending the multiple textuality of "Writing." In "Draft #6" a slightly different description of palimpsestic writing is given:

> pairing the letters
> underneath
> sitting   citing
> the writing under writing.
>
> (1988a, 50)

Here, the notion of "underwriting" adds a financial or economic resonance to the palimpsestic text that DuPlessis has been developing. While much of her earlier overwriting focuses on what is added to the page, the more openly elegiac focus of "Draft #6" shifts our attention to what comes up from beneath the surface of the text. In an almost Rilkean perspective (and only almost: DuPlessis's concern is not so much with the spoken word nor with "spiritualized" breath but with the mark and the written word), DuPlessis in "Draft #6" gives space to the surfacing marks of the dead, so that "It is they that speak / silt / we weep / silt / the flood-bound / written over and under with their / muddy marks. // of writing under the writing" (1988a, 53).

DuPlessis thus realizes the poet as anthropologist and archaeologist, brushing the surface and finding where "Always another little something— / a broken saucer flower fleck / unremarkable wedge, except its timing / [is] working itself loose in the rain" (1988a, 53). Or, in another version of the poet, a revision of Emerson's poet as an Adam new naming the beasts, DuPlessis tells of Noah (a second namer?) calling forth stories ("with words in secret twin") from the ark, overlayering and redoubling as he goes:

> Or midrash—
> overlayering stories so,
> that calling out the ark, it's
> Noah hails and harks
> new name and number
> for
> what stinking fur and tuckered feather-fobs
> did clamber forth
> disoriented. Cramped. Half-dead.
>
> (1988a, 53)

DuPlessis's own "Drafts," as well as her overwritten texts such as "Writing," can be seen as a kind of midrash, a layering of story, commentary, and interpretation, with the added disturbance and motion suggested by the turn into "midrush."

In an essay on Susan Howe's work, DuPlessis (1987c) offers descriptions that serve to situate her own writings as well: "The taxing struggle to assemble and maintain a self-questioning (who? how?) cultural position: anti-authoritarian, yet authoritatively provoked by one's female identity" (164). In a more detailed and discerning analysis of Howe's position, DuPlessis (1987c) describes her own double gesture:

> Howe appears to be on the cusp between two feminisms: the one analyzing female difference, the other "feminine" difference. For the latter, she is close to Julia Kristeva, who evokes marginality, subversion, dissidence as anti-patriarchal motives beyond all limits. Anything marginalized by patriarchal order is, thus, "feminine;" the "feminine" position (which can be held by persons of both genders) is a privileged place from which to launch an anti-authoritarian struggle. The female use of this "feminine" of marginality and the avant garde use of this "feminine" of marginality are mutually reinforcing in the work of some contemporary women: Lyn Hejinian, Kathleen Fraser, Gail Sher, Beverly Dahlen and Howe. This mixed allegiance will naturally call into question varieties of flat-footed feminism. (161)

It is this combined or mutually reinforcing use of the "feminine," with particular emphasis on the innovative and transgressive aspects of avant-garde writing, that characterizes the writing community that gathered around the journal *HOW(ever)*. In "Draft #3," DuPlessis (1987a) summarizes (and valorizes) her writing project:

> of words, enormous slant, difficult OF.
> being. Junctures of saturation
> beyond catalogue, yet catalogue HAS TO DO
> do
> syntax; how, why being beyond me. in the
> totality of its relations
> unstatable   the what.
> ice treacherous.
>
> (24)

Crucially, that "totality of its relations," for DuPlessis and most Language Writers, involves a renewed awareness of the communal nature of the writing enterprise, as well as the politics and economics of textual production and distribution.

What results is a poetry by DuPlessis and others that extends the oppositional activity that Kristeva (1984) sees beginning in experimental poetry of the late nineteenth century: "To penetrate the era, poetry had to disturb the logic that dominated the social order and do so through that logic itself, by assuming and unraveling its position, its syntheses, and hence the ideologies it controls" (83). The poems in *Tabula Rosa*, and the more recent "Drafts," provide the reader with "one of the most daring explorations the subject can allow himself, one that delves into his constitutive process. But at the same time and as a result, textual experience reaches the very foundation of the social—that which is exploited by sociality but which elaborates and can go beyond it, either destroying or transforming it" (Kristeva 1984, 67). Poetry such as DuPlessis's, in its disturbance and reconstruction of modes of ordering and self-constitution, "reminds us of its [poetic language's] eternal function: to introduce through the symbolic that which works on, moves through, and threatens it" (Kristeva 1984, 81). That reminder constitutes precisely the risk, bravery, and accomplishment of DuPlessis's poetry.

5. "Singing into the draft"

Susan Howe's Textual Frontiers

Susan Howe has received considerable acclaim, and justly so, as one of the most important poets of our time. Essays by Marjorie Perloff, Linda Rein-feld, Geoffrey O'Brien, Michael Palmer, Bruce Andrews, Charles Bernstein, Bruce Campbell, John Taggart, Rachel Blau DuPlessis, and others have appeared in numerous books and magazines, including two special issues of *The Difficulties* (vol. 3 [1989]) and *Talisman* (no. 4 [1990]), the latter including a superb interview with Howe. Now, with the publication of three books of poetry, a substantial body of her work is for the first time made available to a wider audience. Sun and Moon Press has published *A Europe of Trusts* (1990a), which includes three previous small press releases, *The Liberties*, *Pythagorean Silence*, and *The Defenestration of Prague*; Wesleyan University Press's *Singularities* (1990b) collects three more recent poem-cycles, *Articulation of Sound Forms in Time*, *Thorow*, and *Scattering As Behavior Toward Risk*; and Paradigm Press has published *A Bibliography of the King's Book; or, Eikon Basilike* (1989).

Even the simplest of Howe's sentences involves us in the dilemmas and shifts of her poetry, history, and thinking. *Articulation of Sound Forms in Time*, for example, begins with a seemingly straightforward, elementary textbook story: "Just after King Philip's War so-called by the English and shortly before King William's War or Governor Dudley's War called the War of the Spanish Succession by Europeans, Deerfield was the northernmost colonial settlement in the Connecticut River Valley" (1990b, 3).

Howe's own work positions itself, as did Thoreau's (to whom she pays homage in *Thorow*) by his reassertion of Indian names, within a textual space of rewriting, of partial erasure and correction. Her poetry constitutes a "tribunal of rigorous revaluation" (1990b, 25).

Howe's poetry again and again enacts fractured and fracturing narratives of exploration:

> Untraceable wandering
> the meaning of knowing
>
> Poetical sea site state
> abstract alien point
>
> root casket tangled scrawl
> (1990b, 25)

The textual woods of her wandering exist at a juncture of sense and dissolution, "bond between mad and made" (1990b, 33). The poem's site is a crossroads of recovery and destruction: "Rhyme of Heaven open // Collision with human protection" (1990b, 25). While Heidegger (1971) in "What Are Poets For?" can try to make purely metaphysical the poet's exploration—"language is the house of Being . . . , we reach what is by constantly going through this house (132)"—Howe's textual house acknowledges holocaust as one of its rooms, with destruction intertwined in its construction:

> Home in a human knowing
>
> Stretched out at the thresh
> of beginning
>
> Sphere of sound
>
> Body of articulation chattering
> (1990b, 26)

While Howe's exploration may posit "Author the real author / acting the part of a scout" (1990b, 51), such a scouting party is not romanticized. She returns us to beginnings (though not to origins) so that we may not arrive at our ending:

> Stripped of metaphysical proof
> Stoop to gather chaff

Face to fringe of itself
forseen form from far off

Homeward hollow zodiac core

Omen cold path to goal

End of the world as trial or possible
trial

(1990b, 27)

Howe reenters early American writing of colonial settlement, disturbing the foundations and assumptions of that prior act of appropriation.
She inhabits what has hitherto been a white, male, partriarchal base of
operations. Her father was a constitutional law professor and serious stu-
dent of Puritan history as well as a close friend of Perry Miller and F. O.
Matthiessen. So there is, implicit in Howe's historically oriented poetry
also a story of "home" and "family," a communing with her father as well
as a skeptical investigation of the history that his generation of Harvard
scholars produced. Perhaps this aspect of her work has its residue in a
passage such as "Constant parties of guards / up & down // Agreseror //
Bearer law my fathers // *Revealing traces / Regulating traces*" (1990b, 46)
She resides at the historical headwaters of a line of American descent that
takes us through the lives of Jonathan Edwards, Emily Dickinson, and
Howe herself—the theological/spiritual/conceptual Nile of early America,
the Connecticut River Valley (which, in light of Howe's compositional
fragmentation, might be read as connect-I-cut).

Howe writes books of poems in which textuality is in conflict with
itself. Each book puts into play a spirited fracturing, a willed but also
inevitable and necessary breaking apart. There is, for Howe, no original
that is lamented as lost, just as historical documentation is not presented
as poetry's other nor as some sort of objective truth. A neat arrangement
on the page would fail to acknowledge the gulf Howe perceives between
the word-on-paper and its existence elsewhere: as speech, as document by
someone else; as sound not yet word; as partially articulated thinking.

In *A Bibliography of the King's Book or, Eikon Basilike*, in which Howe
(1989) reanimates a book and its bibliographic controversies, her introduction is aptly named "Making the Ghost Walk About Again and Again."
Howe reiterates the controversies of authorship for *Eikon Basilike*, which
appeared on the day of King Charles I of England's execution in 1649,
by "rewriting" a later document, Edward Almack's *A Bibliography of the*

King's Book; or, Eikon Basilike (1896). She literalizes the position of bibliographer, which her introduction identifies, by way of *Webster's Third International Dictionary*, as "one that writes about or is informed about books, their authorship, format, publication, and similar details." In a search for authority and for an inevitably incomplete original text, Howe writes at a juncture of materiality and invisibility: "Only by going back to the prescriptive level of thought process can 'authorial intention' finally be located, and then the material object has become immaterial." Such a conception of the position of writing rhymes with the title and substance of *Articulation of Sound Forms in Time* (in 1990b).

At times, that juncture receives expression within a relatively familiar lyrical format. As evidenced in these three books, Howe's poetry should put to rest the misimpression that current experimental poetry has abandoned the lyric(al). (So, for that matter, should, in quite different ways, the poetry of Lyn Hejinian and Rae Armantrout put to rest that misunderstanding.) *Pythagorean Silence* begins with a Robert Duncan–like lyrical, pastoral invocation:

we that were wood
when that a wide wood was

In a physical Universe playing with

words

Bark be my limbs my hair be leaf

Bride be my bow my lyre my quiver
(1990a, 17)

Even at the level of the phrase, Howe's work, especially in *Articulation* (in 1990b) and *Pythagorean Silence* (in 1990a) is full of a recognizably beautiful vowel-consonant music: "Throned wrath / I know your worth"; "sorrows are sectors / with actors"; "Sign of sound / sibilant wind // Scanned chronicles clasp edges" (1990a, 27, 29; 1990b, 29). But there is an exhilarating range to Howe's lyricism that goes well beyond the more conventional beauty of mere intensification of the words' music and imagery. In Howe's poetry there are several noteworthy lyricisms: a lyricism of "disturbance" (of syntax and the layout of the page), that concentrates attention on the individual word, or even the syllables or letters in a word, as well as the word's placement on the page; a lyricism of statement in which the "philosophical" or didactic also sings; and a lyricism of historical fact, acting as an image or epiphanic vortex, often intensified by its opposition to accepted or normative historical accounts.

Thus Howe writes a dialectical or oppositional lyricism. Typical of her writing is a page laid out with lines on top of each other, lines overlapping, words partially erased, phrases and fragments going off in many different vectors and directions:

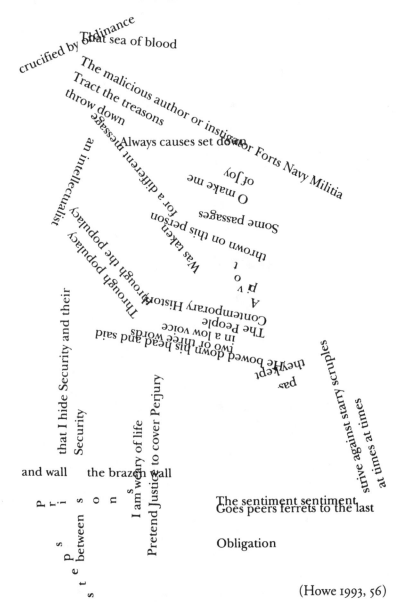

(Howe 1993, 56)

As opposed to a more traditional lyricism, Howe's acts of intensification do not have the function of summing up or swallowing up the text's other directions of exploration. This resistance to unification is also why it is dishonest criticism of her work to cite coherent pithy passages from the poems as if the experience of the poem crystallized with some finality in such remarks. One overall project of her poems, in fact, is to make such reduction impossible (1993 repr. of 1989, 56). Howe's poetry follows in the spirit of John Cage in the specific sense that he seeks "to find a way of writing which comes from ideas, is not about them, but which produces them" (Cage 1983, x).

But Howe's most fragmented writing is not a random expression of a malfunctioning word processor conspiring with a virally infected computer printer. Nor is it, as is often suggested by the unsympathetic or the simplistic, a (naive) celebration and imitation of the alleged fragmentation of contemporary existence (ugh). If, as Howe suggests, there is not a recoverable original, what we have then is a field out of which some de-limited forms of expression get extracted. Howe's work suggests a more radicalized and less demotic version of John Ashbery's (1976) notion (in "Grand Galop") of poetry as palimpsest—where poets "add to the already all-but-illegible scrub forest of graffiti on the shithouse wall" (18). For Howe's Charles I text, that palimpsest includes the *Eikon*, Charles's own Shakespearean posturing, Almack's explanatory decipherings, and Howe's own current responses.

Howe's work represents a revisualization of notions of field-composition. As with similar writings by Olson, Williams, and Duncan, or more recent work by Tina Darragh, Howe expands the notion of field to a composition with the *page* as unit of composition, not a line or a syllable-count or a sentence. We are, then, in the realm of Freud's mystic writing pad, Olson's charged energy field, the palimpsest, and the twentieth-century painter's use of the canvas as a site for deploying not recognizable representations but as a site (in this case a page) for new things. Not original but new things. It is yet one more strategy, growing out of but re-thinking the work of Stein, for rematerializing written expression.

Such writing bears a kinship both to other avant-garde poetic practices and to certain folk forms of expression: the textual equivalent of talking in tongues, similar to the mystical script paintings of Georgia folk artist J. B. Murry, or the realm of clairvoyance in the multiple text-poems of Hannah Weiner's Journals. Such overwriting runs throughout Howe's work and appears in all three of the books here under consideration.

A strength of Howe's writing, though, is that it is *not* an avant-gardism or aestheticism severed from history. Precisely the opposite: Howe's poetry in particular, with its anxious spiritual tracking, constitutes a contemporary version of the Puritan journal. This historical dimension of Howe's poetic thinking marks her poetry (which is of a piece with her prose scholarship, including her superb essays and books on Emily Dickinson, Herman Melville, Mary Rowlandson, and others) as among the most adventurous and accomplished of our present time.

The nature of the relationship of Howe's poetry to history is complex and polyvalent. As my earlier mentioning of her father's interest in Puritan writings and Howe's own upbringing in a circle of family friends that included Perry Miller and F. O. Matthiessen might suggest, there is at once an (often ignored) personal autobiographical element to her revisionist historiography. Too often critics of contemporary experimental writing take too literally the notion of an exploded or dispersed subject. As Howe's work amply illustrates, the death of the author and the death of the personal "I" in poetry are, at best, extremes toward which such writing moves asymptotically; that is, such concepts represent limits toward which the poetry moves, but the poetry also moves in opposition and self-contradiction. Howe's New Historicism radically departs from earlier conceptions (such as the poems of Richard Howard) of historicized poetry, which were based on a kind of voice-mimesis. Howe's poems are not dramatic monologues; indeed, they are not principally based on "voice" as the key feature of poetic expression. Instead, her poems represent a putting into play of the recoverable linguistic elements of a historical expression/situation.

Howe seeks out and inhabits a linguistic frontier on the verge of disorder; at that frontier she begins to remake and renew that order. As such, her poetry allies itself with skeptical, textually innovative feminist writing (such as the community of writers associated with *HOW(ever)*, especially Rachel Blau DuPlessis). While there are collagist elements in Howe's compositional practice, she is formally more adventurous than either Ezra Pound or T. S. Eliot; unlike these predecessors, she does not cling to a hope of essentializing or unifying the fragments she makes and collects.

The chief insistence, then, of Howe's poetry is exploration, as in the brilliant poem *Articulation of Sound Forms in Time*, which, among other things, retells the story of Hope Atherton, a minister who wandered among the Indians immediately after the Falls Fight of May 1676. He, and

Howe's poem, each submit to the "danger of roaming the woods at random" (1990b, 12) Textually, we enter into his break-up in passages such as

> rest chondriacal lunacy
> velc cello viable toil

and

> Posit gaze level diminish lamp and asleep(selv)cannot see

> *is* notion most open apparition past Halo view border redden
> possess remote so abstract life are lost spatio-temporal hum

If this be "antecedent terror stretched to a whisper (17)" (1990b, 14), Howe's task is not to thematize or summarize it, but to enact it textually, so that we are "slipping from known to utmost bound" (1990b, 19).

Howe understands the peril of such exploration: "Migratory path to massacre / Sharpshooters in history's apple dark" (1990b, 22). As a scout and (re)writer, she remains skeptical of her own role as poet-historian, wondering if "I am // Part of their encroachment" (47) and if her own writing is "Collision or collusion with history" (33). As a poet committed to exploring the sociohistorical context of signs, Howe's avant-gardism remains insistently and consciously embedded in history and ideology (particularly foundational American stories); but she proceeds with a rigorous self-consciousness of the medium of language and of her own potential acts of complicity.

Often contemporary avant-garde poets are viewed as creatures of theory, as if their work responded to or grew out of *a* theoretical encounter. (See, for example, the inane reductive reading of Carla Harryman's *Vice* in Lehman 1991, where he dismisses her work as merely repeating Derridean premises.) While it is true that Howe's own poetry, which is continuous with the restless intelligence of her critical prose writing, is informed by New Historicism, particularly the writings of Stephen Greenblatt, Mitch Breitweiser, and Michael Paul Rogin, as well as much earlier works such as Charles Olson's *Call Me Ishmael* (1947, repr. 1967) and William Carlos Williams's *In the American Grain* (1925), her relationship to this body of work remains skeptical. Her prose writings, for example, can be seen in part as feminist correctives to the masculinist biases of Olson and Williams. It would be more accurate to describe her thinking as simultaneous with New Historicism, as sharing with it a project of revision. The model that Lehman and others work out of seems to be a picture of a poet who reads a work of theory and then says, "aha; I'll write poetry like that." It just ain't so. Because the contemporary avant-garde has resisted the dominant form of contemporary professional conduct of the (academic) creative writing careerists (that is, the voice-based, intuitive, lyrical, crafted personal poem, severed from theory and other forms of intellect) contemporary experimental poetry often has an intellectual depth and rigor absent from mainstream poetry. Howe's poetry, among others, makes Clayton Eshleman's (1985) question quite reasonable: "when will critics like Harold Bloom and Helen Vendler start writing on poetry that knows more than they do?" (155).

As *Articulation of Sound Forms in Time* (in 1990b) indicates, rather than locating such fragmented writing within a French tradition of critical discourse—Derrida's *écriture*, Barthes's writerly text, or more likely Kristeva's *chora* (each of which, it seems to me, runs the danger of a restricted notion of revolution in poetry which, mistakenly, seems to culminate with Mallarmé)—Howe's poetic exploration belongs more properly to an American literary tradition of frontier writing, that frontier being understood as both a physical and textual place. She weds a contemporary linguistic frontier to the wilderness of early Puritan writings.

The peculiar accomplishment of Howe's writing is that while the marks of skepticism and intelligence are everywhere in Howe's poetry—"I pick my compass to pieces // Dark here in the driftings / in the spaces of drifting // complicity battles redemption" (1990b, 55)—her work equally retains and makes anew an exuberant spirituality:

> Mind itself or life
>
> quicker than thought
>
> slipping back to primordial
>
> We go through the word Forest
>
> Trance of an encampment
>
> not a foot of land cleared
>
> The literature of savagism
>
> under a spell of savagism

Nature isolates the Adirondacks

In the machinery of injustice

my whole being is Vision
(1990b, 49)

6. Partial to Error

Joan Retallack's *Errata ʃuite*

I came across Retallack's *Errata ʃuite* (1993) under interesting circumstances. I was in Los Angeles in October 1993 to give a salon reading at Sun and Moon Press, and had the chance to visit John Cage's installation "Rolywholyover A Circus" at the Museum of Contemporary Art. The first room of the exhibition consisted of a long table set up for browsing and for playing chess, surrounded by two large cabinets of books and papers (some of which would be changed every day). At first I smiled knowingly and thought that the two people sitting down playing chess were part of the installation, but as we spoke to one another I realized that they were no more installed than I was. I felt as if I had arrived at John Cage's house only to find a note: "I've gone to the country. Make yourself at home. Feel free to browse." The book-browsing was a delight. One of the first books I found was Retallack's *Errata ʃuite*, which apparently had just been published. Then, during my stay in L.A., the poet/editor/critic A. L. Nielsen, with whom I was taping a radio show for KSJS, gave me a copy of Retallack's earlier book, *Circumstantial Evidence* (1985). So, circumstantially, or by chance, my trip to L.A. became a way to realize that Retallack's poetry has now begun to gather in significance, strength, force, and importance. (Such has already been known of her critical intelligence for some time now.)

At once philosophical and playful, intelligent and error-prone, Joan Retallack's *Errata ʃuite* is a remarkable production. Bringing together the errata slip with the five lines of the musical staff, Retallack constructs a space for thinking. Such a space bears kinship to the stanza; that is, it makes a room for thinking. It also asks us to rethink fundamental questions: Poetry is a space *for what?* From the cover art (also by Retallack) to the title (written on a five-line staff) to the series of five-line pages, Retallack's is a book that exhibits proudly an awareness of its own constructedness. As one of Cage's favorites, Thoreau, wrote in *Walden*, "shall we forever resign the pleasure of construction to the carpenter?" In terms of Kandinsky's division of modern art into two polarities—expressionist and constructionist—Retallack's work positions itself decisively in the latter camp. Such a commitment marks a considerable shift in her poetry from the earlier work represented in *Circumstantial Evidence* (1985).

Let me present a sample of a typical page in Retallack's book:

> read for for four last line misting eart aron (of) spoken rhythms untitled
> add a pronoun what it is/has agitated to a strange and not (for) tensor
> analytic reads as reads as follows crossing the ford where Emerson saw the
> sky glad to the brink of fear ybore dislodg-èd enso semiamazia o tics of
> zero sum ergo blather to rush to race to wander
>
> (4)

If poetry, as a heuristic mode of thinking, allows chance, errors, and stammers to figure into its arsenal of what even a compulsively eloquent poet such as Wallace Stevens would call "sudden rightnesses," then the reader of such poetry must learn to inhabit a reading-space that is less rigidly thematized, less linearly insistent than the poetry of most earlier moderns, including Stevens. If there is a recurring "about" in Retallack's book, it is "about" processes of reading—as in the errata slip, recurrently a reading by replacement, "for *x* read *y*" (but also more philosophically, "why read?").

In miniature, the passage I have reproduced from Retallack's book enacts many of the possibilities under investigation in *Errata suite*. It is the reader, in the rushes and stays of path-making, who enacts these possibilities. If we attend to our own processes in sense-making, and in delight at the disturbance of habitual forms of sense-making, our own phenomenology of reading becomes itself a heuristic device. Oddly, there is an authoritative tone to the errata slip; we are ordered into certain directions of reading and substitution. But the reproduction of the errors themselves introduces a humor opposite (or is it apposite) to the command voice of correction. So that, as in the carefully multiple manuscript-poems of Emily Dickinson, the poems and the passages do not stabilize into their singularly corrected print but remain in their multiply noted directions. Retallack's errata suites equivocate: both the "error" and the "correction" are given voice (or, more accurately, space within which to be printed, and recognized). Within such a field of multiplicity, what Marjorie Perloff in an earlier phase of her scholarship might have called a hymn to possibility, one such hymn, but now in a new context, is that old tune of lyrical epiphany, a pleasing trace that haunts much experimental writing, from John Cage's to Susan Howe's. In Retallack's passage, it is the Emersonian moment of the transparent eyeball, glad to the brink of fear, a moment that (by its familiarity) emerges from the welter of Retallack's dense textuality as a kind of comforting narrative release. Emerson, however, retreats suddenly from the moment of insight and self-obliteration, back into the conventions of the forward-moving essay. Retallack's own writing, on the other hand, is not premised on self-expression but is (like Cage's) already built on self-erasure. Paradoxically, Retallack's fractured language allows her/us to enter more substantially and decisively into the realm of Emerson's ecstatic experience and to *dwell* there by means of a language *not* tied to syntactical and semantic correctness. We cross the ford into "ybore dislodg-èd enso semiamazia o tics of / zero sum ergo blather to rush to race to wander." In a sense, Retallack plays Emerson against himself. His own attention to the magical, philosophical properties of the individual word —which Emerson finds to be a fossil holding the traces of certain fundamental truths that we, as inspired readers (and philologists), can decode— now is employed with the attention to the individual word that we'd find in Stein (of *Tender Buttons* or the "Portraits"). If the word does have the resources that Emerson claims for it, then much of twentieth-century experimental writing has been a literalizing and an exploring of those potentials. To put it politically, such poetry reclaims the rights of the signifier. But those rights are *not* claimed on behalf of the word as a vessel of truth but on behalf of the word itself (freed of any preconceived obligation to a "higher" truth other than the possibilities of its own particular being).

Many of the finest sections of *Errata ʃuite* (1993) are built from the writings of others. Similar to Cage's process of writing through others, Retallack's compositions are more a mode of radicalized anthologizing. That is, she exercises more choice in her selections and builds from them more willfully. Here is one such example:

art is a mode of prediction not found in charts & statistics (D1) poetry and religious feeling will be the unforced flowers of life (D1) practical socialism consists rather in a correct knowledge of the capitalist (E1) for the sceptics the ideal was to be optimistic (F1) the methodological preeminence that thus belongs to poetry (G1)

D1-Dewey/E1-Engels/F1-Foucault/G1-Gadamer

(31)

But what *is* "the methodological preeminence that thus belongs to poetry"? Perhaps as David Antin argued in essays and interviews in the early 1970s, the foundational activity for modernist writing is collage. Perhaps, as in some of Retallack's work, that methodological preeminence comes from and illuminates the acts of reading and recomposing: reading as a means to writing (and writing as a means to reading).

I know that for readers already somewhat attuned to postmodernist premises it is not necessary to ask that typically conservative, xenophobic question, But is it really poetry? Nevertheless, in relation to Retallack's work in *Errata 5uite*, I find it profitable to engage some of those square questions again. For example, what do we gain by calling it "poetry"? I think that the term improves our chances of hearing certain kinds of musical relationships among the sounds of the words (as in Retallack's "courage to err and Guess that Mess for read thru authors deranged / chronologies foretasta alphabeta foreven were earth's inner discontent / assuaged" [36]). And the term "poetry" seems like a fit occasion for a perhaps vanishing mode of attentive reading, a sort of hyperalertness. In his provocative and seminal book, *Word Perfect: Literacy in the Computer Age* (1992), Myron Tuman (by way of George Steiner) describes the changing scene of reading:

> "To much of the planet," writes George Steiner in the essay, "The End of Bookishness" (1988), "what I have called the classical act of reading, the private ownership of space, of silence, and of books themselves, never represented a natural or native formula." For Steiner, changes in our use of space and silence, brought on by changes in electronic technology, all spell the end of a certain book culture, except perhaps as an object of nostalgic yearning. Gone, for example, is the "circle of silence which enables the reader to concentrate on the text." And for this Steiner is not entirely sad, for he sees that we have already lost most of the appreciation for the wondrous things contained in books. Book culture, he speculates, may exist in the future as it once existed in a more distant past, as the expression of a coterie, in what he calls "*houses of*

reading—a Hebrew phrase—in which those passionate to learn how to read well would find the necessary guidance, silence, and complicity of disciplined companionship." (10–11)

But the entire argument about the end of book culture, and its replacement by a culture of digitalization and the video display terminal, often is staged within a very limited conception of the reading processes possible *within* a book culture. Many of the most productive transgressive reading/writing deeds within the book culture have occurred within the poetry texts of the past one hundred (post-Mallarmé) years. And Retallack's own *Errata ʃuite*, in its celebration of "error" as a means to renewed, defamiliarized expression and in its playfully intelligent collagist fusing of multiple texts, creates a hyperspace *within* the domain of book culture. What is so remarkable about Retallack's book is that the presumably nostalgic gesture of constructing a mode of writing out of contact with the bookish, scholarly errata slip leads into a fractured, playful space of intelligent, speculative thinking. (I am also struck by the irony of my proofreading my own essay; Retallack's work makes me feel funny as I try to get her cited errors "right.")

Retallack's world of playful substitutions, of crazed phrasing and conflicting semantic intersection, stands in opposition to an expressionist (and distinctly Emersonian) dream of reading as a transcendental moment of pure correspondence. The latter—a romantic myth of reading—is best represented in Wallace Stevens' poem "The House Was Quiet and the World Was Calm":

> The house was quiet and the world was calm.
> The reader became the book; and summer night
>
> Was like the conscious being of the book.
> The house was quiet and the world was calm.
>
> The words were spoken as if there was no book,
> Except that the reader leaned above the page,
>
> Wanted to lean, wanted much most to be
> The scholar to whom his book is true, to whom
>
> The summer night is like a perfection of thought.
> The house was quiet because it had to be.
>
> The quiet was part of the meaning, part of the mind:
> The access of perfection to the page.

And the world was calm. The truth in a calm world,
In which there is no other meaning, itself

Is calm, itself is summer and night, itself
Is the reader leaning late and reading there.

(1947/1954; repr. 1982, 358–59)

Stevens's dream is of a world (via reading) of pure correspondence, of such correspondence (presumably of the reader's consciousness with the external world) as constituting an ultimate truthfulness. Retallack's "truthfulness" or fidelity is to a world of much greater contingency—a world of expressive error. Or, in Charles Bernstein's terminology, a world of dysraphism—the stitching together of mismatched parts (to produce a new form of rhapsody). Thus, Retallack composes in what Stein calls the time when the work still is taken to be ungainly and "ugly," a time in which many contemporaries fail to realize that a (truly contemporary) work is still beautiful even when and while it is jarring and odd. In fact, more generally, I would argue that our relationship to eccentric texts enacts a more generalizeable political/social relationship to "otherness."

But to return more directly to the specific excellence of Retallack's work: her poetry is one of intersecting musics, where the rhetoric and phrasing of good old Robert Frost meets a critique of mainstream contemporary poetry's twin dullnesses—predictable scenic writing and predictably sincere expression:

> read ignomine domine flushed with sincerity's ergo sooner or later along
> the horizon o creaking smiles to go to sleep to rest is history read for an
> age not so much wrong as abstracht and preliminary the coastal scenic
> drive to scenic points with almost all left out to know to read the blind
> reed urgent moist and smooth fore rough & civil

(38)

As I read it, the scenic and the sincere profit immensely from erasure, interruption, and discontinuity—else we read only a boring correctness, "o creaking smiles to go to sleep." And as I reread Retallack's book, I found a passage from Pascal's *Pensées*—a passage I was forced to memorize over twenty years ago—bubbling up into impertinent pertinence. Pascal claims, "L'homme n'est qu'un roseau, le plus faible de la nature; mais c'est un roseau pensant." Retallack's passage, and her recurrent juxtaposition of "read" and "reed," makes me think again of Pascal's version of man as "a thinking reed." Retallack's work too offers a thoughtful read, verdant reed/read as, eyes close to the page, we learn "to know to read the blind reed urgent moist and smooth fore rough & civil."

Retallack's *Errata suite* provides us with a reading experience of choices. I begin to hear in my head these kinds of transformations: "the road not taken" becoming "he rode not talkin" becoming "the road knot talking." But my form of wordplay differs from Retallack's. *Errata suite* celebrates the play of printed exchanges (whereas my passage, and much of my own writing, indulges in puns and other oral/aural forms of replacement). In Retallack's invigorating stew of playful and sustaining print, we find

> to read read real denied being there at all that is to cause to follow these
> the choices that make us defacto human bacchae melanesia cafeteria ergot
> cert to be included a error for mirror interroregnum regulaterrrata p. 8
> forementioned bag-O-bugs the gardeners friends late evenings
> inadverdant soar remarks to others to mak ammendes

(48)

We see the Pleiades better by looking slightly away from them; in Retallack's book we read, not exactly in Emily Dickinson's truth told slant, but askew; as in the erotic play of Stein's tender buttons, we touch around and slightly off. And with each particular reading—"inadverdant soar remarks"—we, greenly, make amends, pass amendments, read through various emendations "to follow these/ the choices."

As the last fragment of Retallack's composition (from Wittgenstein's *Remarks on Color*) asserts and/or asks: "phenomena of seeing.—For whom does it describe them? *What* ignorance can this description eliminate (W2)." Hers is an infectious world of textual play. It does not eliminate ignorance; instead, she compounds error, and thus earns interest on the original casual investment. Divested of the anxiety of correctness, her suite-music (read: sweet music) tolls for the (read thee). It is, then, a phenomenon of seeing we would do well to listen too.

7. "To make equality less drab"

The Writing of Bruce Andrews

I am puzzled by the fact that Bruce Andrews's poetry is not better known. Perhaps I too have contributed to a pervasive academic practice of tokenizing and domesticating innovative writing. The term Language Writing may at one time have allowed (in Ron Silliman's words in *Paradise*) for increased market penetration. But the term now also masks the considerable variety of writing practices that fall under that label as well as the fact that a few writers, presented as the worthy examples, receive nearly all of the critical attention: Charles Bernstein, Ron Silliman, Lyn Hejinian, and Susan Howe. The amount of attention accorded Bernstein's writing compared to that given to Andrews's writing, when Andrews was in fact the co-editor for the journal $L=A=N=G=U=A=G=E$, is doubly puzzling. In a remark applicable as well to processes of engaging the present, Cary Nelson (1989) reminds us, "Custodians, of course, concern themselves not only with conserving the past but also with selectively disposing of much of it, though the two impulses become deceptively conflated in the imagination of academic disciplines—so that a self-congratulatory process of conservation remains primarily in view" (4).

Tokenizing provides one explanation for a lack of critical attention to Andrews's work; the particular difficulties of Andrews's writing provides another. Deleuze and Guattari (1983) contend, "Interpretation is our modern way of believing and of being pious" (171). Andrews's work denies us professionalized piety and comfort. Andrews's poetry presents a per-

sistent intensity of resistance. It deserves consideration as an instance of
what Foucault calls (in his preface to Deleuze and Guattari 1983) the
"art of living counter to all forms of fascism," an art Foucault sees as
freeing "political action from all unitary and totalizing paranoia" and preferring "what is positive and multiple, difference over uniformity, flows
over unities, mobile arrangements over systems" (xiii). If we look at a passage from "Praxis," one of Andrews's earlier poems, we begin to see what
Andrews's nomadic, multiple poetry can do:

> many read fine
>
> many so that do not
>
> the tissue of contradiction is pictured
> as a criss-cross
>
> she inadvertently omits
> on a windmill
>
> actually two-thirds
>
> shows the sum was nothing extraordinary
>
> though the saying
>
> with everything in their favor
>
> expected once again
>
> as prey
>
> which exactly describes the habits of a weasel
>
> withdrawn
>
> there
>
> for government
>
> does not refer to music
>
> of bees
>
> I think the little kingdom
>
> so that there should be continual stimulus
>
> to effort

the end of all being
obedience

(1988, 42–43)

First, Andrews's writing is not "pretty." Descriptions such as "flows over unities" and "mobile arrangments over systems," when applied to a literary context, are susceptible to a neutralizing aestheticism. For example, I can imagine the same phrases being used to describe the following passage of poetry, written roughly at the same time as Andrews's "Praxis":

> That time faded too and the night
> Softened to smooth spirals or foliage at night.
> There were sleeping cabins near by, blind lanterns,
> Nocturnal friendliness of the plate of milk left for the fairies
> Who otherwise might be less well disposed:
> Friendship of white sheets patched with milk.
> And always an open darkness in which one name
> Cries over and over again: Ariane! Ariane!

(Ashbery 1976, 33)

This second example, from John Ashbery's "Hop o' My Thumb," might also be described as full of flows and mobile arrangements, but Ashbery's are more readily identified as familiar "literary" flows. His tone and rhetoric are "high": soothing, mannered, decorous, "accomplished," and, above all, "literary." He has mastered (and remixed) a late nineteenth-century tone of wistful lament. These are the kinds of flows about which Helen Vendler (1988) can write confidently: "It is our wish to isolate the line as touchstone which makes us at first find Ashbery baffling; once we stop looking for self-contained units we begin to feel better about our responses, and soon find a drift here, a meander there that feels, if not like our beloved stanzas or aphorisms, at least like a pause in the rapids" (233).

An aestheticized version of "flow" depends on an implicitly soothing pastoralism—a poeticized canoe ride, a readerly meandering over accomplished if shifting tones of literary address. We are dazzled by the "accomplished" if varied surface that such a poet has crafted. But Andrews's flow is more in keeping with the nomadism of Deleuze and Guattari (1983), who claim that Andrews's writing is a form of "desiring-production [which] is pure multiplicity, that is to say, an affirmation that is irreducible to any sort of unity" (42). In more recent work, in "Swaps Ego," Andrews (1987a) writes:

Authors Dear Mom Logic Can Missile Crisis Ellipse
Impeccable Showed Nothing Authority Rock 'N Roll Our
        Physical Glottis
Determine Signal Peppy Ever
Be Platters Tighter Lucky
                Semivowels My Wazzoo Architectural
Tee Gee Institutional Populations
Complex Deep Structured Coffee Indeed What A Shrub
Found Here And Now Heat Pit
Words Diplomatic Fate Rubs Another Tune
        Flight Small
Zap Man Say Barb Coint

                                                (114)

Deleuze and Guattari (1983) begin to equate such literature (of a disruptive, innovative mode) with desire: "That is what style is, or rather the absence of style—asyntactic, agrammatical: the moment when language is no longer defined by what it says, even less by what makes it a signifying thing, but by what causes it to move, to flow, and to explode—desire. For literature is like schizophrenia: a process and not a goal, a production and not an expression" (133). But Deleuze and Guattari are only moderately helpful in providing a vocabulary and an orientation for theorizing Andrews's writing. The match is not exact. As seen in the passage from "Swaps Ego," Andrews does not give up or evade the social structuring and social acts of signification and meaning-making, certainly not to the extent that Deleuze and Guattari idealize as a kind of purified or completely resistant writing. As other sections of *Anti-Oedipus* reveal, Deleuze and Guattari (1983) heroize, in the figure of the schizo, a purified and purifying alterity that verges on an apolitical transcendence of the political by means of a kind of psychosis: "As if the great voices, which were capable of performing a break-through in grammar and syntax, and of making all language a desire, were not speaking from the depths of psychosis, and as if they were not demonstrating for our benefit an eminently psychotic and revolutionary means of escape" (134). We should bear in mind that Andrews (1990), on the other hand, is self-consciously wary of "ontologizing the arbitrary" (104).

    Deleuze and Guattari (1983) *are* quite helpful in theorizing a writer who is able "to disengage himself from familialism" (95). Especially when compared with the hegemonic American poetries of the 1960s, 1970s, and 1980s, Andrews's writing—even more so than the work of Bernstein, Hejinian, and Susan Howe—is remarkably disengaged from familialism. This disengagement may be yet another reason why his poetry is so difficult to assimilate into more conventional conversations and interpretations of contemporary poetry. Like Ron Silliman and a number of other contemporary innovative writers, Andrews has developed a writing that is "productive rather than expressive" (Deleuze and Guattari 1983, 110). As critical vocabularies develop that apply terms such as flow, discontinuity, and dispersed subjectivity to a range of (often relatively conventional) contemporary poetries, we might do well to heed Deleuze and Guattari's (1983) question: "Isn't the destiny of American literature that of crossing limits and frontiers, causing deterritorialized flows of desire to circulate, but also always making these flows transport fascisizing, moralizing, Puritan, and familialist territorialities?" (277–78). Such a question, when paired for example with Susan Howe's brilliantly empathic investigations into early American captivity narratives, makes most mainstream critical activity merely a redundant act of containment and totalization.

The difficulties of Andrews's poetry offer us a realm for productive thinking. Even as I acknowledge Stein's writing about processes of assimilating experimental writing, I find her narrative to be riddled with romanticizing and sentimentalizing. (Of course, much of her own work has resisted assimilation; *Tender Buttons*, for example, in spite of countless recent critical interpretations, remains resistant to easy thematized reading.) Some acts of defamiliarization remain unfamiliar for extended periods of time. I predict that that will be the case for much of Andrews's poetry: instead of "news that stays news," something more like "difficulties that remain difficulties." That time perspective—of decreasing levels of difficulty and defamiliarization—is an interesting and often ignored feature of the avant-garde. Some difficult writing, such as Ashbery's or Eliot's or Pound's, under the onslaught of domesticating, totalizing, and/or explanatory critical writing, ceases to be difficult, ceases to be upsetting. Some writing, and in differing ways of difficulty, persists in its difficulty and remains productively recalcitrant to assimilative and mastering reading practices. Andrews's best poetry pushes this process of unassimilability. In part, he is able to do so because his writing springs, to a significant degree, from sources and motivations outside professionalized literary/poetic training and decorum (1987b, 1–2).

In the course of "Praxis," one of Andrews's (1988) earlier poems, I find the phrase "as idle spectators" (55), and I begin to wonder about the possibilities for a reader's activity in relation to Andrews's poetry. Jackson Mac Low has suggested that we think in terms of reader-centered writing, and much has been made (so much so that the concept itself verges on the platitudinous) of such writing as seeking out a collaborative relationship between reader and writer in the production of meaning. I agree with Volosinov's (1986) argument that "a generative process can be grasped only with the aid of another generative process" and that "therefore, there is no reason for saying that meaning belongs to a word as such. In essence, meaning belongs to a word in its position between speakers; that is, meaning is realized only in the process of active, responsive understanding" (102). But the utopianism of a description of reading-as-collaboration evades the fact that the writer, even in a chance-determined process of text-generation, has chosen the (always finite) materials that the reader will collaborate with. I cite from "Praxis" a somewhat typical passage:

> turrets
> but does not use the words
> by two consecutive lines
> strung, glass
> for the outward
> omits
> yet everything else will be forgotten
> how much do we
> late events do not obliterate the former
> am not surprised, am surprised
> isolate it significantly
> made a great show
> but cannot
> it is still with us

(1988, 56)

Volosinov (in 1929) writes about the ways in which "the physical object is converted into a sign. Without ceasing to be a part of material reality, such an object, to some degree, reflects and refracts another reality" (1986, 9). Andrews's poetry often takes place precisely at this moment of transition from thing to sign:

> eye sophist
>
> / tools

                    & misc. explosions everything
                        skin before

                                sleep of
                            thought
            that means like I wanna get a portable flame thrower
                                    conniption
                    without coquettish

                black spiders of such government
                                            (1987a, 84)

While there are moments in Andrews's poetry that tempt a reader into
totalizing summaries, such acts of extraction run counter to both the
poem itself and experiences of reading the poem. If we were to "isolate
it significantly," we would also realize that such isolations are strictly our
own attempts to make one kind of sense out of a text that moves in many
more directions. Andrews's poetry attunes itself to what Coward and Ellis
(1977) see as a chief characteristic that demarcates Marxism from idealist
philosophy: "the primacy of contradiction" (86). The disconcerting nature
of Andrews's poetry, its resistance to our unthinking pieties of "natural"
interpretation (which stem from a literary tradition that Andrews himself
did not absorb as a primary given), is in keeping with a fundamental observation made by Marcuse (1978): that "it is not the business of art to
portray the world as the possible object of domination" (36).

But Marcuse's (1978) notion that "literature can be called revolutionary
in a meaningful sense only with reference to itself, as content having become form" (xii), is in fact reversible. That is, in a great deal of the most
interesting poetry of our own era, form becomes content, enacting in our
relationship to the text a revolutionary politics. In "Plex," Andrews (1988)
presents us with a barrage of codes and partial codes:

                    b. c. back blue does incites
                        narrate daughter ideaed universe
                alm dire tenting crystal go biography
                        whicker whim pape coalesce
                    blue of lube stooge senators

                six of alkaline redeem
                        not physical violet triumph toyed
                    weepless suturee disbelieved cargo

unrevealing veered potassic welter weakness
warmed so fief — largest passive

(109)

Coward and Ellis (1977) cite a passage from Kristeva's "L'Anarchie sociale de l'art," where Kristeva suggests that we often overlook "what it is in the poetical process which falls outside the realm of the signified and the transcendental ego and makes what we call 'literature' something other than a 'knowledge'; in other words making it, 'the very place where the social code is destroyed and renewed' " (148). Coward and Ellis (1977) conclude that Kristeva's "analysis demonstrates that in poetical language and therefore, in varying degrees, in all languages, there is something which is heterogeneous to sense and signification" (148). Andrews's writing calls into question the automaticity of signification and enacts revolutionary and utopian potentials of the heterogeneous. His writing may well be out of control; that is, resistant to the kinds of controls suggested in lines such as "American History Dubbed In Dicatation Dictation Dicatation" and "Accidents Culmination Drift Toward Articulation Minister" (1987a, 91, 92). Andrews is involved in a (hopeful) social praxis, akin to the affirmations made by Raymond Williams (1977) at the end of *Marxism and Literature*:

> Writing is often a new articulation and in effect a new formation, extending beyond its own modes. But to separate this as art, which in practice includes, always partly and sometimes wholly, elements elsewhere in the continuum, is to lose contact with the substantive creative process and then to idealize it; to put it above or below the social, when it is in fact the social in one of its most distinctive, durable, and total forms.
>
> Creative practice is thus of many kinds. It is already, and actively, our practical consciousness. When it becomes struggle — the active struggle for new consciousness through new relationships that is the ineradicable emphasis of the Marxist sense of self-creation — it can take many forms. (211–12)

One of those forms, broadly conceived, may be what Andrews means by the enticing phrase "widened idealism" (1988, 76).

In addition to his eschewal of familialism and his writing of a poetry that does not come from within the domains of the professionally institutionalized "literary," Andrews's writing constitutes an important investigation of the understanding that the individual herself is a socioideological construction. As Volosinov (1986) argues:

> The individual, as possessor of the contents of his own consciousness, as author of his own thoughts, as the personality responsible for his thoughts and feelings, —such an individual is a purely socioideological phenomenon. Therefore, the content of the "individual" psyche is by its very nature just as social as is ideology, and the very degree of consciousness of one's individuality and its inner rights and privileges is ideological, historical, and wholly conditioned by sociological factors. (34)

Or, as Andrews (1991) asks, "Does the text's *address* need to be built on a rhetoric of authorship?" (6). Andrews's author is a subject whose individuality is thoroughly embedded in productive activity. It is "a subject who is produced in this movement of productivity. Man is constructed in the symbol, and is not pre-given or transcendent" (Coward and Ellis 1977, 23). As Volosinov (1986) points out,

> Signs can arise only on *interindividual territory*. It is territory that cannot be called "natural" in the direct sense of the word: signs do not arise between any two members of the species *Homo sapiens*. It is essential that the two individuals be *organized socially*, that they compose a group (a social unit); only then can the medium of signs take shape between them. The individual consciousness not only cannot be used to explain anything, but, on the contrary, is itself in need of explanation from the vantage point of the social, ideological medium. (12)

Volosinov (1986) is correct to underscore the "role of language as the specific material reality of ideological creativity" (xiv), but most Marxist literary critics are demonstrably unequipped to read contemporary innovative writing. Perhaps this is because most Marxist literary criticism, not unlike the more formally inclined theme-criticism, relies heavily on positivist and essentialist assumptions about content. In reading and rereading various Marxist critics as a kind of background or simultaneous reading with my reading of Andrews's poetry and essays, I have been struck again and again by the conservatism of most Marxist critics' reading habits in poetry. Consider Adorno's (1974) insistent turning to Goethe, or Marcuse's (1978) equally backward-looking glances to Goethe and Mallarmé, or the near absence of attention to poetry in Raymond Williams (1977), or Fredric Jameson's (1984) notoriously silly analysis of a Bob Perelman poem. It is not difficult to find Marxist critics whose theorizings about language and signification *are* helpful and generative for a reading of contemporary poetry. But it is almost impossible to find such critics who are also at home in the reading of innovative, and thus truly revolutionary or transgressive, contemporary writing. (Of course, the big exception to such a characterization comes from the writing of the poets themselves, particularly Steve McCaffery, Bruce Andrews, Charles Bernstein, Ron Silliman, Barrett Watten, Andy Levy, and a few writers known principally as critics such as Andrew Ross, Jerome McGann, and Cary Nelson.)

A section from "Getting Ready to Have Been Frightened" (1988) presents us with

onan

on

& on

(84)

whereby, as in work by Stein, or more recent writing by Melnick, Davies, Howe, Cole, Darragh, and others, the materiality of the word and the syllable predominate over any other more accumulative sense. In this particular instance, Andrews's sound and graphic play is underscored by a running section at the bottom of the page which enters into a fragmented explanatory realm: "Am I fitter sounds before word filtering Do filter something words before filtering mean?" (1988, 84). Such writing represents a tendency "in which literature becomes auto-analysis, an implicit research into the rules of its own construction, exposing its components and its laws. In opening onto this process of construction, and in fragmenting the unity of the subject, these texts are no longer instruments of communication, but signifying practices which show the subject understanding and organising the real" (Coward and Ellis 1977, 149). One of the disconcerting features of Andrews's poetry, if we expect poetry in some sense to be consoling, is that the subject, as discussed by Coward and Ellis, is not a transcendent figure who organizes and serves up to us, as reader/consumers, a form of textual productivity that tames or dominates the real. Volosinov (1986) explains: "Individual consciousness is not the architect of the ideological superstructure, but only a tenant lodging in the social edifice of ideological signs" (13).

But, as Andrews shows us, such tenancy need not be passive nor obedient. We might read a passage from "Plex" as both an instance of careful registry of recurrent sounds and as a socially active resistance:

countries laying down in our brain tissue
pretzel but really mints truly cathect
it's cholera — chameleon choreless
to yatters dote christ
chocolate shake tricked froze hymns
will off sentiment on one's laurels
wallet cake with refugees
to prefer semen to water
eloquence if you crush punctualism

(1988, 114)

A fit description of some of the premises enacted in such writing comes from Volosinov (1986): "Countless ideological threads running through all areas of social intercourse register effect in the word. It stands to reason, then, that the word is the most sensitive *index of social changes*, and what is more, of changes still in the process of growth, still without definitive shape and not as yet accommodated into already regularized and fully defined ideological systems" (19).

Within a literary climate in which poetry and lyricism are misunderstood as nearly synonymous, Adorno's (1974) remarks on lyric poetry bear attention. Adorno redefines the lyric as containing within itself an oppositional element, a rupture, a protest. But, crucially, he argues that "that resistance to social pressure is not something absolutely individual. Rather, through the individual and his spontaneity, objective historical forces rouse themselves within the poem, forces which are propelling a restricted and restricting social condition beyond itself to a more humane one" (61–62). Adorno's conception of language is doubled: "For language itself has a double aspect. Through its configurations it submits to all possible stirrings of emotion, failing in so little that one might almost think it is language which first produces feeling. On the other hand, language remains the medium of concepts and ideas, and establishes our indispensable relation to generalities and hence to social reality" (62). Adorno concludes that "the most sublime lyric works, therefore, are those in which the subject, without a trace of his material being, intones language until the voice of language itself is heard" (63). I bring up Adorno's version of pure poetry in relation to Andrews simply because of the peculiar and specific nature of Andrews's anti-individualist expression. (As an aside, it would be quite useful to consider Andrews's dissolution of individual expression in contrast to that of poets such as Cage and Mac Low whose self-erasure is accomplished through chance-driven procedures of composition. Paradoxically, their differences form the basis for a kind of personal signature, even for a poetry in which traditional bourgeois subjective expressiveness is banished.) Adorno (1974) grants that "Lyric poetry, therefore, shows itself most thoroughly integrated into society at those points where it does not repeat what society says—where it conveys no pronouncements—but rather where the speaking subject (who succeeds in his expression) comes to full accord with the language itself, i.e., with what language seeks by its own inner tendency" (62). But it seems to me that one of the chief purposes of Adorno's investigation of lyric poetry is to provide him an opportunity to critique Heidegger's mystical fusion of language, thinking, and Being: "On the other hand, language cannot be raised to the position of an absolute voice of existence, as some current ontological theories of linguistics would have it. . . . The moment of self-forgetting in which the subject submerges in language is not a sacrifice of himself to Being" (62).

Andrews's poetry presents an interesting case of a subject's dissolution in language. Andrews avoids the idealism (and, ultimately, sentimentality) of an imagined merging with Being (and such a conception's displaced theologism). Andrews's dissolution remains *into* the realm of the social, into the realm of language as social coding and social organization. Adorno wants both to critique Heidegger and to establish a more thoroughly social and materialist conception of language, especially language in poetry. But his conception of language is nowhere so thoroughly social and ideological as Volosinov's. And so Adorno (1974) can conclude,

> In order that the subject may truly resist the lonely process of reification he may not even attempt anymore to retreat to himself—to his private property. He is frightened by the traces of an individualism which has meanwhile sold itself to the literary supplements of the marketplace. The poet must, rather, by denying himself, step out of himself. He must, so to speak, make of himself a vessel for the ideal of a pure language. (70)

But for Andrews "pure language" is not an ideal. There is no language beyond or outside of social organization and ideology. Poetry may, though, provide an opportunity for an oppositional praxis (however "impure" and socially implicated). A key premise for Andrews (1989) is that there is an analogous relationship between language and society both in terms of explanation (of how those things are understood) and also in terms of praxis and prescriptions deriving from that explanation.

First, in terms of explanation, the link is between conceptualizing the nature of the social order and how it's organized and trying to conceptualize the nature of the material of writing. (53)

That is, Andrews (1990) works out of "a conception of writing *as* politics, not writing *about* politics" (24). But his writing *as* politics depends upon certain crucial disruptions, perhaps the most important of which is an effort to "define comprehension as something other than consumption" (1990, 28). Such an exploration seems to me to be at the intersection of many of the most intensely productive strains of current reading, theorizing, and writing in the broadly reconceived domain of poetry. To interrupt comprehension-as-consumption, Andrews suggests that "what is called for is writing as a *counter*-reading—that is, as counter-socialization" (1990, 32), a premise that again speaks to the difficulty and disconcerting nature of Andrews's poetry. (As an aside, I would add that there is very little poetry that is truly disconcerting. Much of Andrews's is.)

In its oppositional function, there is, in poetry, an element of indictment. But, as Marcuse (1978) notes, "The indictment does not exhaust itself in the recognition of evil; art is also the promise of liberation" (46). Though some of Andrews's writing *does* seem to me to exhaust itself in the process of indictment, there is a kind of "widened idealism" implicit in Andrews's writing, implicit in the kind of labor that he (and it) put forth. But it is not a utopianism that is the most prominent feature of Andrews's writing; I am more immediately struck by Andrews's confrontation with the "literary" expectations of cheerfulness and consolation.

"Confidence Trick," one of Andrews's (1987a) most remarkable poems, begins in a tone of confrontation and in an address designed to rub the reader the wrong way:

Intentionally leaderless — Recite this alphabet; body never *ends*, little bits of plastic come-on, recite catatonia chic — Up anyway I Say Yes re-writing the body systematic sex cult thing; contrite — Don't give a shit *what* you think; it s all we do — Not to mention everyone is a bigot, wheels so good; how s your ambient buddy system? — If I understand these words, then I find them disgraceful — Camera obscura don't give a damn about my bad reputation — (142)

Andrews (1987a) is well aware that "thinking positive is the tradition" (145), and his writing—its anger, its uncompromising dismantlings—makes us aware of the extent to which poetry as entertainment (no matter how sophisticated) depends upon a possible and probable recuperation, a negation of its negations. But that is precisely what makes reading Andrews at his best a difficult experience: his writing does not point us toward a negation (or synthesis) of his negations. Andrews (1987a) can be blunt ("The given totality sucks" [163]) or even moderately authoritative and proverbial ("Destiny is just another structuralism" [161]). And even in such instances a simple identification of a statement as *belonging* to Andrews is an obvious oversimplification and a potential misreading. Andrews's writing, as Nelson (1989) observes of Stein, is often "wholly unassignable to a humanizing persona" (179). Andrews consistently avoids some illusory but allowed realm of artistic transcendence. Marcuse (1978) contends rather cheerfully that "Art breaks open a dimension inaccessible to other experience, a dimension in which human beings, nature, and things no longer stand under the law of the established reality principle. Subject and objects encounter the appearance of that autonomy which is denied them in their society" (72). Andrews (1987a) concludes, on the other hand, that "even doing what you want takes on a note of desperate escapism" (156).

In a world-time where CNN claims to televise a war, the Gulf War, in which we mainly see correspondents agonizing over their personal safety but never challenging the news blackout and never showing images of the 150,000 killed, in which Ted Turner gets named Man of the Year (by a magazine owned by a parent company which also has substantial investments in CNN) for bringing news to the entire world, Andrews's (1987a) level of attack and critique feels fully justified:

> Debt debt, lovely lovely, lovely lovely, zeitgeist acquiesce debt, spiral scratch, blah blah blah blah; successful cure tends to affirm the entire edifice; we are not talking about terminal experience — Live in a dream world so you congenitally mutilate key citizens with ultimatums reduce your sick bite as seen on TV, catch the plague quiz show S.O.S. now you can bomb at home — (173)

The "hope" of "Confidence Trick" is hardly consoling:

> Culture is cowpie drainage — This country is totally fucked I hope somebody takes us over maybe the Japanese will take us over (1987a, 165)

Though even in this discussion, I am extracting what seems like a co-herent content, a point of view, and a voice, and thus domesticating a field of more conflicting vectors (especially the self-conscious antagonisms, the manipulation of responses, and anticipated reactions figured into and countered by the text). Andrews (1987a) seems aware of what he "should" do: "what they expect me to do is turn the stigma into a rousing slogan" (180). And I am beginning to believe that that is what we expect too often of poetry: a totalizing gesture of some wisdom or poise, the wisdom of wry acceptance, or of sufficiently humorous and/or skillful display. (Or the resolution and hope offered by an image of justice?)

Volosinov (1986) suggests that the "sign becomes an arena of the class struggle," with the ruling class striving "to impart a supraclass, eternal character to the ideological sign, to extinguish or drive inward the struggle between social value judgments which occurs in it, to make the sign uni-accentual" (23). Andrews' (1987a) work exposes that conflicted arena, en-acting rather than repressing that struggle:

> little working dentures intimates
> transparent astral spine passes for knowledge
> pronunciamentos of
> ENC RYPT
> unbosoming
> History Credits
> Say wont'cha   The king of thing
> & We What Unless
>
>   (82)

Or, more concisely, "Dark Your Side Pretense Chili Con Shoot Little Luke" (1987a, 94). Andrews (1987a) is ever aware (and resistant to) the suggestion that "derivative form plus prepackaged content would be enter-tainment" (145).

Though much of Marcuse (1978) remains a nostalgic rehabilitation of the transcendent possibilities of bourgeois inwardness, Marcuse does offer a helpful response to the criticism that much experimental art is elitist:

> If "the people" are dominated by the prevailing system of needs then only the rupture with this system can make "the people" an ally against barbarism. Prior to this rupture there is no "place among the people" which the writer can simply take up and which awaits him. Writers must rather first create this place, and this is a process which may re-

quire them to stand against the people, which may prevent them from speaking their language. In this sense "elitism" today may well have a radical content. To work for the radicalization of consciousness means to make explicit and conscious the material and ideological discrepancy between the writer and "the people" rather than to obscure and camouflage it. (35)

While never acceding to Marcuse's simplistic distinction between "the writer" and "the people," much of Andrews's (1987a) "Confidence Trick" is situated in such conflicting expressive demands:

Desultory info totally wired, his political seltzer went flat, so? — I am learning the language earnest or saint that s hot damage acts like drainage; politics control addict is fashion seconds late — A misterioso of why don t you instead do riffs?; a misterioso of so who cares so much? — Do you want to see what to want do you want to see what to mean I want what I want for you to mean? — To make equality less drab; when your body speeds up it just makes more xerox — Evil want to be his friend & I *am* his business, how influenced by blacks — Born to be a cowboy, blank generation ah shit, trade union disney testcard dance movements, not in *my* car, to make equality less drab — I don t have the questionable challenge of an oral audience; he runs his life like a metaphor for a corporation that fails to connect with a mass — Born to be a cowboy — There are rewards other than financial (145)

As Marcuse (1978) reminds us, "The critical function of art, its contribution to the struggle for liberation, resides in the aesthetic form. . . . The truth of art lies in its power to break the monopoly of established reality (i.e., of those who established it) to *define* what is *real*" (8, 9). Andrews's mode of doing so acknowledges Marx's (1964) observation that "labor produces not only commodities: it produces itself and the worker as a *commodity*" (107). So too does Ron Silliman's (1987b) observation apply to Andrews's writing: "Among the several social functions of poetry is that of posing a model of unalienated work: it stands in relation to the rest of society both as utopian possibility and constant reminder of just how bad things are" (61).

Andrews's poetry exists in part as a kind of prefatory praxis, an exuberant act of (preliminary) destruction, because "the overall shape of making sense needs to be reframed, restaged, put back into a context of 'presense'—to reveal its constructed character; to reveal by critique, by demythologizing. Otherwise, its apparent immediacy dupes us: the lack of distance is a kind of closure" (1990, 32). It is not that Andrews's poetry lacks immediacy; a transparent, "naturalized" immediacy is replaced by an immediacy of breakage:

> Infinity—or paradise—leads us to its home, our reference, outside of the confines of any tight system. A decriminalizing of all the minute particulars of word by word movement (inching) forward as read, to be read—these motions of lexical & acoustic intimacy. Immediacy returns—as breakage. Chargings & rechargings & dischargings are subject matter—to shake down identity into a diaspora, a multiplicity, an evanescing. An experimental choreography of the sign. (1991, 2)

Within that breakage, a utopianism remains, a hopefulness, for we are in the midst of an investigation of "the arrangements that make knowledge possible" (1989, 55). Paradoxically, Andrews's difficulties and obstacles to comprehension "try to create a kind of impossibility—so that you'd be able to restage the preconditions of being able to say . . . everything" (1989, 63). Andrews claims that "this writing which seems to be 'about' meaning also takes as its goal the challenging of existing frames and the widening of this social realm of possibility" (1989, 62). Rather than presenting us with an instance of authorial didacticism (and thus an occasion for, no matter how complex, comprehension-as-consumption), Andrews (1989) hopes that such writing "would allow desire to register as a kind of community-building and put writing at the forefront of envisioning what a positive social freedom and participation might look like" (64). But such writing involves, especially initially, an illegibility and a transgressiveness: "Radical praxis—at this level, or within this first concentric circle—here involves the rigors of formal celebration, a playful infidelity, a certain illegibility *within* the legible: an infinitizing, a wide-open exuberance, a perpetual motion machine, a transgression" (1990, 25).

Cary Nelson (1989) suggests that "literary history is never written from the vantage point of a secure and stable distance. It is always written in the midst of—and constituted by—the multiple social determinations of literariness. We can never be anything other than participants in the stories we are driven to tell" (17). As I have been arguing, a chief value of an encounter with Andrews's poetry is the way in which he calls into question preconceptions of literariness. As a participant in the telling of this story, I avow the value of engagement with (and response to) Andrews's versions of breakage, playful infidelity, and community-building. Though Nelson's

(1989) concern is with American poetries of the first half of this century, his fears—and the processes he describes—bear on the present, and on our efforts to support, engage, and hold in memory productions of the present:

> First, no texts are merely erased from our memory in a neutral and nonideological fashion. There are no innocent, undetermined lapses of cultural memory. The possibility of their erasure may initially be set in motion by their being stigmatized or scandalized (whether as outrageous, trivial, or inferior), and the scandal itself—even if it is no longer linked to exemplary texts—often remains in place as part of the institutional structure of what we do remember. (52)

Andrews's writing offers us a valuable "widened idealism," but it is an idealism that is peculiarly disconcerting.

Nelson (1989) explains that

> We have often convinced ourselves that the idealizations available in literature are largely or wholly positive forces, but this disciplinary self-persuasion not only obscures the discriminatory filters for idealization built into the canon; it also ignores the complex social and political struggle over idealization that takes place continually in the culture and defines the possibilities for idealization we are able to recognize in literary texts. (130)

My own essay, to the extent that it is persuasive, is an argument on behalf of a "widened idealism" that promises community based on the discomforts it provides. As Andrews (1991) puts it: "Writing then can work as a counter-disguising-a resistance to the resistance *against* explanation found in customary language use: a counter-counter-explanation; a contextualizing which contests, which spars & spurs" (12).

8. Thinking About It

David Antin's *Selected Poems: 1963–1973*

In our time, the professionalized discipline of "poet" has become an increasingly narrowed craft-activity, identified almost exclusively with lyrical narratives of personal experience. David Antin's poetic enterprise, as seen in *Selected Poems* (1991), offers a different paradigm for poet and poetry. Antin (1976) begins

> i had suggested that i had always had mixed feelings
> about being considered a poet   "if robert lowell is a
> poet i dont want to be a poet   if robert frost was a
> poet i dont want to be a poet   if socrates was a poet
>   ill consider it"

(1)

Antin's (1991) work in *Selected Poems* lays the groundwork for a Socratic identity, one in which poetry is paired with philosophical inquiry and in which the poet, to use Richard Rorty's term (1979), occupies the position of an edifying philosopher.

Antin (1991) allows us, indeed compels us, to reconsider two narratives of literary history: the story of American poetry's development in the 1960s and the more general story of literary/poetic modernism. Antin tells a challenging version of those two intertwined stories:

> In fact it was the sixties that saw the great explosion of American poetry.
> If there were perhaps twenty or thirty strong poets among the Black

Mountain, Beat poets and the first generation of the New York school, it is probable that the number of impressive poets to appear in the sixties is more than double that. For those of us who came into the arena of poetry at the end of the fifties and the beginning of the sixties, the Beats, the Black Mountain poets, the New York poets represented an "opening of the field." (1972, 132)

That opening depended upon an extension of an innovative tradition: "The poets of the sixties simply went about the business of re-examining the whole of the modernist tradition. By now we have had to add to the fundamental figures Gertrude Stein and John Cage, both of whom seem much more significant poets and minds than either Pound or Williams" (1972, 133). Though Antin wrote such a history with complete assurance more than twenty years ago, it is only over the past few years that poets and critics such as Marjorie Perloff, Cary Nelson, Charles Bernstein, and Ron Silliman have been at work substantiating and reinforcing such a revisionist and reinvigorating history of modernism. In his own calculatedly audacious manner, Antin (1974) adds,

> Of all the writers in English only Gertrude Stein seems to have had a thorough understanding of how profoundly Cubism opened up the possibilities of *representation* with this analysis. But then she was the writer in English with the deepest interest in language, the only one with an interest in language as language. I know almost everybody will object to this, but I've never understood why anybody thought Joyce, Eliot, Pound, Stevens, or Williams were innovators in language. Essentially all of their interest was concentrated at the level of rhetoric. (13)

Antin's story of modernism is one that makes a current revival, the New Formalism, sound like a bad joke. In debunking the implicitly moralistic arguments of the increasingly conservative and dominant academic branch of high modernism—Eliot, and his successors such as Tate, Ransom, Lowell—Antin claims, "The idea of metrics as a 'moral' or 'ideal' traditional order against which the 'emotional' human impulses of the poet continually struggle in the form of his real speech is a transparently trivial paradigm worthy of a play by Racine and always yields the small set of cheap musical thrills" (1972, 120). For Antin, as *Selected Poems* convincingly demonstrates, poetry's principal identification with verse-metrics had ceased to be viable and had in fact become merely a form of nostalgia:

The return of collage modernism in the fifties had both semantic and musical implications. If it meant a return to the semantic complexities of normal human discourse in the full "hyperspace" of real language, it also meant an end to the ideal of "hurdy gurdy" music, finishing off once and for all the "dime store" eloquence of Yeats and the "general store" eloquence of Frost, along with the mechanical organ of Dylan Thomas, as anything more than shabby operatic genres that might be referred to out of nostalgia or an equivocal taste for falseness and corrupted styles. (1972, 121)

Antin's version of the sixties and of modernism, written long before the writings of French theorists such as Lyotard, Foucault, or Derrida had any currency in American literary circles, makes postmodernism unnecessary, deeming it an erroneous misperception of the force and/or completion of modernism. Further, Antin (1974) establishes a philosophical/theoretical milieu for poetic practice:

As for the general theory, if you like you can construct a single tradition of Modernism going back to the end of the 16th century, characterized by the serious questioning of traditional representations of reality. You could push it back further, if you want to include the assault on Ciceronian rhetoric. If you don't want to go to that extreme and if you're prepared to discount the fact that their questioning largely concerned the representation of physical reality rather than humanly experienced reality, you could situate your point of origin in Galileo and Gilbert. But if that seems pushing it a little, it's easy to pin the whole "movement" on Bacon and Descartes, the twin theorists of experimental modernism. (29)

In light of the wrongheaded separation of creative and critical faculties that was taking place in American English Departments by the late 1960s, with the proliferation of Iowa-inspired degree programs in creative writing, Antin offers a paradigmatically challenging and radically different conception of poetry, poet, and poesis—a paradigm that is at odds not only with American disciplinary and professional formations of the late 1960s (and on into the present), but is also at odds with deeply rooted Western cultural separations of philosophy and poetry that go back at least as far as the *Republic* and Plato's imagined expulsion of poets from an ideal polis.

Antin's work in *Selected Poems*, especially in *meditations*, most resembles the work of Descartes, whom Antin (1974) argues "invents himself as an exemplary experimental man" and whose *Discourse* "is very much like many other novels, *War and Peace*, say, and it is certainly more intelligent" (30). What Antin (1974) finds in the writings of Bacon and Descartes is that "an art of representation gives way to an art of 'exemplary' presentation, and Bacon and Descartes father the process pieces, not only of Kandinsky and Arp, but John Cage" (31). And, I would add, Antin. It is in this context that *Selected Poems* must be read: as a series of experiments, a restless poesis of exemplification rather than *re*presentation.

Antin's work, particularly in *Selected Poems*, exists in a space between two sets of conventions that he rejects. The first is an assumption that has dominated American poetry of the latter half of the this century: the identification of poetry with personal(ized) expression. Antin understands that such poetry amounts to nothing more than the mastering of a rhetoric (of sincerity): "what we can expect of speaking sincerely is an elevation of feeling that we can equate with sincerity" (1991, 156). The other is the equation of thinking with principles of clear expository writing. The latter misunderstanding is one that Charles Bernstein (1986) in "Writing and Method," obviously drawing on assumptions and figures central to Antin's argument, sets aside: "as a mode, contemporary expository writing edges close to being merely a *style* of decorous thinking, rigidified and formalized to a point severed from its historical relation to method in Descartes and Bacon. It is no longer an enactment of thinking or reasoning but a representation (and simplification) of an eighteenth-century ideal of reasoning" (221).

Antin's *Selected Poems* offers us, in his preface "A Few Words," an uneasy phenomenology of a writer/speaker's relationship to books as deceptive artifacts. Antin's own principal affinity as a poet lies with poesis as process. He begins *Selected Poems* with the following observations:

> I don't usually reread my past work once it's published; and because for the last fifteen years I've been working at a kind of improvisation and go to a reading to work out a new poem instead of reading several old ones, my older poems are now almost as unfamiliar to me as to anyone else.
>
> But not in the same way.
>
> Because for me they've been changed by time and by the way they've appeared in books. Books have a very definitive appearance. My books anyway. Because I tried to make them that way. In spite of the fact that there is a sense in which the work of poetry is an ongoing process, a

book is a self sufficient object, obdurate even, as it gives decisive shape through selection and ordering to a cluster of attitudes and ideas, enclosing them in a definite space and time.

Too definite maybe, or at least now for me looking back at the poems I wrote between 1963 and 1973, with a view to publishing them in a new book that I hope will show somewhat more loosely and truly the body of work that I did then and its clear connection to the apparently very different work I am doing now. (13)

A book offers a temporary appearance of definitiveness. The vast majority of American poetry books offer roughly the same appearance: page after page of half-filled pages; recognizably "poetic" lines and poetic sentiments within certain accepted poetic vocabularies; conventional stanzas (to professionalize the writing and to mark an alleged difference from prose); a series of discrete (usually no more than one page long) single-voiced, visually precise mini-narratives. For Antin, the deed of a book is always in some conflict with his love of improvisation. It is not only that the forms he has chosen to make and to explore contest boundaries; they must also submit to, test out, and display the boundaries he finds in his own newly made forms.

When Antin writes that with his *Selected Poems* he hopes to show the older body of work's "clear connection to the *apparently* very different work" (my emphasis) he is doing now, he lets us know what *Selected Poems* discloses: the earlier poems are of a piece with his more recent talk-poems. Those talk-poems, particularly the pieces collected in *Talking at the Boundaries* (1976) *Tuning* (1984), and *What It Means to Be Avant-Garde* (1993), stand as one of the most important and fundamentally innovative (if least assimilated) contributions to American poetry in the latter half of the twentieth century. Though the poems of *Selected Poems* are not talk-poems in the mode of Antin's principal works of the 1970s, 1980s, and 1990s, they share the inquiry of the talk-poems into definitions and into new ways of thinking. As a collection, they enact a reorientation of poetry as investigation and inquiry. *Selected Poems* is the best place to begin a sustained relationship to David Antin's work, since 1963 marks a fundamental, decisive break in his poetic activity. In fall 1963, Antin (1991) explains, "I had given up writing a particular novel and put behind me a way of writing poetry—a kind of image poetry that I was finding more decorative than meaningful and incapable of addressing the kinds of things that were coming insistently to my mind then" (13).

Antin, in his rejection in 1963 of the decorativeness of an image-based poetry, turned away from what would become America's dominant poetic idiom for the next twenty years. Nineteen sixty-three marks the year of James Wright's image-oriented transformation in *The Branch Will Not Break*; it is also the year for similar shifts in emphasis in Louis Simpson's *At the End of the Open Road* (which won the Pulitzer Prize for poetry in 1963) and W. S. Merwin's *The Moving Target*. An image-based poetry, in a poetic movement called the poetry of the Deep Image, became a means for an internationalized (principally through Spanish and South American poetries, with some influence of French surrealist and Eastern European poetries) lyrical mysticism in the hands of poets such as Bly, Merwin, Kinnell, and Wright. Such image-based writing also governs the poetry of personal epiphany and self-investigation as seen in the poetry of Plath, Sharon Olds, Gregory Orr, and many others.

For Antin, an alternative to the crafted concision of an image-based poetics came from an investigation of language and acts of meaning-making: "Language and politics, as it seems from reading the poems that I went on to write then. They are of course not the same thing, but they are very close, because language is the cultural matrix in which the value systems that determine politics are held" (1991, 13–14). When Antin returned to New York City in 1963, his attention shifted to an interest in poetry's (and art's) constructedness:

> So it was a new beginning in New York City, in a landscape surrounded with old ideas and things falling apart or being torn apart to be replaced by shiny new ones that might themselves soon start to fall apart, in the midst of all this constructing and reconstructing I began to work with prefabricated and readymade materials, recycling materials, recycling texts and fragments of texts, enclosing valuable and used up talk and thought and feeling, hoping to save what was worth saving, liberate it and throw the rest away. So those were my first three books, *definitions*, *autobiography*, and *Code of Flag Behavior*. (1991, 14–15)

As Thoreau asks in *Walden*, "shall we forever resign the pleasures of construction to the carpenter?" Antin's emphasis on the pleasures and necessity of construction, of invention, in poetry, aligns him with innovative artists whose work crosses genre and disciplinary boundaries: Gertrude Stein, John Cage, Robert Rauschenberg (whose collage-painting is the cover for Antin's *Selected Poems*), Marcel Duchamp, Jackson Mac Low,

Jerome Rothenberg, and Blaise Cendrars. Antin's rejection of an image-based poetry anticipates (by nearly fifteen years) the complaints of critics such as Robert Pinsky (1976), Charles Altieri (1984), and Marjorie Perloff. Each of these writers have pointed out the serious limitations of an image-based writing. Of Antin's contribution in *Selected Poems*, Perloff (1991–92) has observed, "Indeed what a reading of *Selected Poems* suggests is that for Antin, the much discussed dichotomy between speech and writing or between improvisation and the made object is not nearly as important as is the dichotomy between a poetics of image and one of *language*, of the 'word as such,' as the Russian futurists called it" (8). Antin's work, especially as it offers and enacts a different paradigm for the poet as one engaged in serious issues of philosophy, linguistics, cultural criticism, and anthropology, offered an example for the many diverse poets lumped under the category of Language poetry. But ultimately Antin's speech-based poetics diverges significantly from the syntactical disturbances of many language poets (such as Charles Bernstein, Bruce Andrews, and Alan Davies).

What is crucial, for the innovative American poetries of the 1980s and 1990s, is Antin's identification of poetry with thinking, an identification that reverses prejudices, turf warfare, and bifurcations as old as Plato's *Republic*. As Richard Rorty (1979) points out, "Plato defined the philosopher by opposition to the poet" (370). Antin does not see the value of such a definition-by-opposition; his version of a poet is engaged in the fundamental activities of a philosopher.

A few years after the writing in *Selected Poems*, Antin (1976) is able to identify more fully his discomfort with books as such, declaring that his preference is

> to improvise something   because as a poet i
> was getting extremely tired of   what i considered an unnatural
> language act   going into a closet   so to speak   sitting in
> front of a typewriter   because   anything is possible in a closet
> in front of a typewriter and nothing is necessary a closet is no
> place to address anybody   or anything   and its so unnatural
> sitting in front of a typewriter   that you dont address any-
> one   what you do is you sit at the typewriter and you bang out the
> anticipated   . . .
>
> the whole problem of our literate and literal culture has

been   to some extent   the problem of the totally dislocated
occasion   that is in this case the book   which goes out into a distributional
system unknown to us

(56)

Selected Poems is continuous with such fundamental questioning as a heuristic poetic practice. The core element of Antin's questioning, as seen in *Selected Poems*, is an investigation of key definitions: What is a poem? What might a poem be made of? What materials and vocabularies might a poem include? How might poetry and thinking overlap? It is this last question, which Antin states as "to keep the work to my idea of a truly meditational discipline and to avoid tasteful arrangement" (1991, 19), that reaches fruition in *Selected Poems* in works such as *definitions* and *meditations*. In describing the scope and nature of Antin's investigations in *definitions*, Sherman Paul (1986) writes,

> Definitions aren't language, that is, the words defined in the dictionary have not yet found their human use, their occasion. By bringing words to their human use, Antin gives us a representation of reality.
>
> The definitions of *loss* and of *value*, from which "Definitions for Mendy" unfolds, come from an insurance handbook and Webster's dictionary. They have the neutrality of the words in Schwerner and Kaplan's *Domesday Dictionary*. They themselves are not *the* definition of *death*, though they help to define it. That is, *loss* is so general a case, and *value* so valuable, these definitions do apply. They enter the language system, and it is within this all inclusive system that they help us define what especially needs defining: what it means to be human. (26)

What Paul's comments hint at is Antin's ability to conduct philosophically serious and emotionally intense investigations within an innovative practice of collagist poetry. Throughout his writing career, Antin has spoken through a variety of found texts and vocabularies, from insurance handbooks to codes of flag behavior to textbooks for non-native speakers to popular novels. Rather than the more narrow goal of mainstream poetry's lyric mode of production, which it can be argued becomes a field for a rather limited and stylized version of self-expression, Antin's poetry becomes the site for investigating how sense and meaning are constructed and for what Marjorie Perloff (1991–92) calls "the poet's Wittgensteinian concern with ordinary language" (8). Antin's investigation is conducted within discourses that more mainstream poets have banished as unpoetic.

While Wordsworth declared in 1800 in the preface to the "Lyrical Ballads" that the language of poetry "is, as far as possible, a selection of the language really spoken by men," no one then took such a remark literally nor does anyone (except for perhaps Antin) today take such a remark literally. Even the most celebrated of twentieth-century plainspoken poems are recognizably based on professionalized and restricted poetic rhetorics. As Hugh Kenner (1975, 60) reminds us of William Carlos Williams's "Red Wheelbarrow," in spite of claims for Williams's poetry as speech-based, we cannot imagine a context in which someone actually approaches us and says, "so much depends upon a red wheel barrow glazed with rain water beside the white chickens." Wordsworth himself was uncomfortable with the implications of his own claim for poetry's closeness to actual speech. In order to maintain a class-based distinctiveness for poetic language, Wordsworth immediately adds the following clarification to his more famous assertion of poetry as "a selection of the language really spoken by men": "that this selection, wherever it is made with true taste and feeling, will of itself form a distinction far greater than would at first be imagined, and will entirely separate the composition from the vulgarity and meanness of ordinary life; and, if meter be superadded thereto, I believe that a dissimilitude will be pronounced altogether sufficient for the gratification of a rational mind." On the other hand, Antin (1991) in an epigraph to *November Exercises* in *Selected Poems*, asks, "If someone came up and started talking a poem at you how would you know it was a poem?" (260). In blurring the boundaries between talk and poetry, Antin does not so much rein in poetry's possibilities as make us aware of (poetic) qualities already present in speech. The "false" voice of the (usual) poetry reading— the introduction to the poem in "normal" speech, then the more tentative precious delivery of the reading proper—is not necessary. Antin asks us to consider: *Is* poetry a different language than speech? If so, how and why must it be so? Is poetry different by some process of intensification and condensation? Or, are such properties already *within* speech? Antin dares to explore the possibilities of a talk-based poesis, though admittedly Antin's own talking is idiosyncratic and complex, incorporating a range of knowledge and rhetorics, from storytelling to engineering, linguistics, art criticism, philosophy, psychology, and anthropology. In poem after poem, beginning with the work in *Selected Poems*, Antin endeavors to engage in makings that do not repeat what is already known.

Early on, one of Antin's (1991) most productive discoveries (in "poem found in the street") is that "everything is relation" (32), and much of

Selected Poems can be understood as Antin's investigation of the possibilities, à la Duchamp, Rauschenberg, and Cage, of collage as a basis for poetic composition. As Antin explains in "10th separation meditation," "performance / depends on knowledge / of relations" (1991, 232). By the latter stages of his meditations, in "12th separation meditation," Antin offers a series of axioms regardings relation: "relations / connect the central mind / with the pupil of the eye," "maintain fitting relations with other men," and "spirit / inclines to what moves it" (1991, 244).

In early poems such as "who are my friends," with its virtuoso deconstruction of the term *friend* (which Antin accomplishes by interrogating Lyndon Johnson's famous remark "we must help our frehnds in veetnaehm") the political subversiveness of Antin's skepticism is fully apparent, especially in the poem's conclusion:

> i think i have a foe in washington   a number of foes
> all of whom have friends in viet nam
> if i have friends in viet nam they should send me mail
> ive never been to viet nam
> its too far away and costs too much to get there
> i dont even know how to pronounce viet nam   though i thought
>   i knew how to pronounce it
> but if my friend in washington knows how to pronounce it
> then i dont
> probably neither of us pronounces it the way our friends in
>   viet nam pronounce it
> we must all be talking about a different place
>
> (1991, 35–36)

"Code of flag behavior," made from exactly such a manual, shows too the emotional intensity (just the opposite of an anti-experimentalist's misconception that innovative work is emotionally arid) that empowers such a construction, which begins "the flag should never be displayed with the union down except as a sign of distress" (1991, 37). Similarly, Antin's "a list of the delusions of the insane / what they are afraid of" reaches a comprehensiveness that makes paranoia seem prudent and prophetic:

> that disgusting things are being put into their food and drink . . .
> that all of the nutriment has been removed from food that evil chemicals
> have been placed in the earth
> that evil chemicals have entered the air

that it is immoral to eat
that they are in hell
that they hear people screaming
that they smell burnt flesh

.   .   .   .   .

that there are unknown agencies working evil in the world

(1991, 39)

By reinhabiting cultural "truths"—that we know who our friends are
and that we must help them; that we should treat the flag with respect;
that the insane have fears which are groundless—Antin's early poetry is
political, subversive, and resistant, a position he comes to identify with an
artist's function as an obstacle:

the idea of the artist as
obstacle   how perhaps instead of giving a more precise
   or glamorous form to the platitudes of the culture
   the artist might propose himself as a sort of impedi-
ment   like sticking out a foot in a corridor and changing the direction of traffic

(1976, 52)

Such a definition, as well as Antin's varied use of found materials, provides for a radically different (personal) expressiveness than that of the
poetic or artistic mainstream. Furthermore, mainstream poetic or artistic
accomplishment is mostly based on a model of individualized, recognizable voice or style that can then be imitated or repeated by the artist
who, having achieved a recognizable (and therefore repeatable) identity,
has reached this commodified plateau of producing a thing recognizably
his. Antin's model, as he indicates in a note to his poem *The Black Plague:
Parts I-IV*, is generative and exemplary (but *not* at all directly concerned
with *personal* expression):

(Part III of the *Black Plague* is pretty much an arrangement of words
taken from a translation of Wittgenstein's *Philosophical Investigations*.
About the words, nobody owns them—not Wittgenstein, or the trans-
lator, or me—and anyone who wants them is welcome to use them
again.) (1991, 93)

The third part of *The Black Plague*, the part written partly in Wittgenstein's words, becomes a complex meditation on definition, naming, and

the relationship between sensations and the name for a sensation, and the extent to which such naming can be a way of knowing and/or a way of being lied to. Antin begins,

> a man cries out he is in pain   we want to say we know
> what that means   what does that mean
>
> how do words refer to sensations   how do we learn the
> meaning of pain
>
> (1991, 85)

But the portion of *The Black Plague* that identifies what will be a lifelong concern for Antin occurs, typically, in an interrogatory mode:

> the words "i am afraid" are they a description of a state of
> mind   someone asks me "what was that?   a cry of
> fear?   or do you want to tell me how you feel?   or is it a
> reflection of your present state?"   can i always give a clear
> answer?   can i ever?
>
> (1991, 87)

In Antin's quest—what I see as an ethics of poesis or an ethical responsibility to an honest phenomenology of present-creation—to work "swiftly to make [his] kind of sense" and to keep "to [his] idea of a truly meditational discipline and to avoid tasteful arrangement" (19), Antin obligates himself to a serious relationship to the present. Such an honoring of the present should not be confused with so-called stream of consciousness writing, which becomes over time a decorous, formalized, and conventional representation, a period style really, of what one generation of early twentieth-century writers stylized as a seemingly spontaneous *re*presentation of consciousness. It is the ethical nature of this relationship to the present that motivates much of Antin's behavior, including his choice (for approximately the past twenty years) to talk improvisationally rather than to read (from already completed pieces) at poetry readings:

> but the reason
> im not tempted to read is different i think than most people
> suppose   the reason   my reason   is the sense that i
> have in looking at a book   my book   not somebody
> elses book   but in looking at my own book and feeling
> that as i look i lose my sense of the present   my sense
> of the present disintegrates for me as i read
>
> (1984, 84)

As Sherman Paul (1986) observes, "Antin is a moralist (so is Cage), and he may be experimental for the good reason that nothing is so difficult in our time as to credibly speak moral truth. To attend and speak such truth is one of the eminently *human* things to which he devotes his work" (38). As Antin continues,

> the present is a difficult thing to have a taste
> for   its very difficult because   in satisfying it the question
> i always have to ask myself is   what is the present and
> how long is it?   how long is the present?
> thats a question
> i take very seriously as a poet   i have a very strong commitment
> to the idea of the present
>
> (1984, 84)

In such remarks we can also see why Antin (1972) entitled his ground-breaking essay on postmodernism "Modernism and Postmodernism: Approaching the Present in American Poetry." For Antin the crux of making, of poesis, is an inhabitation of the present, which is often radically and antagonistically different from mainstream craft-oriented versions of the poem as a lyrical-narrative form to be learned, repeated, modified, and perfected.

Antin's (1974) definition of poetry is a broad one:

> As far as I'm concerned there is the language art. That's poetry. All of it. There are genres within it. Like narration. And there's a subform of narration. Called fiction. . . . "Prose" is the name for a kind of notational style. It's a way of making language look responsible. . . . As with all notations it has conventions, writing rules and the like, that will prevent you from saying a lot of things, or at least make it difficult to get those things notated clearly, or in their full energy and perspecuity. It will also encourage you to talk in such a way as to make it easier for you to use the notation. (27)

At a fundamental level, Antin's identification of poetry with meaning-making (rather than with the appearance or tabulational features of verse or with poetry as personal expression) allows the poet a paradigmatically different intellectual site. So too is Antin's setting aside of the *line* as poetry's fundamental unit one of the most important premises for twentieth-century innovative poetry, linking Antin's poetry to oral poetry traditions (from the paleolithic to the present, as in the anthologies of

Antin's good friend Jerome Rothenberg), to writers as varied as Blake and Wittgenstein, and to a range of twentieth-century writers such as Stein and Cage. As Hugh Kenner (1987) argues that William Carlos Williams's poetry must, in part, be understood (especially in terms of layout) in relationship to the capacities of the typewriter, Antin's poetry, especially *after Selected Poems*, must be thought of in relationship to the (audio) tape recorder. For Antin, perhaps the sixty-minute tape becomes a unit of poetic composition. For the immediate present, it remains to be seen how, as in Laurie Anderson's work, the videotape shapes poetic activity or how in many different directions the video display terminal (as the new page) shapes compositional practices.

"scenario for a beginning meditation," one of the most important poems in *Selected Poems*, reads now like a storehouse for many of Antin's concerns for the last twenty years:

> this is probably the beginning
>
> don't you think it was the right place to begin?
>
> well what would have been a better time?
>
> if you can tell when it's time to begin how can it be the beginning?
>
> i wanted to begin for a long time
>
> or more correctly i had thought about beginning for a long time
>
> but everything that preceded the beginning was not over yet
>
> what i meant to say was that nothing that had preceded the beginning was over yet
>
> supposing you think of your life
> where does it begin?
>
> (143)

Antin is perpetually blurring and unsettling boundaries (and bear in mind that this scenario precedes familiarity with Derrida's problematizing of origins). As with his monumental yet impermanent skywriting-poems, Antin's meditations and subsequent talk-poems have about them a lightness and contingency. The scope of the poet's ambition is always circumstantial: "i'm doing the best i can under the circumstances" (1991, 146). Antin's work assumes (or hopes for) a response: "in doing this i find it hard to imagine that it will not / be someone else who will answer me" (145). In the case of *Selected Poems*, Antin (in the preface) returns to answer himself as he revisits his earlier work. More often, we are asked to answer, by objection or rejoinder or, better yet, by our own compositional acts as responses to Antin's work. Such responses amount to the continuation of a long tradition of philosophy-as-conversation, articulated variously by Kenneth Burke (1973, 110–11), by Michael Oakeshott (1962), Richard Rorty (1979, especially 365–79), and others. Indeed, Antin's presumption of a response, and thus a conversation, is the cornerstone for Plato's *Dialogues*.

As Antin himself explains in "what am i doing here?": "i see thinking as talking   i see it as talking   to a question   which may give rise to another question" (1976, 20). Thus, Antin's philosophy-as-conversation may be an internal dialogue, or (over a period of time) an individual inquiry that involves different responses, and/or a conversation between different conversational partners. The danger posed by a book is that its appearance of decisiveness may put an end to conversation (rather than promote conversation), may foreclose further talk by the book's peculiar form of authority. As Antin explains in "is this the right place?":

> writing is a form of fossilized talking   which gets put
> inside of a can   called a book   and i respect that can   its a
> means of preservation   or maybe we should say in a frozen food
> container called a book   but on the other hand if you dont know
> how to handle that frozen food container that icy block will never
> turn back into talking
>
> (1976, 45–46)

Antin has gone to great pains to make his own books of sufficient tentativeness and circumstance (along with intensity and provocativeness) that we (and he) are encouraged to talk back.

Selected Poems, 1963–1973 provides the foundation by which we can see Antin for what he is: one of twentieth-century America's most important poetic innovators. Antin's talk-poems, arguably his most important accomplishment, may represent a culmination of his inquiry, but *Selected Poems* adds significantly to our sense of the range of his inquiry. What we await to complete the picture is the publication of Antin's long-overdue collection of essays.

9. Mouth to Mouth

Douglas Messerli's *Maxims from*
My Mother's Milk/Hymns to Him: A Dialogue

Messerli's first poem in *Maxims/Hymns* (1988) begins

> Start and you have . . . a jar to leave open
> that can release whatever was
> within

and ends

> waiting for the weight
> of whatever might
> be strong enough to hang
> from that hope.
>
> (9)

What hangs from that hope weighs enough to de-form (and thus re-form) our ways of saying. Wit and pun double and redouble the sentence's attempted movement toward a singleness of articulation. *Maxims/Hymns* is heady in its optimism; the overall book ends with a command to move out: "Still we stand. / Let's get going."

A guiding sensibility for *Maxims/Hymns* is Roland Barthes, whose importance Messerli signals by a lengthy epigraph. The long quote from Barthes I offer now, for its pertinence to Messerli's remarkable skills with puns and a wide range of acoustical play, is not that exact epigraph, but a passage from Barthes (1986). As I move us through the Barthes passage, I interrupt it now and then to interpose passages from Messerli's *Maxims/Hymns*, not simply as illustrations but as collaborations and elaborations, as enactments, and as the putting into play of Barthes's (1986) pronouncements:

> . . . the rustle of language forms a utopia. Which utopia? That of a music of meaning; in its utopic state, language would be enlarged, I should even say *denatured* to the point of forming a vast auditory fabric in which the semantic apparatus would be made unreal;

> talent to take the man
> into the tent, to divest
> the proper pants
> gasp at the grasp and ache to tell
> the time that tests the ease
> of all our tries
>
> (64)

> the phonic, metric, vocal signifier would be deployed in all its sumptuosity, without a sign ever becoming detached from it (ever *naturalizing* this pure layer of delectation),

> a gain to part, read as scarlet
> , let her drape the pun
> across the nuptials, there to wake
> the rash from the bushes
>
> (33)

> but also—and this is what is difficult—without meaning being brutally dismissed, dogmatically foreclosed, in short castrated.

> Halt sings into lapse
> to further the after
> shock, laughter
> can't erupt until safe has opened
> up the inheritance
> of what has been
>
> (31)

And just as, when attributed to the machine, the rustle is only the noise of an absence of noise, in the same way, shifted to language, it would be that meaning which reveals an exemption of meaning or—the same thing—that non-meaning which produces in the distance a meaning henceforth liberated from all the aggressions of which the sign, formed in the "sad and fierce history of men," is the Pandora's box.

This is a utopia, no doubt about it; but utopia is often what guides the investigations of the avant-garde. (1986, 77–78)

Messerli (1988) begins with "Pandora's Box." His is a poetry that hopes to leave open the box precisely for the reasons articulated by Barthes in "The Rustle of Language." Or as Rod Smith (1988) claims, "In Messerli tension between sound's sped momentum and ideation's drag" (65).

Instead of echoed vowel-consonant sounds as background music, that music is perpetually on the verge of gobbling up what is signified. As Barthes (1986) has it, a utopic process of signification, a sumptuous saying. Messerli's pun-play becomes not a disturbance of a more significant textual process but a primary constituent of the text, as in the second stanza of "Pandora's Box":

> and everything that's not
> 's tied round the neck
> as smack drives a buss
> into the mouth of another

Why pun upon pun? Messerli: "The pun offered me a possibility of getting two, three, four levels going in different directions at one time and allowing the poem a greater richness of meaning and density" (quoted in Perloff 1988, 37). But mere complexity and multiplicity is not all. Messerli's punning, as in "smack drives a buss / into the mouth of another," links to an erotics of the poem, its sumptuousness, a thing made/shared on the mouth. Barthes (1975):

Does writing in pleasure guarantee—guarantee me, the writer—my reader's pleasure? Not at all, I must seek out this reader (must "cruise" him) *without knowing where he is*. A site of bliss is then created. It is not the reader's "person" that is necessary to me, it is this site: the possibility of a dialectics of desire, of an *unpredictability* of bliss. (4)

In "On the Face of It," Messerli (1988) announces, "The cost of experience is minding/ your mouth" (50). Barthes (1975):

Due allowance being made for the sounds of the language, *writing aloud* is not phonological but phonetic; its aim is not the clarity of messages, the theater of emotions; what it searches for (in a perspective of bliss) are the pulsional incidents, the language lined with flesh, a text where we can hear the grain of the throat, the patina of consonants, the voluptuousness of vowels, a whole carnal stereophony: the articulation of the body, of the tongue, not that of meaning of language. (66–67)

> The thicket's in the thick of what
> the civet cat & krait snake have
> in common, the sea & the ca-
> ve in which the swimmer's caught, not
> as in a twist
> of some plot, but as a cemetery can become
> a crematorium.
>
> (46)

More to the point, there is an erotics, a polymorphous pleasure to Messerli's wordplay and transformations. An erotics the reader shares by mouthing, by attuning to, the pleasures of a Messerli text. "As smack drives a buss / into the mouth of another" (9) might well be glossed by Barthes's (1977) evolutionary (and utopian) history of *Parler / embrasser*:

> According to the Leroi-Gourhan hypothesis, it was when he could free his upper limbs from the task of locomotion and, in consequence, his mouth from predation, that man could speak. I would add: *and embrace*. For the phonatory system is also the osculatory system. Shifting to upright posture, man found himself free to invent language and love: this is perhaps the anthropological birth of a concomitant double perversion: speech and kissing. By this accounting, the freer men have been (with their mouths), the more they have spoken and embraced; and logically, when progress will have rid men of every manual task, they will then do nothing but discourse and make love! (140–41)

‖

Bring down the clouded reign of the iron-fisted one; lift a stein aloft to the celebrated unaligned skies.

But for Messerli, in *Maxims/Hymns* particularly, poetry is a dialectical way of going. Not simply an exaltation of the multiplicities of speech-music-pun defeating a message- or meaning-dominated discourse that would weed the field of language back into a single crop of expression. Sound goes in alliance with and at cross-purposes with grapheme, only the latter able to "say" (or let us see) the poem "defining as its end / its readers' (s)a(ti)s / factions" (15). The chief factions (and satisfactions) of Messerli's book being mother and lover, each known through/by the mouth. Overall, *Maxims/Hymns* proceeds by insistent doubleness: each Maxim-poem (rich in pun and wordplay) is followed by a Hymn-poem (usually somewhat less devoted to these particular multiplicities). Within each Maxim-poem, each poem-field is doubled by virtue of its layout: a maxim (in italics) at the top of the page, separated by a thick line from the poem, which takes place below the line. Even, or especially, within each maxim there is a doubling back on the principle of the maxim itself. One good example of this double impulse within Messerli's made-up maxims is "Meaning meets at the weave of word and frays" (17). Typically, a maxim presents an observation in a tone of certainty. But this very act of authority, subject-verb in quick succession, frays, unravels, a little at the level of the phrase, but more at the level of the multiple possibilities within the syllables' sounds. Meaning only exists at a site of fighting, in the midst of frays, a fracas that attempts to bounce, toss out, what prevents singularity of expression.

Such a deconstructive relationship to the maxim bears a close relationship to Messerli's particular notion of manifesto. In the special Manifesto Issue of the *Washington Review* that Messerli edited in 1983, his own contribution undoes the singularity and sureness of the typical manifesto, replacing it with the manifesto as at least a dialogue and more likely as the site for many voices:

> As a dialogue, the manifesto—strange as it may seem—seldom posits a single viewpoint. Generally speaking, manifestos are documents of contradiction and inconsistency. The vast majority of manifestos subvert the normative patterns of grammar and rhetoric. Sentence fragments, leaps of logic, italicized words and phrases—these are the stuff of manifestos. For they reveal the panoply of voices in the world as reconstructed by the individual or group who signs the document. (Messerli 1983, 3)

Messerli begins *Maxims/Hymns* with a long epigraph from Barthes:

> Now the maxim is comprised in an essentialist notion of human nature, it is linked to classical ideology: it is the most arrogant (often the stupidest) of the forms of language. Why then not reject it? The reason is,

as always, emotive: I write maxims (or I sketch their movement) *in order to reassure myself*: when some disturbance arises, I attenuate it by confiding myself to a fixity which exceeds my powers: "*Actually, it's always like that*": and the maxim is born. The maxim is a sort of *sentence-name*, and to name is to pacify. Moreover, this too is a maxim: it attenuates my fear of seeking extravagance by writing maxims. (from Barthes 1977, 179)

As the poem "under" the sign of this maxim enacts, poetry for Messerli is an inquiry conducted along the lines of insistent doubling, a doubling that shared by a reader becomes a coupling, as this book becomes an homage to mother (and mother-tongue) and lover (his tongue too). But in my own idealization of the function of sound and wit in Messerli's poetry, I begin to neglect that horizon toward which, as Barthes asserts, those sounds move: meaning. As Joe Ross (1988) correctly cautions: "It is crucial to note that sound [in Messerli's poems] is not the subject, but rather the aesthetic embellishment of a fine ear. Yet this is not only a simple embellishment with Douglas' work, it too is the meat: the meeting in accord, or a chord, of perfect balance/harmony of sound and meaning, intwined inextricably in the work" (60–61).

Perhaps that interplay of sound and sense (as well as the overarching dialogue structure of the book) is best experienced by reading closely two of the book's shorter paired poems, "Aller Et Retour" and "On Edge." I suggest that the Maxims, often in a tone of command or admonition, more typically explore an anxiety of separation, an edginess about edges, an unease in the presence of gaps. The Hymns tend to be more self-assuredly playful, more readily and confidently displaying their spirit, more openly celebratory of play and disjunction.

Here, from the Maxims, is "Aller Et Retour":

Meaning meets at the weave of word and frays.

Aller et Retour

Write often the bat insists. It doubles its lips
and slips into something said. It can never be
natural to wing a sentence when a word might
work for instance, blink and the ball spins
into the glove.

(17)

As all of *Maxims/Hymns* attests, Messerli's interest lies with meaning's barely achieved ability to emerge from (by remaining attached to) the weave of sound and sense. At the particular site of the word, we arrest motion into/of the phrase. And so a fight, a fray, many frays. As the word accumulates into the phrase, meaning too begins to accumulate; but so too does that meaning or accumulation begin to fray and unravel, especially if that crucial juncture is a pun ("frays") and thus a site for multiple departures.

Such duplicity is critical to Messerli's playfully destabilized thinking. Whether the poem is a tug of war between maxim and lyric, or going and returning, or sound/music versus the accumulation of a sentence-based coherence, Messerli's poem at its most fundamental tension arrests itself at the level of the word. If the poem begins as a duty ("write often the bat insists") even that old authoritarian "bat" may soon become the bat of baseball games and sudden hits. Its first base hit quite rightfully should be a "double"—Messerli leads the league in doubles. But the poet evades opportunities to invent and create if the poem gets limited, as in much mainstream writing, to a reduced coin of the realm, a lowest common denominator: poetry as a "natural" way of slipping "into something said"— the reductiveness of slipping into something comfortable (and usually something that takes for granted its own transparency). Messerli's best work, as in the word "frays" for this poem's maxim, "a word might work for instance," apprises us of the fresh possibilities available at the site of the word that resists a singular accumulation. Blink and we miss the entire hit, the trajectory, the flight of the ball, and find the play over and the ball already in the glove. So it is in our reading experience of most "natural," plainspoken mainstream verse (where that naturalized theme plops into the glove before we *know* it). Or so we are admonished in "Aller Et Retour," or at least in one (partial) reading of it.

"On Edge," the companion poem in dialogue with "Aller Et Retour," celebrates the edge upon which Messerli would have us live:

On Edge

Appreciation is to precipice like
what makes the edge so
loose beneath the shoe, the rocks ready to
have, been swallowed by the gorges!
Valleys are always hungry
for the mountains, the valet waits

on the suitor. Love is like that
break between where
it emanates and is
highly regarded.

(18)

"On Edge" can be read as a hymn to edges and breaks, and to the crum-
blings and collapsings that consume and reassemble what lies on edge. The
formulaic A is to B as C is to D—that staple of the analogy exam—has
its tone of surety undone by the immediately mysterious relationship between "appreciation" and "precipice," a relationship that must be sounded
out before it is understood (and thus anticipates the similar kinship of
"loose" and "shoe," "valley" and "valet"). It is the poem's tone, the exuberance of the initial exclamation (which helps us to hear the closeness of
"gorges!" and "gorgeous"), that marks "On Edge" as a brief lyric of/on the
sublime. But this prospect or precipice is not mastered but felt. Love itself
is understood as that feeling whereby we feel a break, an edge, a precipice; and that break exists *between* its emanation (in the language of the
previous poem "aller"?) and its regard (or "retour"?). For love, as Messerli
presents it, is not self-contained but exists as a relationship *between* but
also predicated upon and through a break. At first, love may seem to be
(merely) an attending: "the valet waits / on the suitor. Love is like that."
But as we extend beyond the end of the line (and go over the edge), love
is also (and more aptly) "like that / break between," that edge and precipice around and over which Messerli's own amative play turns, verse itself
being principally (and at root) a turning and a turn of phrase. Such a
use of line break illustrates Joe Ross's (1988) observation that in Messerli's
poems we move "toward the conviction that language properly exercised
not only allows but is indeed the thinking process itself" (62). Thus in this
particular pair of poems the most maximlike statement occurs at the end
of a Hymn and not at the beginning of a Maxim.

III

*As the maxim eyes the most within the shortest span, sew the poem, a playful
cross-stitch.*

Messerli writes what Wallace Stevens (1947/1954; repr. 1982, 240) called the
poem as the act of the mind, though Messerli does not thematize that act

with the closure and tidy theatricality of Stevens. Messerli's maxim is "To think is to place words in motion, to act is to race them to devotion" (13).

As this book's first maxim announces, "Sometimes a sentence ends in imprisonment." And in the third poem of the book: "Assign a period to it and you've put an end to destination" (11). So, one half of Messerli's dialectical ambition is to resist and subvert the constraints of sentencing. An odd ambition for one drawn to the maxim, an essentializing, self-contained, sure-sounding pronouncement, but precisely Messerli's own Barthesian form of reassurance.

Within Messerli's poems we sometimes find a kind of literary criticism, a poetry of statement:

> Poetry is always seeking something special. To men with
>   leashed dogs leave
> everyday life. A poem is not a window but a door
>
> (19)

And: "Since conception some have stayed in bed and said 'I can't understand // why anyone would want to go so far'" (19). But Messerli's poetry and poetics are on the side of flow. As his earlier trilogy *River to Rivet* (1984) suggests, part of poetry's dialectical tension comes from opposing and yoking flow and stasis.

Pun, typographical disturbance, and line break all are enlisted on behalf of Messerli's resistance to closure and enclosure. Frost, in "Mending Wall," writes that "something there is that doesn't love a wall"; but Frost, for the most part, thematizes and makes metrically correct those forces of disturbance. Messerli's form of play is more radical, as in "Night Train":

> The world in some sense must—break
> the floe—summer breezes. the mourning
> doves into its own after—coo
> ling the fire
> flies—& frees us.
>
> (22)

Such a poetry of motion and fragmentation seeks a multiplicity by way of music and line break, by pun and by transformation, particularly by blurring syllable boundaries, setting phonic continuity against the cut of a line break.

One danger of such wordplay is that it may be perceived as an irrelevant or decadent, decorative art. Messerli is not unaware of such accusations:

I'm like that, snorting
hog hunting trifles for the rich.

                            (43)

One answer is to side with and to seek out forms of disturbance that are
containable as mere trifles, as baubles for the tongue and taste of the rich:

But here in the Teutons
there's nothing so expansive
as the roar
of an avalanche. Even
the edge may be nothing
more than cicatrices, still
upon the brace I rest
my face. It's a manner
of peaking in the greater
of volcanoes
before they corrupt.

                            (43)

There is, as Barthes (1986, 78) suggests, an ethics of the signifier, an ethics
of signification. Messerli: "The proposition is to sign away your life, to
leave no terrain // untouched" (19). And in one sense, Messerli's entire
business life, as editor, publisher, and distributor, can be seen as a devotion
to an ethical dimension of signification, an allegiance to a signification
that disturbs dominant habits of expression.

Thus I would argue for a socially engaged, politically progressive position for Messerli's work. As Theodor Adorno (1984) concludes, "Among
the links that mediate art and society, subject matter is the most superficial and fallible one" (326). When I say Messerli's work, I mean both
his business (Sun and Moon Press itself, as well as Messerli's equally significant activity in editing, anthologizing, publicizing, and distributing a
wide range of avant-garde writing) and his writing. The former ("if we
want to determine the nature of the relation between art and society, we
must look not at the sphere of reception, but at the more basic sphere
of production" [Adorno 1984, 324]) marks Messerli commitment to a life
and circulation for alternative, oppositional writings. The latter ("what it
[art] contributes to society is not some directly communicable content
but something more mediate, i.e., resistance" [Adorno 1984, 321]) by its
steady subversion of a mainstream, plainspoken poetry of "sincerity" and

unified voice/narration, enacts a purposeful (and playful and compassionate and *political*) resistance. As Messerli observes, "when it comes down to our own times, a great many of the poets who are most praised or adulated by the general public don't have much interest in language: they're more interested in story or sentiment or self-expression" (quoted in Perloff 1988, 32). By contrast, he professes, "I'm really interested in the constructive aspect of language: the minute-to-minute, second-to-second building up of a structure which therefore can (and often does) 'bridge' something" (quoted in Perloff 1988, 33).

If "When we Calypso the mind creates a floor on which to dance" (25), then Messerli is partial to a shifting dance floor, one where the steps are not marked out, where the footprints get moved around, where the dance is a testing out, an attesting to possibilities of playful utterance and thought:

> A particle
> from plain seizes
> stout as poised
> ploughs a race easy
> as if planned
> surfaces abrupt
> ly retract.
>
> (67)

As one of Messerli's early maxims suggests, "To think is to place words in motion" (13). Thus, as other maxims have it, "The word spoke makes the reel man's greatest invention" (50), and "A verb should never be applied to curb" (19).

IV

Though he dug less, depths resulted: generative, and foxy, were his digs.

But one obvious danger of my own habit of reading Messerli, or at least this line of approach, is that in my thematizing of this aesthetics of flow I neutralize it. Messerli's is a poetry of breaks and gaps: its meanings are not separable from its play, its line breaks, its careful soundings. Consider "En Route (Narcissus)":

> Rising just
> a little under
> the weather

```
        's cold
        the cat
        atonic man in the mirror
        for making him come
        from such a sweet sleep
        er to sink
        & revive with his hand
        upon the hand
        dle of the raz
        or he shaves within
        an inch of his life.
                        (13)
```

Such a poem can be explored in juxtaposition with William Carlos Williams's exploration of the line and the line break in *Spring and All* (first published 1923), where we find

```
            of death
            the barber
            the barber
            talked to me

            cutting my
            life with
            sleep to trim
            my hair—
```

and

```
            That sheet stuff
            's a lot of cheese.
```

and

```
        What

        The place between the petal's
        edge and the

        From the petal's edge a line starts
        (W. C. Williams 1986, 212, 216, 195–96)
```

as well as the better known (and now trivialized) "Red Wheel Barrow." Such examples begin to hint at the tradition(s) behind Messerli's writing (though Gertrude Stein's writings of the same period would be more to the point).

Messerli's poems provide us with many pleasant points of departure. As Howard Fox (1987) argues for the virtues of postmodern art, such experimental work allows "a myriad of access points, an infinitude of interpretive responses" (30). As we learn to say and savor this multiplicity, in works such as Messerli's, we affirm the resistant play of the most adventurous writing of our present moment. Barthes (1975): "Whence, perhaps, a means of evaluating the works of our modernity: their value would proceed from their duplicity" (7). If so, the contagious play of Messerli's writing, in this doubled book, *Maxims/Hymns*, a devotional book of (h)ours, speaks doubly well for him and for the poetry of our day.

Of course, what
many have regarded as a liberating permission
to write in otherwise unsanctioned ways
will provoke professional sanction-takers to see
only red.

—Bernstein, *Dark City*

10. Charles Bernstein's *Dark City*

Polis, Policy, and the Policing of Poetry

Charles Bernstein's writing, particularly his poetry, tends to generate two kinds of response. First, the mere mention of his name occasions a metonymic substitution: "Bernstein" becomes the means for an evaluation (or attack on or summary or advocacy) of Language poetry, and his poetry recedes into a more general discussion of the sociology of American poetry-culture. Second, his poetry gets discussed principally in terms of its stylistic features and poetic assumptions, somewhat in accord with Bernstein's (1986) own critical pronouncements:

> There is no escape in writing (or 'elsewhere') from structures/forms, they are everpresent—'de'forming and 're'forming. To *see* them—to *hear* them—as inseparable from 'content'. . . . All writing is a demonstration of method; it can assume a method or investigate it. In this sense, style and mode are always at issue[.] . . . [A] "constructive" mode would suggest that the mode itself is explored as content, its possibilities of meaning are investigated and presented, and that this process is itself recognized as a method. (72, 226, 227)

Indeed, in this essay I continue some aspects of those two projects of critical consideration. But, after an initial lengthy detour, I shall try a different approach to Bernstein's poetry, an approach that, quite improbably, owes its genesis to a strategy undertaken by Helen Vendler in relation to John Ashbery's poetry.

Fifteen years ago, when the name "John Ashbery" occasioned similar critical anxiety as the name "Charles Bernstein" today, Vendler (1981), with great directness, brushed aside the tendency to write (merely) about Ashbery in terms of style:

> It seems time to write about John Ashbery's subject matter. His *As We Know* will, of course, elicit more remarks on his style—a style so influential that its imitators are legion. It is Ashbery's style that has obsessed reviewers, as they alternately wrestle with its elusive impermeability and praise its power of linguistic synthesis. There have been able descriptions of its fluid syntax, its insinuating momentum, its generality of reference, its incorporation of vocabulary from all the arts and all the sciences. But it is popularly believed, with some reason, that the style itself is impenetrable, that it is impossible to say what an Ashbery poem is "about." (108)

Vendler proceeds, in an essay of considerable lucidity and influence, to discuss precisely what Ashbery's poems are about. Similarly, I wonder if it is possible or even desirable to discuss Bernstein's poetry in terms of content? Would such an approach inevitably deform and domesticate (as it thematized and demystified) Bernstein's poetry? Certainly, over the past few years, that is one thing that has happened to Ashbery's poetry: once the cutting edge and the flashpoint for debates about poetry's direction and function, Ashbery's poetry is now seen as an elegant, somewhat wistful, poetically nostalgic but easily thematized poetry on the passage of time, on the phenomenology of dailiness, and on the indirectness and instability of self-portraiture. There is, then, a cost to such an approach: thematized or content-based criticism, in the manner of the New Criticism, inevitably pretends to a unification of material. In the case of Bernstein's poetry, a thematic or content-based approach may falsify his poetry, which is quite insistently based on difference and on a collagist practice of dysraphism, which Bernstein (1987b) in a footnote to a poem given that same term as its title defines as

> a word used by specialists in congenital disease to mean a dysfunctional fusion of embryonic parts—a birth defect. Actually, the word is not in Dorland's, the standard U.S. medical dictionary; but I found it "in use" by a Toronto physician, so it may be a commoner British medical usage or just something he came up with. *Raph* literally means "seam", so dysraphism is mis-seaming—a prosodic device! But it has the punch

of being the same root as rhapsody (*rhaph*) — or in Skeat's — "one who strings (lit. stitches) songs together, a reciter of epic poetry", cf. "ode" etc. (44)

Nevertheless, acknowledging the liabilities of a thematic approach, it does seem worthwhile to ask, especially after twenty books, What are Bernstein's recurring concerns? After an initial consideration of the reception of Bernstein's writing and its place in recent representations of American literature, I shall begin a thematic reading of Bernstein's most recent poetry.

An inquiry into the recurring concerns in Bernstein's poetry may also begin to answer a recurring criticism directed at his poetry. Interestingly enough, this particular line of criticism has been leveled at Bernstein from opposing critical quarters. In a letter written to me seven or eight years ago, Helen Vendler acknowledged that while some of Bernstein's ideas (or poetics) were of interest, she asked (both about Bernstein's writing and about Language poetry more generally) What was memorable about the poetry? What lines or passages were memorable or beautiful? To answer Vendler in her own terms would require a detailed (re)consideration of the memorable and the beautiful (see Gertrude Stein 1926). Certainly the form of much Language poetry — from Lyn Hejinian's (1987) *My Life* to Ron Silliman's *Tjanting* (1981) to Bernstein's "Standing Target" (1980, 39–47) — is memorable and, arguably, beautiful. From a position that, unlike Vendler's, is generally sympathetic to innovation and experimentation, Richard Kostelanetz in his *Dictionary of the Avant-Gardes* (1993) discusses Bernstein in terms of complaint remarkably similar to Vendler's:

> BERNSTEIN, Charles (1950). The most conspicuous of the language-centered poets who gained a precarious prominence in the 1980s[.]
> . . . Trained at Harvard in philosophy and thus rhetorically skilled, Bernstein's writing is derived from early Clark Coolidge and middle Gertrude Stein. Though his experiments in poetry are various, there is not enough consistent character, even in the kinds of experimental intelligence, for many (if any) poems published under his name to be immediately recognizable as his, which is to say that they lack signature. The second, perhaps related problem is that few, if any are individually memorable. Ask even his admirers which poems they like best, and you will find them unable to identify anything. Thus, Bernstein's career raises the radical question of whether a purportedly major experimental poet can be someone whose *poems*, apart from his or her theories, lack signature and are not remembered. (21)

First, those of us who have been reading Bernstein's poetry over a number of years *can* identify particular poems as favorites: "Standing Target" (1980, 39–47), "The Only Utopia Is in a Now" (1987, 34–36), "Amblyopia" (1987, 112–29), and "Emotions of Normal People" (1994, 85–101) among them. But the complaint of a lack of signature (which my essay will show to be a dubious claim) is particularly odd. Such a complaint comes close to a mainstream poetic assumption: that poetic accomplishment must be marked by the achievement of a singular, recognizable, individual "voice," following the commodified artworld's insistence that an artist develop a conceptual signature and/or a repeated, recognizable style. But Bernstein's work resists such simplistic commodification; he produces instead a varied poetry based more on principles of difference. But, as with the (paradoxically) highly personal and individual manner of self-erasure in John Cage's work, Bernstein's poetry of difference—in spite of or *through* his resistance to a poetry of (mere) self-expression—*does*, over a long period of time, develop individualistic modes and manners. What Bernstein's poetry involves is a resistance to (but *not* absolute evasion of) self-expression and the poetics of signature, voice, and a homogeneous style. Indeed, Bernstein's work does not ignore but is in constant dialogue with such forces.

Putting aside for a moment the conflicting evaluations of Bernstein's poetry—in part because as Dana Gioia (1992, 3–9, 15–16, 23) and others have noted, we live in an era in which a genuinely critical debate and a seriously engaged critical writing about poetry are virtually nonexistent—I find it shocking that Bernstein's poetry is unrepresented in virtually every "major" anthology of American Literature and nearly every "major" anthology of contemporary American poetry. *Dark City* (1994) is Charles Bernstein's twentieth book of poetry. In conjunction with *Dark City*, Sun and Moon Press has also reissued Bernstein's groundbreaking first collection of essays, *Content's Dream: Essays 1975–1984*. As co-editor with Bruce Andrews of the important journal $L=A=N=G=U=A=G=E$ and as one of the leading figures of Language poetry, Bernstein entered debates over the role and direction of contemporary American poetry as a serious, provocative critic of the poetic mainstream, decrying the limitations of what he labeled official verse culture:

> What characterizes the officially sanctioned verse of our time, no less than [William Carlos] Williams's, is a restricted vocabulary, neutral and univocal tone in the guise of voice or persona, grammar-book syntax, received conceits, static and unitary form. . . .

Let me be specific as to what I mean by "official verse culture" — I am referring to the poetry publishing and reviewing practices of *The New York Times*, *The Nation*, *American Poetry Review*, *The New York Review of Books*, *The New Yorker*, *Poetry* (Chicago), *Antaeus*, *Parnassus*, Atheneum Press, all the major trade publishers, the poetry series of almost all of the major university presses (the University of California Press being a significant exception at present). Add to this the ideologically motivated selection of the vast majority of poets teaching in university writing and literature programs and of poets taught in such programs as well as the interlocking accreditation of these selections through prizes and awards judged by these same individuals. Finally, there are the self-appointed keepers of the gate who actively put forward biased, narrowly focussed and frequently shrill and contentious accounts of American poetry, while claiming, like all disinformation propaganda, to be giving historical or nonpartisan views. In this category, the American Academy of Poetry and such books as *The Harvard Guide to Contemporary American Writing* stand out. (1986, 245, 247–48; from a talk delivered in 1983)

That narrow-mindedness and xenophobia continue today in mainstream publishing, including the most recently updated American Literature anthologies of Norton (4th ed., 1993), Heath (2d ed., 1994), Harper-Collins (2d ed., 1993), Prentice Hall (1991), and McGraw-Hill (8th ed., 1994). The exclusion of Bernstein's writing by the editors of these anthologies has no credible basis. These anthologies all include many poets of similar age with far fewer books of poems, fewer awards, and far less international recognition. In addition to being one of the leading figures in the Language poetry movement, Bernstein has published twenty books of poetry and two books of essays (one with Harvard University Press); he has edited numerous books and special journal issues; his work is widely translated, published, and read in Argentina, China, Spain, Australia, New Zealand, France, Switzerland, Germany, Italy, the Netherlands, Portugal, England, Canada, Mexico, Finland, Yugoslavia, and Japan; he has received a Guggenheim Fellowship and an NEA Fellowship; and, since 1990, he has been the David Gray Professor of Poetry and Letters at the State University of New York, College at Buffalo. Bernstein is the subject of a great deal of critical writing by critics as diverse and distinguished as Marjorie Perloff, Jerome McGann, Rachel Blau DuPlessis, Alan Golding, Keith Tuma, Bob Perelman, Pierre Joris, Henry Sayre, George Hartley, Linda Reinfeld, and Geoffrey O'Brien, among others.

Bernstein's poetry does get into Norton's *Postmodern American Poetry* anthology (Hoover 1994). But his absolute exclusion in the "major" American Literature anthologies points to an aesthetic conservatism (or xenophobia) that calls for additional consideration (and correction). While the "new" American Literature anthologies—led by the ostensibly ground-breaking Heath (Lauter 1994)—lay claim to a greater range of inclusive-ness, that inclusiveness, as Bernstein's case points out, is, in spite of a valid and important multiculturalism, still exactly as Bernstein claimed in 1983 of official verse culture: narrow, stylistically rigid, and aesthetically xeno-phobic. It is precisely this stylistic and formal narrowness that is most alarming about *all* of the "new" American Literature anthologies. If we were to use an ecological analogy, the range of (poetic) species exhibited in these anthologies is frighteningly narrow.

The "new" American Literature anthologies make Gertrude Stein's (1926) lament equally pertinent today: "it is very much too bad, it is so very much more exciting and satisfactory for everybody if one can have contemporaries, if all one's contemporaries could be one's contempo-raries. . . . If every one were not so indolent they would realise that beauty is beauty even when it is irritating and stimulating not only when it is accepted and classic" (515). As with Stein's own writing (which, similarly, baffles most makers of American Literature anthologies), Bernstein's writ-ing presents us with, to paraphrase William Carlos Williams, difficulties that stay difficult. These difficulties, *if* presented to readers of American Literature, would prove quite worthy of consideration, for they are pre-cisely the difficulties that call into question our most ingrained habits of reading. The situation for Language poetry (and Language poets) within the academic practice of creative writing is roughly the same as the situa-tion in the anthologies: Language poets are kept outside the walls of the institutionalized practice of Creative Writing. Interestingly enough, the principal pressure for the situation to be otherwise comes from students in these programs who are often more democratic and adventurous readers than their teachers (who, for the most part, were raised on the institution-alized divide between poetry and criticism, creativity and theory).

While Bernstein's poetry does not provide an easy or steady target for quotation nor for the simple summary-by-quotation that would assure us that these are Bernstein's essential views and themes, there are recurring concerns (even if enmeshed in the play of ever-shifting tone and form and even if freed from the false innocence of direct self-expression). The first

poem in his 1994 collection *Dark City*, "The Lives of the Toll Takers,"
establishes a consideration of the state of poetry today as one such recurring concern for Bernstein. If we ignore the complexities of voice and
advocacy, we find some seemingly simple and straight-forward axioms or
conditions for poetry: "There is no plain sense of the word, / nothing is
straightforward, / description a lie behind a lie: / but truths can still be
told" and "No 'mere' readers only / writers who read, actors who inter /
act" (24, 20).

Bernstein's poetry, like nearly all of the significant innovative poetry
of this century, takes its place against poetry as a simple form of self-
expression. As John Cage has it, an art of "self-alteration not self-
expression" and "a way of writing which comes from ideas, is not about
them, but which produces them" (1993, 15; 1983, x). While Bernstein rejects
today's mainstream activity—"Poetry: the show- / me business" (17)—the
notion of a self or an individuated writer of poetry remains a complex issue
that will not, even with the magic wand of the phrases "the death of the
author" or "the fragmentation of the self," disappear. For Bernstein, one
distinctive and idiosyncratic form of self is an insistence on his presence in
poems as a kind of besidedness, a besidedness (as in the root of the word
ec-stasy) that is manifest in alternative or multiple phrasings:

<blockquote>
(I

pride myself on my pleonastic a[r]mour.)   {ardour}

(Besides.)

Love may come and love may

go

but uncertainty is here forever.
      {profit?}

(14)
</blockquote>

The entire poem ends with the word "Besides," and as in Bernstein's earlier
poem "Standing Target," there are disruptive syntactic forms that undermine any traditionally unified voice or version of stock expressiveness.

But even a process of self-erasure (as in Cage's chance-generated compositions) or self-dissemination bears with it personal traces. Bernstein
asks and claims, "*Then where is my place?* / Fatal Error F27: Disk directory
full. / The things I / write are / not about me / though they / *become me*"

(15). The humor, vocabulary, and rapidity of shifts are all idiosyncratically Bernstein's. In other words, it is important to recognize that all collaging is not the same nor is it of equal interest, durability, or intelligence. All experimentation, even if premised upon the displacement of self-expression, is not the same. While it most certainly would be wrong to think of (current) poetic expression apart from its community, cultural, historical, and economic contexts, there remain ways in which Bernstein's writing differs decidedly even from the writing of other Language poets. That is part of why Kostelanetz's (1993) remarks are so wrong in two fundamental ways: a personal signature is *not* a goal for Bernstein's writing (in fact, the blunting of such through a poetry of sustained difference *is* one of Bernstein's chief accomplishments); and besides, Bernstein's writing *is*, as I hope to demonstrate, distinctive.

In *Dark City*, humor—slapstick, punning, low humor, the humor of an associative stand-up comic (à la Lenny Bruce or Jackie Mason), a self-critical Jewishness—grows more and more important to Bernstein's writing. His poetry of play deforms the common and the clichéd, whether the source be nursery rhymes (and, obliqueley, Bernstein's role as father and as reader to his two children figures into his writing again and again): "There was an old lady who lived in a / zoo, / she had so many admirers / she didn't know what to rue" (11) and "There was an old lady / who lives in a stew" (14–15). Or the humorous rephrasing of banal music lyrics (in this case, variations on Bob Dylan's "Knocking on Heaven's Door"): "Take this harrow off / my chest, I don't feel it anymore / it's getting stark, too stark / to see, feel I'm barking at Hell's spores" (24). Before we assume that serious, difficult poets lack a sense of humor, we might recall that T. S. Eliot was a devoted fan of Groucho Marx. In fact, one might conjecture that the example of the stand-up comic contributes significantly to the multivoiced productions of modernist and postmodernist poetries.

One joy in reading Bernstein's poetry comes from his uncanny ability simultaneously to spoof a given discourse—in "The Lives of the Toll Takers" the rhetoric of investment calculation and market penetration—and to investigate an issue in poetry of considerable seriousness:

Our new

service orientation

mea

nt

not only changing the way we wrote poems but also diversifying
into new poetry services. Poetic
    opportunities

        ,

        however, do not fall into your lap, at least not
very often. You've got to seek them out, and when you find them
            you've got to have the know how to take advantage
of them.
        Keeping up with the new aesthetic environment is an ongoing
process: you can't stand still. Besides, our current fees
        barely cover our expenses; any deviation from these levels
would
    mean working for nothing. Poetry services provide cost savings
        to readers, such
    as avoiding hospitalizations (you're less likely
to get in an accident if you're home reading poems), minimizing
wasted time (*condensare*), and reducing
        adverse idea interactions
(studies show higher levels of resistance to double-bind
political programming among those who read 7.7 poems or
more each week

).
Poets deserve compensation
for such services.
For readers unwilling to pay the price
we need to refuse to provide such
service as alliteration,
        internal rhymes,
        exogamic structure, and
        unusual vocabulary.

                                (1994, 22–23)

A recurring topic for Bernstein has been Poetry as/and/is Business. Within
the inherent humor of presenting poetry as a kind of small business investment opportunity, Bernstein's counsel does raise serious questions:
Isn't poetry a small business with plenty of indirect economic benefits
(prizes, reading fees, academic positions, grants, residencies, publication)
that usually go unacknowledged? What are the significant trends in poetry

today? (Is the wise investment in performance-oriented poetry? In computer or CD-based texts? In multicultural identities?) What are the benefits of reading poetry? What is an efficient way to distribute poetry? (Free through e-mail? Or through the hierarchies of prestige and "major" [hardcopy] publishing houses?) What service does a poet provide and how is she to be compensated? In such matters, Bernstein has throughout his career been influenced by the thinking of Thoreau (1989), who insisted that "trade curses every thing it handles; and though you trade in messages from heaven, the whole curse of trade attaches to the business" (70). Bernstein and others, especially experimental poets who resist the trends and habits of the mainstream, face a serious issue: how to commodify poetry (for publication inevitably constitutes commodification) without destroying poetry's oppositional potential and the poet's position as a player in the enterprise of cultural criticism.

The avant-garde is, as Bernstein realizes, not exempt from the deforming pressures of a market economy. While David Antin contends that poetry is essentially "an advertisement for nothing," most poetry in fact is an advertisement for a community of writers, for itself (as a worthy object of attention), and for the writer (as "competent" and "professional" and worthy of "compensation"). While Shelley's idealism contains some element of truth—we all are working on one big poem (collectively, over time)—anyone who has tried to get published also knows that poetry too is an intensely competitive business. Knowing Stein's description of the movement of innovative poetry from outlaw to classic, a wise poet-investor might wish to venture into the new but might also do so in a savvy manner: "What if / success scares you so much that at the point of some / modest acceptance, midway through / life's burning, you blast out / onto the street, six-shooters smoking, still a rebel. / For what? / Of course new ventures always require risk, but by carefully / analyzing the situation, we became smart risk / takers" (1994, 21). And such may in fact be both Bernstein's own position—as the "rebel" who now holds an endowed professorship and who *is* published in *American Poetry Review*—and that of Language poetry generally, the latter now being a frequent topic for university-based critics writing about contemporary poetry, as the central school in recent anthologies such as Hoover (1994) and Messerli (1994); and as the object of some anxiety among younger innovative poets (see for example Nash [1994], with its implicit question "what next after Language poetry"?) who seek both to extend the work of Language poetry and to differentiate themselves from it. Also, over the past five to seven years, many of the leading Language poets have, for various reasons, written less and less in the way of manifestoes or adversarial critical essays. The era of market penetration and of positioning by way of antagonism is over for Language poetry. The risks being taken by most Language poets today may be "smart risks" or risks that occur within an established domain (of market consolidation or risk repetition). Just as the term "risk" (used as a form of praise) within the domain of a mainstream poetry of personal experience and singular voice now sounds absurd, the same may be true for most forms of innovation in Language poetry. In *Dark City* Bernstein addresses, albeit humorously, this sense of having reached some sort of plateau: "Voyage of life / Getting you down? Felt better when things / Were really rocky & now there's smooth / Sailing but it's lost its meaning?" (133–34). Perhaps it is fair to say that Bernstein's writing—particularly the essays—is less adversarial than it was ten years ago (and a rereading of *Content's Dream* [1986] confirms such a sense). Bernstein's work is more widely read; Language poetry is a movement and a variety of poetry that has achieved a certain level of visibility. But there has also been a cost for such citizenship, a cost for participation in a broader (institutionalized) literary discussion for both Bernstein and Language poetry: a politeness and conciliatoriness that go along with a quest for greater acceptance. In rereading Bernstein's earlier essays, though, I must also conclude however that most of the complaints he lodges in *Content's Dream* (against the narrowness and exclusions of the mainstream) are still, for the most part, valid.

But the more serious question to ask is not What comes *after* Language poetry? Rather, we should ask, Does Language poetry, or more specifically the work of Charles Bernstein, represent (merely) an extension of earlier developments in modernism? Or is there something fundamentally or seminally distinct about Language poetry's contribution? My own sense is that such questions must be answered with attention to the specific cultural and historical circumstances in which Language poetry and the writing of Charles Bernstein appeared. In answering in the affirmative— that Language poetry and Charles Bernstein *do* make important contributions to American poetry—that contribution may, oddly enough, *not* be principally based in formal innovation per se, but in altered professional conceptions of the poet and in redirecting (and re-imagining) relationships between reader and writer and in rethinking earlier modernisms. (In the latter regard, the New Formalism, by contrast, is fundamentally a nostalgic and regressive phenomenon: it makes no claims for undiscovered or unknown forms in its predecessors, nor for a significantly altered perspective in the rereading of prior poets. Its primary claim seems to be that poets should return to those already accomplished forms and learn to do them again.)

To return though to the specific poems in *Dark City*, we find that Bernstein is quite skilled at taking a common phrase or proverb and deforming it. In "Locks Without Doors" the phrase about "the quality of mercy" becomes "The quality of Hershey's is not / too great although I always preferred / Skippy's smooth to crunch" (55) and "Then again the quality of Jersey is not / much to wriggle your teeth about" (56). Or, in the same poem, more substantive transformations occur such as "not for you / the hullabaloo"(54), "Books can be deceiving" (57), and "I can't but make it con / fluesce" (52), the latter (with its assertion of the inevitable running together of all writings) stands as an important corrective to Pound's lament late in the *Cantos* that he could not make it cohere. The high modernist quest for unity—Pound's quest for closure and unification in the *Cantos*, Eliot's attempt in *The Waste Land* to shore fragments against his ruin—gives way to a postmodern understanding more attuned to Cage's relativist assertion: "that two notations on the same / piece of paper / automatically bring / about relationship" (1993, 22). Or, if Bernstein's writing were to be called a new kind of realism then that realism would be premised not upon closure and (thematic) unification but upon resistance to these particular overused poetic devices.

One particular register in Bernstein's (1994) compositional arsenal is, in addition to a wide-ranging vocabulary (which contrasts with the more narrow claim of an anti-poetic diction by William Carlos Williams's 1960s descendants, whose claim really amounted to the reintroduction into poetry of slang and of some elements of vernacular "common" speech), the recurrence of a peculiarly clotted sound effect, a kind of line and sound that is deliberately but interestingly difficult to say, a kind of anti-mellifluousness: "Slump not lest slip, slumber, swagger into / indelicacy, delirious indolence" (50) and "Sustenance evaporates in subsequent / slumber. Amulets emit armatures" (42). When Kostelanetz (1993) laments the lack of a signature to Bernstein's poems, I would counter with this peculiar sound quality in Bernstein's work. Admittedly, such a feature of sound is not established with the consistency or reductiveness to constitute Bernstein's "personal voice" (ugh), but it is a recurring idiosyncratic marker in his work. As is his odd inhabitation of a late nineteenth-century iambic Swinburnian mellifluousness:

For long have I entombed my love
Less fleck than flayed upon
Who quaint and wary worry swarms
In tides lament nor laminations ore
As stare compares a bellys tumble
Have I awaited by the slope
Of lumined ledgers lumbering links
Foregone though never bent

(51)

When, as he often does, Bernstein makes apparent the mode or form of construction for a given passage of his writing—as in the following example where a process of word association from one word at the end of one sentence to the same word used with a different meaning at the beginning of the next sentence—we must ask if that display of conscious construction (cf. Thoreau 1989: "Shall we forever resign the pleasure of construction to the carpenter?" 46) is the only content of the passage:

Not that I mean to startle just
unsettle. The settlers pitched their tents
into foreign ground. All ground is
foreign ground when you get to know
it as well as I do. Well I wouldn't agree.
No agreement like egregious
refusal to hypostatize a suspension.
Suspension bridges like so many
drummers at bat, swatting flies in
the hot Carolina sun. No, son, it
wasn't like that—we only learned we
had to be proud not what's worth taking
pride in.

(51)

First, it is tempting to answer no and to back up such an answer by isolating assertions that do indeed have a substantial resonance for Bernstein's poetry and poetics: "Not that I mean to startle just / unsettle." Such a process of isolation amounts to a repetition or reapplication of New Critical methods of reading-as-thematizing. (The third sentence may also be subjected to a similar act of thematization-by-isolation.) But what such a method fails to take into account is the deliberately ambiguous status of the authoritative proverbial pronouncement in Bernstein's writing. In this section, each such self-assured pronouncement is immediately undone or at least made dubious by the next sentence, which stands as a literal counter to its partner sentence, exposing the rhetoric that allows the illusion of unchallenged authoritativeness (folk wisdom) to come into being in the first place. To "No, son, . . . ," we must answer, "right, we don't know what to take pride in, including this authoritative tone that allows us to make such a negative declaration." Bernstein thus mixes irony, pastiche, play, and serious declaration in a conscious act of theatricalized dysraphism. And, as Bernstein's previously cited discussion of dysraphism points out, there is a rhapsodic element to such writing. Bernstein's poems also demonstrate some of the range available to a collagist writing practice that as David Antin (1972, 107) has argued, may be the single most important critical principle of twentieth-century innovative poetic practice.

Though Bernstein's work, and that of Language poets generally, tends to be presented in opposition to many of the projects and styles of mainstream poetry, there is an important overlap. Among mainstream poets (and poets of the plain style), Louis Simpson and Philip Levine (in different ways) typify attention to "the ordinary" or to "the common life." Bernstein (1994) too is interested in "the ordinary": "As if the / ordinary / were just there answering / our call but we / won't sound it / out, or find the work / too demanding (de- / meaning), too extra / ordinary" (62–63). Whereas Simpson and Levine thematize that ordinariness, by relegating it to the position of the poem's subject matter (presented in a thoroughly unself-conscious language that pretends to a nondistorting transparency), Bernstein, like Ashbery, is concerned with the ways in which different modes of language fashion our conceptions of the ordinary, indeed the ways in which different modes of language *are* the ordinary in which we live:

> Every syllable stings. & that's the
> hardest thing to stomach on a low-noise
> diet, if you can sink your teeth into
> the
> thought that all that sound gotta be
> digested. Anemic
> poetry—or roughage?—for the health-
> continent society? But

why prize distraction over direction, song over
solemnity? The times detail a change of
pockets & everybody's loopy, mind made
up with hospital corners, while the leaves
of our lives unsettle their occupation.

(64)

Like the music of Charles Ives—a collage of avant-garde dissonances
alongside immensely popular elements of band music—Bernstein's collagist poetry increasingly involves the language of movies, the style of
stand-up comedy, and the language of business. At times, along with the
camp citation of cartoon characters, there is even a quaint, Ashberian sentimentality to Bernstein's most recent poetry:

> Popeye
> no longer sails, but Betty
> Boop will always
> sing sweetlier
> sweetliest
> than the crow who fly
> against the blank
> remorse of castles made
> by dusk, dissolved in
> day's baked light.
>
> (1994, 81)

One of the most important poems in *Dark City* is "Emotions of Normal People," an extended collage-poem that invites comparison with
Bernstein's earlier classic "Standing Target" (in *Controlling Interests*, 1980).
Though, overall, *Dark City*, as all of Bernstein's larger books, is built on a
principle of difference—each poem different from those that surround it
and a book of poems that offers conscious resistance to signature and the
cults of personal voice, personality, individualized-instantly-recognizable-
style, and poetry-as-personal expression—long composite poems such as
"Emotions of Normal People" recur throughout Bernstein's twenty-book
output, and constitute his most important, distinctive, and most fully realized contribution to American poetry. The poem begins in the language of
computer sales:

> With high expectations, you plug
> Into your board & power up. The

Odds are shifted heavily in your
Favor as your logic simulator comes
On-screen. If there's a problem
You see exactly where it's located
& can probe either inside or
Outside with a schematic editor.
English-like commands make
Communication easy.

(1994, 85)

As in the earlier poem "Standing Target," Bernstein's concern is with the world of words and concepts in which we command and are commanded. While the sales-rhetoric—consistent with an American ideology of individualized choice—insists that the product will be "Compatible with target-embedded / Resident assemblers & wet-wet / Compilers. & the fact that you can / Configure it yourself means you / Get exactly what you want" (86), Bernstein calls our attention to the recurrent elements of control, standardization, and normalization in the technologies that shape our thinking. The ways in which we are sold on computers—with their "controllers," "a family of workstations," an "external trigger," "low-loss mating," "debugging," and "remote-error sensing terminals (RESTS)" —resell us on embedded American ideologies as "several vendors [attempt] to control the marketplace by promoting standards that especially benefit their computing architecture" (89). In "Emotions of Normal People," where computer/business transactions are juxtaposed with thank-you notes, psychological analyses, descriptions of marital difficulties, market surveys for personal products, and book advertisements, Bernstein is concerned with the ways in which we are targeted in the processes of social and technological normalization—a process of narrowing possibilities with obvious ramifications for poetic expression. The consumer-oriented world that Bernstein lays out—a world of complete commodification, from computers to self-esteem—where exchange and sales are endless, the one certainty is that all of the time "operators are on duty."

True, there is a truism or cliché at the heart of such a poem: that we today are bombarded and manipulated by many messages (that is, that the Marxist term "overdetermination" names an alarming omnipresence). But Bernstein explores that truism and focuses attention on the particular language-terms and rhetorics that may foreclose thinking and standardize our options if such forces are not resisted. Thus, poems such as "Standing

Target" and "Emotions of Normal People" embody both a pedagogy and an implied primer of/on resistance.

The final, extended section of the poem begins "Are you a normal person?" Of course, some deviance from the norm is perfectly normal: "Probably for the most part you are [normal]. / Your sex complexes, your fears and furies and petty jealousies, / your hatreds and deceptiveness, only serve / to secure your normalcy" (96). Nearly all of us remain fit targets for the consumerist bombardment detailed earlier in the poem; thus Bernstein's aside in the flat discourse of a scientific news release — "Dr. Cuit P. / Tichter of the Johns Hopkins University / found that Norway rats / died quickly if their whiskers were clipped / and they were put into a / tank of water" (96) — rhymes with the other modes of manipulation and targeting detailed throughout the poem. As targets, we are warned in the appropriated language of pop psychology that "there are no adequate emotional outlets / for many stresses and people who depend completely / on their emotions frequently find themselves / in jail" and "the intestine is / as sensitive to bombardments / from the brain as the skin of some people to sun rays" (97). In Bernstein's characteristic mode of self-cancelling irony, the end of the poem warns, "In any case, sarcasm / is evidence of a sadistic trend in one's / personality" (101). So, if sarcasm is not appropriate — and Bernstein's collage-poems of social and consumerist manipulation rarely descend into a simplistic sarcasm or superior scorn — what strategies are available to us? Bernstein's entire poetic output answers that question by embodying modes of writing and thinking that resist simple commodification and that undermine most forms of normalized, standardized "communiciation." The political dimension of Bernstein's "opaque" writing thus, in its subversion and defamiliarization of the "transparent" communication used in the world of commodification and consumption, bears an important relationship to what Michel Foucault, in his preface to Deleuze and Guattari's *Anti-Oedipus*, calls the "art of living counter to all forms of fascism." Foucault advises, "Prefer what is positive and multiple, difference over uniformity, flows over unities, mobile arrangements over systems. Believe that what is productive is not sedentary but nomadic" (Deleuze and Guattari 1983, xiii). Such advice pinpoints the ideological implications of Bernstein's poetic practice.

One form of resistance or subversion that Bernstein has worked on for years is a humorous writing based on a series of rapid shifts and replacements. As an example of this kind of intellectual poetic slapstick, I cite the opening lines of "Debris of Shock / Shock of Debris":

The debt that pataphysics owes to sophism
cannot be overstated. A missionary with a horse
gets saddlesores as easily as a politburo
functionary. But this makes a mishmash of overriding ethical
impasses. If the liar
is a Cretan I wouldn't trust him
anyway—extenuating contexts wouldn't amount
to a hill of worms so far as I
would have been deeply concerned about
the fate of their, yes, spools. Never
burglarize a house with a standing army,
nor take the garbage to an unauthorized
junket. Yet when I told the learned
ecologist about my concern for landscape
she stared unsympathetically into the
carbon. Mr. Spoons shook his head, garbled his
hypostases. To level with you we'd have
to be on the same
level. Then, with all honesty, we can
only proceed to deplane.

(1994, 105–6)

Later in the same poem, Bernstein writes, "Fool's / gold / is the only kind
of gold I / ever cared about." But only an uncritical reading would take
Bernstein at his word, as if his aphorisms had some sort of transcendent
"truth" value, as if they were somehow the "essential" part of a poem. Humor (often of the pun, the replacement [of one word for another similar
word], and of association) and a perpetual shifting of perspective become
Bernstein's vehicles to an absolute contingency—the nomadic flow that
Foucault idealizes in his preface to *Anti-Oedipus* (Deleuze and Guattari
1983). Bernstein achieves a dizzying kind of poetic variancy. By contrast,
for a poet such as Emily Dickinson such compressed variancy focuses on
and creates a perpetually elusive meaning (or theme). For Bernstein that
variancy displays the slipperiness of a constantly shifting tone.

A poem such as "Heart in My Eye" goes a long way toward illustrating
some of the peculiarities of Bernstein's "unpoetic poetic" (113) ear. He has
always toyed with an encrusted, alliterative sound, as in these lines from
"How I Painted Certain of My Pictures": "The lorry has left the / levy lest
the sandwiches lay / lost, looted" (62). We can zero in on some of Bern-

stein's particular unpoetic poetic sounds in the following passage from "Heart in My Eye":

> —or hate
> the boom-shebang effect
> fostered at time
>
> interlock, station flayed by
> inoperable hampers, obsequious
> swoops, as pulp bumps
> plop, thingamawhoseit buffle
>
> joint, glassed in gradually
> gestures of gerrymand
> origin, jitters jocose oblong—
>
> (114)

Bernstein is increasingly drawn to the odd demotic word such as "boom-shebang" (or, as elsewhere in the same poem, "higglety pigglety" and "slumpy"). He has established a well-developed ear for a peculiar dissonance in word-sounds, a kind of deliberately clotted, awkward, technical language that has its own percussive music. I dare say that no one else is writing lines such as "voids convivial handtray intubation" (114), and that no one else is as attuned to such a peculiar music. The very deliberateness of such a music—indeed, it must be a conscious craft—baits the reader in several ways. The regularity of stanzaic appearance (in this poem, alternation of three- and four-line stanzas, with alternating three-word and four-word line lengths) combined with this odd music may bring into play outmoded habits of reading, particularly the seeking out of theme and unified meaning. In such poems, the sound itself and the form itself become the poem's content; deliberately, they do not yield to some meaning beyond their appearance. The words and sounds refuse the more habitual or mainstream poetic task of carrying meaning. Instead of sacrificing their "thingness" to the allegedly greater task of expression (of a message), Bernstein's words do their work at the level of sound and appearance. These words exercise their full rights in an act of oddly pleasant autonomy, what Bernstein hints at (earlier in the poem) as "coddling codices in / endoskeletal humor mongering" (113).

Nevertheless, in Bernstein's poetry I feel an element of encodedness. His poetry does not arise out of an absolute rejection of meaningfulness nor even an absolute rejection of thematization; the milieu of the literary in which Bernstein's writing comes into being is too fully situated in these particular tasks. As a reader, I feel baited to crack a code or in some way to tame or domesticate the poetry by means of some seemingly more coherent form of restatement. One such method would be the New Critical hangover of compulsive meaning/theme-making, which takes any writing, no matter how fragmented and dispersed, and creates the fiction of unification (often by means of an overarching idea). Such cherry-picking— selecting choice quotation-morsels—achieves a readerly sense of mastery (by an assured tone of restatement) but utterly falsifies the reading experience of such a text. Another alternative would be the personalizing (or, more accurately, biographicalizing) of the text. This second approach has proved to be a "successful" approach to both Eliot's *Waste Land* and Pound's *Cantos*. In the latter case, the painful personal story of Pound's experience in Pisa and subsequent time in Saint Elizabeth's is used as a substitute narrative that makes "accessible" the more complicated poem by graphing the poem's language in terms of the poet's personal experience. Of course, such an approach misses the poetry's adventurous formal consciousness (and replaces it with the more familiar contour of personal narrative). Such an approach also verges on becoming a *People* magazine version of criticism. Bernstein's work—with its occasional references to his father's clothing business, to his children and family, to Bernstein's many years of writing medical digests, and so forth—offers some similar temptations. But the rigor of his poetry of difference (his conscious resistance to a poetry of personal expression) adequately short-circuits such reading approaches. Like the more radical phases of Gertrude Stein's writing, Bernstein's poetry successfully resists reductive recuperative reading strategies. He writes "difficulties that stay difficult." Thus, along with Stein, he shares an important place in American innovative poetry with his contemporaries such as Susan Howe and Bruce Andrews.

One of the most intriguing poems in the collection is the concluding title poem, "Dark City," which begins with a movie epigraph, Lizabeth Scott to Charlton Heston in *Dark City*, "We're a great pair—I've got no voice and you've got no ear." While throughout *Dark City* (and earlier collections as well), Bernstein engages in a kind of genre writing, inhabiting the language of various cinematic genres, in this concluding poem the epigraph points more decidedly toward (simultaneously) issues of poetics, Bernstein's poetry decidedly being a writing that eschews the mainstream essential of a recognizable individual "voice." Oddly, this poem leads into two sections—"Apple-Picking Time" and "Early Frost"—that are obliquely in dialogue with a conventionally voice-based poet, the (metaphysical) Robert Frost of the folksy vernacular. The opening lines, though, do not bear any obvious relationship to Frost (nor to Frost's "After Apple-Picking"):

> A transom stands bound to a flagpole. Hard
> by we go hardly which way is which
> lingering somewhere unsettled where evidence
> comes harder by sockets, stems
> etched in flexed omission like osmotic
> molarities flickering edge and orange at flow
> rates unrepresentative of ticking or torpor
> any child or person requires for, well
> against, that remorse remonstration
> brings. It's cold outside, maybe
> but the heart sinks daily in
> slump of sampled parts and *I*
> *feel like* carelessness, disowning what's
> acquired in indifferent
> animation, no body swaps to—
> not as if elevated or cut down
> to size up, like layers of lost
> boys, like aspiration in a tub
> at sea, lists all the scores and
> scares at measures twice the fall.
>
> (139)

Instead, they point more toward both a kinship with John Ashbery's sumptuous sentences and Bernstein's idiosyncratic difference from such eloquence. What I have referred to as a clotted sound or a difficult percussive music is reflected in phrases such as "etched in flexed omission like osmotic molarities" and "that remorse remonstration brings" (139). His long sentences are like Ashbery's but with lumps and clots in them: sumptuous, sinuous sentences partial to a strangely pleasant awkwardness, sentences that stage a deliberate conflict between mellifluousness and a clunky scientific quality. The epigraph leads us to wonder whether such writing does indeed constitute both a voice and an ear, albeit a deliberately "off" version of both.

In a manner similar to his self-canceling irony, Bernstein in "Dark City" plays (both quaintly and movingly) with aspects of the iambic English lyric tradition:

> *I loved my love with gold*
> *She loved me with her smile*
> *But I took no possession*
> *Then / Had no taste called mine*
> *I knew I wept alone that night*
> *As sure as sheep in folds*
> *The I has ways the arm betrays*
> *For now my lance is warped*
>
> (140)

If it is the "I" that is perpetually being reconstituted, critiqued, burlesqued, and dismantled in his poetry, we may do well also to keep in mind Bernstein's injunction earlier in the book, "Our jailers / are our constipating sense of self" (127).

Bernstein's poetry remains self-consciously a poetry of venture and adventuring: "I think it's time we let the cat out / its bag, swung the dog over the / shoulder, so to say, let the hens / say 'hey' to the woodpeckers, doled / out some omniaversions to the / too-tapped-upon, the tethers without / toggles, the field-happy expeditioneers / on the march to Tuscaloosa, Beloit, / Manual Falls, Florid Oasis" (142). That adventure remains one of deformation and transposition—a destruction of the automatic and habitual and the clichéd: "The Czech / is in the jail (the wreck is / in the wail, the deck is in the / sail, the Burma shave's shining over the / starry blue skies, Waukeegan, New Jersey, / 1941)" (142). But it is a transposing that is serious too:

> A poem should not mean but impale
> not be but bemoan,
>   boomerang
>   buck(le)
>   bubble.
>
> (141)

Bernstein's altered aphorisms (like Fractured Fairy Tales?) offer up the unsettling "truth" of transposition and deformation. They mark and remark upon the perpetual (and inevitable) metaphoricity of poetic expressiveness:

Love is like love, a baby
like a baby, meaning like
memory, light like light.
A journey's a detour
and a pocket a charm
in which deceits are borne.
A cloud is a cloud and
a story like a story,
song is a song, fury
like fury.

(145)

In the midst of his play, Bernstein has the poem swerve toward a more seemingly direct consideration:

This is the difference between truth
and reality: the one advertises itself
in the court of brute circumstance
the other is framed by its own
insistences. Truth's religious, reality
cultural, or rather
truth is the ground of reality's
appearance but reality intervenes
against all odds.

(145–46)

But the book itself ends with a critique and a reminder: " 'The words / come out of / her heart / & into the / language' / & the language / is in the heart / of that girl / who is in the heart / of you" (146). As he claims in "Thought's Measure," one of the most important essays in *Content's Dream* (1986), for Bernstein (via Wittgenstein) there is no allowance for thoughts apart from language:

An analogous idea to that of language not accompanying but constituting the world is that language does not accompany 'thinking'. "When I think in language, there aren't 'meanings' going through my mind in addition to the verbal expressions: the language is itself the vehicle of thought." (1986, 62)

So, too, for Bernstein does the expression of emotion, and the creation of meaning in and through emotional experience, take place in and of language. Perhaps that is why this poem begins with references to Frost, whose poetry, crafted and self-conscious as it is, pretends to truths apart from the nature of language itself and pretends to a voice of wisdom that somehow transcends the contingencies of rhetoric and theatricality. It is this same poetic naïveté in Frost that David Antin, at greater length and more vituperatively, complains about in his talk-piece "the death of the hired man." Bernstein, though, does not himself eschew voice nor rhetoric nor theatricality. Instead, he insists on the constructedness of poetic writing, speaking/writing through it with necessary contingency, humor, and a peculiarly accomplished grace:

> Boxers
> can't live by punching alone, but
> stay clear of such as possible—a
> Divine Swerve will still land you
> in Hell's cauldron. *Thus*
> make your peace with yourself at
> your own risk for peace with the Devil
> costs everybody more than you could
> hope to destroy. *Holy is as holy does.*
> Essence precludes existence.
>
> (143)

Bernstein's poetry, with its odd humor and its calculated resistance to repetition and personal narrative, provides us with a rich exploration of new modes of meaning-making in poetry. His poetry, particularly the new work represented in *Dark City*, makes a substantial contribution to the ever-developing and perpetually unstable genre of American poetry. Bernstein's poems challenge our most ingrained reading habits, particularly the thematizing of poetry that has dominated American critical reading methods for poetry since the advent of the New Criticism nearly seventy-five years ago. The particular irritation, difficulty, pedagogy, and beauty of Bernstein's poetry ought rightfully to occupy a significant place in current representations of American poetry.

11. Atomic Epistemology and Constituent Knowledge

James Sherry's *Our Nuclear Heritage*

If poetry is, as Charles Bernstein (1987a) asserts, "epistemological inquiry" (1992 repr., 17–18), James Sherry has recently conducted one of the most thorough acts of such inquiry. As in the practice of many other (innovative) poets, that questioning is conducted primarily at a level of linguistic, stylistic, formal, and meaning-making inquiry. James Sherry's (1991) radical gesture is to insist on a pivotal subject matter as well: *Our Nuclear Heritage*, which carries with it not only the peril of our self-destruction but also an investigation into the way in which knowledge is organized. Sherry's radical skepticism — at once tonal and intellectual — denies self-congratulatory poetic thinking. His book is one of the most self-critical I have ever read; in its stripping away of its own comforts, Sherry's book resembles, particularly in temperament, the so-called dark or tragic side of American Renaissance literary consciousness: that of Poe, Melville, and especially Hawthorne.

What marks Sherry's writing as in the spirit of Melville and Poe is a rigorous self-cancelation, in *Our Nuclear Heritage* accomplished principally via the book's appendixes, which are at once concessions (to the reader) for information as well as an undercutting of the truth-status of the text's and/or author's explanatory and expressive capacities. *Our Nuclear Heritage* begins with a preface that "Appendix D: Pony" identifies as in the style of a high school history text: "Atoms existed before people and will exist after" (9). Sherry continues:

> We humans see this, now; we think we see it. We see an image of ourselves echoed and distorted by the countless times and forms this image of the universe projects on the screen of our life. These atoms are everywhere—in the sky we see, in the sky we carry around with us, in the unremembered scenes which we feel as vague and urgent pressures on our every step, in the societies and families we build, and in the selves which are regulated by them. (9)

The atom then exists for Sherry as a governing metaphor, as a structural fiction, operating with the pervasiveness of ideology and the unconscious: "And on self-reflection, individuals are charged in turn by its [the atom's] presence" (9).

Sherry is serious about restoring seriousness to literature. That seriousness has been destroyed by unreflective self-interest, fragmentation, professionalized posturing and careerism, the ghettoization of literature as a merely decorative mode of knowledge (subordinated to the project of individualized bourgeois sensitivity and personal development). Though Sherry writes in different modes of discourse—in modalities and genres (which are more fundamental than "style")—his book is *not* a reveling in a postmodern play of signifiers.

Like Poe's "Man of the Crowd," Sherry's (1991) "characters are impelled from the movement of ideas" (11). The characters of *Our Nuclear Heritage*—Carpaccio and Graceland—are only minimally and sporadically present. They occupy orbitals; they move according to laws of motion. But so too do we and he, and Sherry knows it. In *Our Nuclear Heritage*, Sherry is willing to map "us" in ways that are none too flattering.

From the start, mono-voiced narrativizing or philosophizing is rejected. The first section of *Our Nuclear Heritage* begins, "Go ahead, press it. Humanity's defective" (13) in the voice "of a soldier in the missile silo" (250), though even that voice ends in a strangely Whitman-like invitation, "for you too with me here stand finding out how to decide" (14). That is one of Sherry's particular strengths: though derisive and sarcastic, he is never simply so; he subjects himself and his friends and fellow artists to his scathing humor and skepticism. Sherry's principal enemy is an unselfcritical and unself-conscious self-interest.

In writing *Our Nuclear Heritage*, Sherry has created an odd book, one that might be described as Sherry does in "You Can Bank on It": "To avoid falling into the trap of myself becoming a control-seeking entity forced to vie with their competing logics, my first method was to list all of the inter-actions between the constituent elements involved. So rather than a story I wrote a matrix, so we do not have to speak of the aesthetic of compara-tive value systems" (1991, 78). Sherry's *Our Nuclear Heritage* thus gives up a unifying authorial position that would (pretend to) control or oversee its constituent elements. In this way, *Our Nuclear Heritage* oddly bears an interesting relationship to the chance-operations of Cage or Mac Low, as a way of attempting to make writing other than an ego-dominated form of expression.

Our Nuclear Heritage is thus, for me, a book that is hard to raise (after reading it) to consciousness, hard to hold in mind, hard to re-member, though it is a book that is quite memorable. What carries over is the *matrix* of the reading experience. It is not a developmental reading process (of argument or emotion or narrative or self-revelation). It definitely *is* an in-stance of exciting thinking.

Sherry is peculiar both in his self-critical perspectives (especially on experimental writing communities) and in his investigation of systems-oriented thinking. His is a rare and important intelligence.

Toward a Sociology of Knowledge/
The Writings of Habermas

Sherry's overriding concern is with the atomization of knowledge. In theory, that atomization should provide a stockpile for building other re-lations:

> Even Democritus
> would concede that whether all units are equal
> isn't as important as once he decides
> to emphasize the unit, its relations
> with other units becomes paramount.
>
> (15)

Though equally likely, and perhaps exactly our current condition, is for atomization to take place as sequestered, narrowed self-regard:

> Now we are engaged in a great
> atomic, in this sense war
> where one's ideas are pitted against every other one's,

each the property of a unique and desperate
individual cunningly inscribing signatures
on the underbellies of conjunctions that connect them,
replete with all the rules of our life in one.
The ideas we agree with are morally correct.

(15)

The connections—implicit and explicit—between *Our Nuclear Heritage* and the writings of Jürgen Habermas are quite interesting. Peter Dews (1986) claims that

> Habermas accepts that philosophy can no longer sustain its claims to reveal the fundamental nature of reality; but he also denies that contemporary thought is obliged to choose between trivialized technicality or a gradiose arbitrariness. Philosophy *can* continue to deal with substantive questions, but only by acknowledging that it can no longer do so alone, through a collaboration with empirical disciplines. (3)

We could substitute "poetry" for "philosophy," and Sherry's thinking is remarkably parallel. Sherry is *not* a believer in a mystico-religious perspective on poetry/literature as the great revealer of truth. Within the realm of postmodern theorizing, Sherry may seem to begin at a point similar to Lyotard, who "follows Nietzsche through to a drastic pluralism, suggesting that the 'grand narratives' have been irreparably fragmented into a multiplicity of 'language-games' whose truth-claims are localized, and which are played with an ironic consciousness of their own relativity" (Dews 1986, 7). But Sherry, like Habermas, is not merely ironizing, nor is his writing given over "only" to play. (Though, to his credit, Sherry *is* immensely playful, dandyish, and accomplished—great humor, of a Melvillean deconstructive variety, against which and through which Sherry works toward comprehensiveness and system-building.) Like Habermas, Sherry is skeptical of postmodernist or theory-based claims of "revolution" and "emancipation."

Sherry's systematic thinking marks an important affinity with Habermas and an important critique of postmodernism. If there is to be a lasting importance to the work of contemporary innovative poets, it is that we will have reinvigorated modernist writing (through rereading and re-creating it) without succumbing to an "aesthetic modernism." Habermas correctly characterizes most poststructuralist thinking as blind to its own totalizing aspirations (encoded in such master concepts as "desire," "power," or even "language-games") and most postmodern thinking as prone to a melodramatic narrativizing (of twentieth-century historical tragedy). For Sherry and Habermas, fragmentation itself (as a mode of expression) is not an adequate or complete response to our times:

> It is true that Habermas's work does not hold up a mirror to contemporary experiences of fragmentation, loss of identity, and libidinal release, in the manner which has enabled post-structuralist writing to provide the "natural" descriptive vocabulary for the culture of advanced consumer capitalism. But neither does it pay for its expressive adequacy and immediacy with a lack of theoretical and historical perspective.
>
> The importance of such perspective is, of course, most clearly underlined by the contrast between postmodern theory's melodramatic portrayal of the grand finale of modernity, and Habermas's contention that modernity is necessarily subject to recurrent crisis, insofar as it is the first form of society which cannot draw uncritically on the resources of tradition, but is obliged to unfold its fundamental norms from within itself. (Dews 1986, 33)

But the principal basis of Sherry's affinity with Habermas is as an evaluator and investigator of modes of developing knowledge and of the possible interrelationships of those modes of knowing: "If we imagine the philosophical discussion of the modern period reconstructed as a judicial hearing, it would be deciding a single question: how is reliable knowledge (*Erkenntis*) possible" (Habermas 1986, 3). Sherry's *Our Nuclear Heritage* weighs in as testimony at that hearing—enacting and investigating difficulties of reliability, while trying to investigate systematically its own subject matter (that is, our nuclear heritage).

With Habermas, Sherry acknowledges and savors the shared root assumptions of science and philosophy that if not an immediately healing perspective (of the modern breach between scientific and philosophic thinking), at least allow for the possibility of conversation and communication between the two. Habermas (1986) points out "the ethos that modern science owes to the beginnings of theoretical thought in Greek philosophy: psychologically an unconditional commitment to theory and epistemologically the severance of knowledge from interest" (303). Habermas's (1986) particular definition of theory as well as his conclusion about how theorizing establishes its importance are worth noting: "Theory in the sense of the classical tradition only had an impact on life because it was thought to have discovered in the cosmic order an ideal world structure, including the prototype for the order of the human world. Only as cosmology was *theoria* also capable of orienting human action" (306). Sherry, as Habermas, is recurrently concerned with knowledge and/as self-interest. For Sherry, such an investigation has ramifications for poetry/writing communities (which I shall discuss later), as well as in broader, more worldly forms of knowledge. For Sherry, such an orientation will demystify and demythologize many of Poetry's greatest (self-interested and exaggerated) claims to Truth and to comprehensiveness. Sherry explains, "Shelley's dictum [that we are all at work on one great poem] is a sad one for us because it attempts to subordinate all knowledge to poetry. I think we need a more collaborative model" (1992, 3).

Habermas (1986) claims:

> However, as long as philosophy remains caught in ontology, it is itself subject to an objectivism that disguises the connection of its knowledge with the human interest in autonomy and responsibility (*Mündigkeit*). There is only one way in which it can acquire the power that it vainly claims for itself in virtue of its seeming freedom from presuppositions: by acknowledging its dependence on this interest and turning against its own illusion of pure theory the critique it directs at the objectivism of the sciences. (310–11)

It is precisely such a critique of its own interests that Sherry directs (sympathetically) at contemporary innovative poetic practices. That single gesture makes *Our Nuclear Heritage* noteworthy. Habermas (1986) contends: "From everyday experience we know that ideas serve often enough to furnish our actions with justifying motives in place of the real ones. What is called rationalization at this level is called ideology at the level of collective action. In both cases the manifest content of statements is falsified by consciousness' unreflected tie to interests, despite its illusion of autonomy" (311). *Our Nuclear Heritage* is constructed without the illusion of autonomy; it is a socially constructed text, in spite of, or even more oddly by means of, Sherry's virtuosity in displaying different modalities of expression and thinking. (I say more oddly because stylistic pyrotechnics are usually offered up as evidence of individual talent and individualized genius.)

Sherry's appendixes to *Our Nuclear Heritage* make explicit the socially derived nature of his text. They acknowledge the indebtedness of the writing, with humor; the appendixes are themselves a serious attempt at the impossible task of disentanglement via awareness. "Appendix D: Pony," for example, offers a section-by-section "guide" to *Our Nuclear Heritage*, but that guiding function (which includes identification of source materials) consistently gets complicated by tonal developments within each explanation. For example, the note for the chapter "The Limits of Form in a Context of Accuracy" reads: "Of course I agree with Stein; it's not the bomb itself in fact. Some superficial information (facts) presented in the style of a 'nature' video to convince the unwary reader about some crackpot ideas I have stumbled on" (252–53). Thus, the flatness of explanatory notes themselves get called into question by Sherry's awareness of the potential (and inevitability) of manipulativeness in the style of that similarly explanatory, factual mode known as the nature video. Section after section in Appendix D, in different tones and different styles, demonstrates the impossibility of a fully disinterested, flatly factual divulging of information.

The battle of styles that runs throughout Appendix D takes a different turn in "Plane and Fencing Rhetoric." Sherry speaks of a "war / where one's ideas are pitted against every other one's" (15); that war is inseparable from the atomization of knowledge that Sherry seeks to counter. Organization of knowledge by discipline and professionalized specialization contributes to such atomization, and ultimately plays into the hands of managers and leaders: "the political leaders can maintain their power as broker of knowledge and use it as a wedge between groups. In a country that pays lip service to communication, there is no consistent effort to bridge the gap of the ways of knowing among fields of endeavor" (81).[1]

Sherry desires to question and to purge the self of its (self-)interested bases for expression, yet he does not wish to negate all value and valuing in the process:

> I had the sense that I was remembering these events and not making them up to glorify myself with the imagined breadth of my experience and perfection of my values—so vivid were they that I wanted to have already known them but could not be sure that I had "been there before" even in my most midnight mind, so obscure had my reasons for doing anything become in order to purge myself of values that seemed to me to be the chief cause of misery and pain and among these I include "mercy, pity, and peace." (31–32)

Though Sherry concedes the inherent element of melodrama in his subject matter, even the mockery of an overblown phrase such as "my most midnight mind" does not completely undo emotion (of either his subject matter nor of his attempts at truthful expression). Sherry's cautions, on behalf of truthfulness, turn *Our Nuclear Heritage* at once into a solicitous book, and one full of sarcasm and self-consciousness:

> It would greatly aggravate my dedication to writing about these matters, if I were to stop in the midst of every sentence for the purpose of saying "so-called," or "asserted" in order to avoid all rhetorical inconsistency. And yet how do we write about such matters as assumptions in an assumed language. Besides it would sound ungraciously to both you and their tender ears. I am, however, anxious to be literally true in all that I write that is susceptible to truth. (33)

Sherry's final qualification—all "that is susceptible to truth"—bears the weight of his book's limitations and his passion for truthfulness. Sherry observes and asks: "The critique of the discoveries in one discipline by another discipline results from the lack of acceptance of each other's terms of knowledge and different lexical definitions of the same terms. How can we validate how the different disciplines know things?" (203). It is this last question that preoccupies Sherry, in *Our Nuclear Heritage* and in his subsequent writing. I think of that question as leading into a sociology of knowledge. Or, following on the metaphor of bio-diversity as it is applied to thinking and knowing, the question of reliability leads us to a kind of philosophical ecology.

On Resemblances to the Nineteenth Century/ His Sentences

I began reading Sherry's book in the light of one of my own obsessions: Thoreau's writing. I imagined between the two of them a kinship based on a kind of nineteenth-century sensibility; that is, an abiding interest in the status, nature, and function of facts. I saw, for a time, Sherry's *Our Nuclear Heritage* in the light of one of Thoreau's marvelous sentences in *Walden*: "If you stand right fronting and face to face to a fact, you will see the sun glimmer on both its surfaces, as if it were a cimeter, and feel its sweet edge dividing you through the heart and marrow, and so you will happily conclude your mortal career."[2] That fact has the power to cleave. That fact itself—not trivial facts as mere data—has the power to astonish and annihilate. In *Our Nuclear Heritage*, Sherry claims: "But throughout I wish to deflate fact as not necessarily so and multiply the meaning of fact to reduce a monopoly reliance on it. For even written fact alternatives must constantly be reckoned with" (11).

But Sherry's vision is not Thoreauvian; instead, it is closer to the more tragic or skeptical consciousness of writers such as Hawthorne, Melville, and Poe. Sherry's is an anti-transcendental consciousness, aware at every turn of the dangers of self-interest posing as truth. The rigor of his suspicions resembles Poe and Melville; his sense of scientific writing as compatible with philosophy/poetics bears more than a striking resemblance to Poe's *Eureka*.

At the level of the sentence, Sherry has fully absorbed the potentials of the Melvillean sentence of careful negation and self-qualification. For example, consider the similarities of poise and tone in the following sentences:

Violent irrationals led the way, establishing norms of behavior which even the most husbanded householders held up as heroic, seminal, and centrally human, although such manners hailed from the outer limits of the bell curve of useful citizenry. (Sherry 1991, 27)

It is not seldom the case that, when a man is browbeaten in some unprecedented way and violently unreasonable way, he begins to stagger in his own plainest faith. He begins, as it were, vaguely to surmise that, wonderful as it may be, all the justice and all the reason is on the other side. (Melville 1969, 49)

While I am *not* claiming that *Our Nuclear Heritage* is precisely imitative of Melvillean sentence-making (and both sections in *Our Nuclear Heritage* and all of Sherry's earlier *Popular Fiction* [1985] attest to his ability to imitate and parody various styles of writing), I do call attention to a kinship, in this case of sentence-making where a controlled and elegant tone is in collision with a more horrifying content. Or, as in the following pair of sentences, the two writers share a penchant for offering a self-conscious discussion of craft in a tone and style where the mode of expression does battle with a seemingly didactic content:

My general direction for you to comprehend me thus renders all that I write strictly and actually true, as if I had every time lugged in a formal declaration of the fact of my or others' opinion, and it is only when we forget this particular commonality of truth that we fall into the tyranny of history over our lives or tyranny of a concept of history over our lives, like democracy, or the tyranny of lovers and the wild swings of hope and despair of our anticipation. (Sherry 1991, 34)

> Outwardly regarded, our craft is a lie; for all that is outwardly seen of it is the clean-swept deck, and oft-painted planks comprised above the water-line; whereas, the vast mass of our fabric, with all its store-rooms of secrets, forever slides along far under the surface. (Melville 1990, 404)

I offer one additional example of Sherry's Melvillean sensibility—of the discriminations and capabilities of elegant, extended, carefully qualified sentences:

> The sacred lies in the notation captured by a twist of mind and an individual identifying it with the self in quick down-strokes of the fingers, each one sure and fast, even though a minute or an hour may pass between one stroke group and the next, that one must know just when to strike in a precise and reckless fashion, that one must wait until the real thing comes along, a solid within which motion blurs the edges. The description of how to arrive at it is disappointing to read, but the expectation of more from writing leads to violence. (19)

The beauty of the first sentence is the ingeniously distant, unsentimental description of poesis as computer-based word-processing. Truly, a contemporary description of composition as lyrical (technically assisted) epiphany. But the technical clarity of description, compounded by the second sentence's admonition, simultaneously affirms the act of composition while it warns us against heaping too heavy a transcendental lyrical expectation on it.

A common bias, often one that is voiced by mainstream writers in deriding experimentalism, is that technique is divorced from emotion. Sherry's defense of mechanism in writing is located appropriately in nineteenth-century concerns:

> A common response of appeals to value residing in the individual is to deride technique as having no heart and fear it as inhuman. As Melville wrote to Hawthorne, "The reason the mass of men fear God, and *at bottom dislike* Him, is because they rather distrust His heart, and fancy Him all brain like a watch." (68)

Sherry's connections to the nineteenth century are clear when he cites Melville's technique for *Moby-Dick*: "Melville's technique is most apparent in the structure of *Moby-Dick* where each chapter is titled by an aspect of the whale which acts as a metaphor for an aspect of the self" (69). A parallel statement might be made with regard to the technique of *Our Nuclear Heritage*, where each chapter discusses a different aspect of the book, where that subject matter is metaphorically developed to encompass poetry/literature, cultural activity, a more literal nuclear heritage, and so on, so that Sherry's book presents different aspects of a system or sociology of knowledge.[3] Sherry's call to arms is similar to Emerson's at the beginning of "Nature":

> The influential writers of the past have exercised all their faculties, why not we. Nature and artifice, absorptive and non-absorptive, sound and page, thought and experience, all the polarities that emphasize and position, and that the best poetry blurs the distinctions between, do not need to be reconciled into one "meaning," but rather expanded into the many versions the levels of reality make possible. (Sherry 1991, 70)

Sherry's aim is not then to consolidate or unify conflicting and different poetries or knowledges: "To try to consolidate art work and practice into one theory misses the point about which art is most persuasive" (70). Seeking a utopia of many different constituent elements, Sherry's *Our Nuclear Heritage* is a treatise, with significant roots in the nineteenth century, on behalf of an artistic diversity.[4]

Poetry/Poetics/The Status of Literature

How, then, does poetry fit in to a quest for truthfulness? For Sherry, to make poems is "to construct machines that generate meaning, different for each reader" (45). If there is a new poetry, then

> new poetry means new in a somewhat different way than breakfast cereal manufacturers mean new. We do not want to say that a new shape in breakfast cereals revolutionizes the meal; nor do we want to say that using prosody as a carrier of meaning revolutionizes poetry. In fact the new poetry is nothing more than the emphasis on poetic method rather than an emphasis on poetic subject and yet what a furor is created by this change in emphasis. What are we threatening? (61)

First, such observations, while not casting aside the subject matter of *Our Nuclear Heritage*, place it in a different context, one in which subject matter is not presumed to be of transcendent value: "To start with Nuclear

War, for example, as subject does not insure the value of this to you. Nevertheless I am trying to encourage your attention to these matters under the guise of the overall subject" (61). Principally though, Sherry's poetics severs an idealized and idolatrous relationship to poetry itself by asking "Do we dare to say about poetry what Hawking has said about theory in physics?" (63). The remark by Hawking to which Sherry refers also serves as an epigraph to a section of *Our Nuclear Heritage*; Stephen Hawking's description of theory is markedly anti-transcendental: "theory is just a model of the universe, or a restricted part of it, and a set of rules that relate quantities in the model to observations that we make. It exists only in our minds and does not have any other reality (whatever that might mean)" (60). Paradoxically, Sherry's concern is to map and describe the particular nature of poetry's knowing so that poetry, as a mode of knowing, might again assume a meaningful role in human quests for knowledge. The alternative is to occupy a position of ornamental irrelevance either as a describer/creator of individualized interior emotional space or as a body of language activities with ridiculously grandiose claims for its own comprehensiveness and greatness. Part of the seriousness of *Our Nuclear Heritage* is to ask what poetry can or might be today while filtering out as mere self-interest those remarks that make poetry into a noisy but ignored mode of wisdom.

What marks Sherry's thinking as noteworthy is his ability to critique the self-supporting platitudes of community-friendly theorizing: "There are writers who use this strategy [of difficulty], because they think it will attract the kind of attention they want to the work" (75). I feel a strong affinity to Sherry's view of poetry precisely because his thinking is materialist and social:

> The history of literature is as much the history of legitimizing modes of expression and social needs as it is the order in which the modes of expression themselves were developed. In some cases the writers themselves were the agents of their own distribution. Blake or Pound might be good examples of individuals who handled their own careers and Language Poets and Surrealists of groups whose works included their own commentary. (75)

Our Nuclear Heritage presents a version of the present that begins "as the monoculture tried to finish stamping out local cultures" (110) and proceeds to locate oppositional poetries within the context of resistance to cultural homogenization. Such resistance might also be fought, as in

Thoreau's redefinitions of economic terms at the outset of *Walden*, over definitions, such as the definition of technology:

> Cultural leaders today attempt to limit the definition of technology to electronic hardware, rockets, and better mousetraps, but fail to include the cultural technologies of the alphabet, oil painting, and twelve-tone music. In addition art is at civil war. One side tries to maintain the validity of the interim technologies of poetry and easel painting while the other side makes art and communicates using new technologies. So the technology race goes on in culture as much as in the military. (Sherry 1991, 113)

And it is this view of art as war that is part of Sherry's de-romanticized history of poetry, though with differences: "The difference between the results of military technology and the results of cultural technology is that misuse of military technology results in many lives being lost, while misuse of cultural technology makes everyone's lives miserable and creates an environment for military technology to be misused" (114).

Poetic activity then becomes a form of cultural criticism by means of a language investigation: "The kinds of things poets doubt question the most deeply held cultural beliefs. Just as the scientist is willing to overturn the embedded paradigms of the physical world if the paradigms no longer fit the facts, the poet must be willing to override the most deeply ingrained emotional and spiritual aspects of language if they no longer fit the meaning" (87–88). Of course, one problem of such a version of a poet is that it is nearly impossible for a poet to establish a disinterested vantage point from which to make such judgements. As Sherry acknowledges, "while seeking to write the wrongs of the empowered, the literature of opposition craves their attention" (85).

Sherry declares that "structure is not only the shape and form of ideas and material, but also functions as one of those ideas and events" (117). Such an axiom applies to innovative poetries' emphasis on method (see Sherry 1991, 61), but also to the overall structure of *Our Nuclear Heritage* itself, where the act of equivocation as structure must be understood as an idea itself. The contemporary hegemony of poetry as narration and description, without a self-critical investigation of such "natural" approaches to poetry, ultimately limits and destroys poetry:

> Poetry written as a story of the ideas and experiences of men and women in the past limits meaning to narration and description.

If we allow such boundaries to writing, we cannot hope to write a writing that extends the way we write meaning beyond the scope of narration and description. Even less can we hope to sway readers if we do not practice what we preach except in the narrow confines of "poetry." (121)

Sherry insists both that poetry retain the integrity of its specialized functions as a critique and exploration of meaning-making—poet as language specialist—and break the bounds of its sequestration by engaging in serious relationships and mappings with other modes of knowing.

Within the long "Muslims in Soho" section Sherry offers his most sustained thinking about the new poetry and its relationships to social structures and to utopian aspirations. In "The Boundaries of Poetry," Sherry first offers a definition of the operations of that new poetry:

> in the post-Mallarmean field poetry, space is defined on the page in heterogeneous smooth space. Bruce Andrews' "elusive continent" where "hinges / ride / lava" bodes ill for the linear metrics of the Greeks and English. Length and stress are both mutated and redefined in an open area where language mobilizes a network of meaning using the open space as a kind of time divided by the unquantified movement of the eye and breath while reading—an anabasis. (185)

This new field of poetry, in its presumed relationships to readers and in its fluid spatial existence, implicitly postulates social relations:

> This utopia tantalizes the reader. It idealizes a society where there is no pull between what we want and what we have to do, no conflict between the citizen and the legislator. It postulates an unalienated alternative. It may do so as a critique of contemporary society or it may do so as a sincere proposal, but to date it can only do so as the art of one person or a collaboration among a few. (185–86) [5]

The reader becomes then a citizen empowered to legislate meaning; the reader is a citizen fully entitled to make works of art. Sherry continues,

> Few artists or writers were able to comprehend that structure, by the fact of repetition, implied society. Yet a continuous appeal goes out to all minorities, disenfranchised, terrorists, sub-language groups: "This is your poetry. Join the network to discover new ways of making meaning. Do not fixate on poem, voice, other striated and arbitrary meaning formations. We offer a processual, unbounded methodology that can be applied to any language and can include all languages." (186)

But, as Sherry's sarcastic tone indicates, such enthusiasm and idealistically celebratory social democracy is not in keeping with Sherry's self-critical and skeptical intelligence. Allegiance to such a revolutionary ideal embodied in poetry is taken more seriously by Sherry and is compared, disconcertingly, to the fervor and devotion required by Islam:

> Like the Ayatollah's public version of Islam, poetry demands complete adherence to a redefined world, not one reformed or amended to be co-opted. (Of course I am not supporting Khomeini's absurd position regarding Rushdie. There are, however, difficult changes required if we wish to be thorough about what our ideas imply and we must closely question our motives. If we believe what we have said about new art, we must first implement these changes ourselves or have those changes sweep us away.) (186) [6]

Utopianism and Constituent Knowledge

The utopianism of Sherry's *Our Nuclear Heritage* stems not then from a huge truth-claim for poetry nor from postmodern language-play as a somehow emancipatory resolution of the melodrama of historical crisis. Instead, what Sherry envisions is a participatory form of constituent knowledges, similar to Habermas's (1986) description of an emancipated society: "However, only in an emancipated society, whose members' autonomy and responsibility had been realized, would communication have developed into the non-authoritarian and universally practical dialogue from which both our model of reciprocally constituted ego identity and our idea of true consensus are always implicitly derived" (314). The notion of poetry (and literature) as part of a constituency-based knowledge fuels *Our Nuclear Heritage*. In reflecting on the project begun in *Our Nuclear Heritage*, Sherry (1992) writes (of goals that extend into his work-in-progress, *Sorry*): "The way I'd like literature to be taken seriously is not only by bonding different literatures, but also by establishing an epistemological model that is rhizomic, acknowledging the interdependencies of various modes of thought and practices not just within literature, but for the entire society. Literature is one of the contributing modalities" (2).

When I questioned Sherry about his notion of a constituency-based version of knowledge, I objected that such a notion can become a version of a mushy pluralism, pretending to a tolerance that masks operations of power and exclusion. Sherry's (1992) response involves a lessening of Poetry's claims so that poetry can participate in a broadened (Habermas-like) version of the making of knowledge—a social enterprise involving reciprocity and relationship: "I am not talking about Shelley's notion that we are all at work on one great poem, because Shelley tries to use poetry as a metaphor for all human effort. I don't want to make those kinds of claims for poetry that threaten others' power bases, creating a competitive relationship.

It is the separations between the poems and modes of knowing that I'd like to focus on as the crux of meaning (à la Silliman, but taking it further)" (2).

Through a study of poetry's peculiar position today, Sherry (1991) develops his understanding of the dangers of current forms of specialization: "When doctors talk, they use a vocabulary not tuned to the untrained mind. When lawyers write, it takes a saint to piece together their meaning. When economists prognosticate and computer jockeys rap, no one outside the initiated can make head or tail out of it. Yet poets in our day, the word specialists, are criticized for using more than a tv newscaster vocabulary, because it is elitist" (79).

The simple truth, as Sherry puts it, is that "poetry is not mass communication" (79). But once Sherry has successfully defended poetry's right *not* to be "common speech," he must then turn to the results more generally of specialized vocabularies: "But the result of necessity of specialization is that no one understands anyone outside their discipline unless it is simplified like special relativity, supply-side economics, and beat poetry to the point of losing much of its truth at the expense of being understood by amateurs" (80).

The issue for Sherry is ultimately an epistemological one (and one parallel to those considered by Habermas): "But no profession respects the epistemology of the others so that even where they should be communicating they retreat to their unassailable language citadel when threatening problems arise. Even afore-sectioned Stephen Hawking thinks artists are not to be 'trusted,' because of their methods. Each discipline wishes to invalidate the epistemology of the other disciplines" (80).

"Atomization of knowledge" is complicit with political management, which depends upon such partialized knowledge so that "political leaders can maintain their power as broker of knowledge and use it as a wedge between groups" (81). With Sherry, even as we engage in our specializations, we must wonder, "has specialization passed its usefulness" (82). *Our Nuclear Heritage* itself is a fine example of antispecialist thinking. But in today's cultural marketplace, such antispecialization is perceived (by readers and especially critics trained and professionalized in specialized discourses) as alien. My guess is that *Our Nuclear Heritage* will have lower sales than seemingly more specialized poetic productions and will face a greater difficulty of recognition and appreciation in part because of its serious attempt at antispecialized thinking.

Sherry's hope is not for the resolution of a "one world, one culture" global vision. Instead, it is for an intellectual diversity based on tolerance, reciprocity, and communication: "Perhaps the greatest asset which our species' intelligence ought to give us is adaptability. Not that there should be no structure to our lives, but that it must be flexible enough to avoid our being locked out of common human discourse and basic understanding by a monolithic world view or narrow specialization. Yet these specialties must at the same time be encouraged to allow human progress to continue and to refine its purpose and methods. How to accomplish this is the mystery of dynamics" (83).

To begin the process of moving toward such a utopian reciprocity of knowings, Sherry (1992) proposes first a mapping of current modes of knowing and then a reconsideration of relationships: "Once you have mapped your poetries, there are your other arts, and then how art interacts with science and politics. Once we start mapping art, science, and politics together, we can begin to question why they are divided in that way and finally to redesign the structure of knowledge to reflect the new dependencies and relationships that arise rather than continuing to define only the entities and pretending the relationships don't exist" (3).

It is this willingness to reconsider and redesign relationships among modes of knowing—combined with his jettisoning of the usual (poet's) assumption that poetry is the best, most comprehensive form of knowing—that makes Sherry's (1992) question no longer sound so ridiculous: "Why not have a poet on the National Security Council? This is especially important if we define the primary security issues as health, education, and welfare of the people. Poetry can offer that view to leaders in politics and science. In return we can begin to accept alternatives to our clannish isolation and include more detailed analysis of how we know things" (3).

In other words, Sherry (1992) seeks, as a poet, both to "make poetry and to expand its domain by linking it to other ways of knowing rather than define it in increasing isolation from daily activities, social structures, and the history of science which as Habermas points out is all the epistemology we have left and that needs to be corrected, since art has a contribution to fashion" (5).

Sherry's (1992) contention is that Each poetry is a constituent of Poetry. Each art is a constituent of Art. Art is one of [the] representatives in the legislature of knowledge that informs us daily and which we redraft daily. As poets we have a truly unique opportunity now in that poetry has been freed from its moorings and can move freely among the constituencies, an ombudsman of language. I see this as real, not fantasy. Our tools are prosody, and our goals are integration, not simply a recognition of Relationism" (4).

A goal for Sherry, besides writing a book that enacts a working relationship between science and poetry, is to show "what is connected to what else" because "the vocabularies must find linkages. This is the current problem for me. Determine the extent to which subjects are distinct. I am currently still trying to find out who defined knowledge as art, science, and politics and then to go on to discover why they did that and the extent to which it was conditioned on time and place and . . . Truth needs to be redefined so poetry can approach it as a practice or function not as an ideal" (1992, 4). A matrix of separated (atomized) specializations may mirror a more compelling circumstance: "Has the world been objectified beyond our ability to continue to work with its materials?" (1991, 91). If the answer is yes, then the shifting tones and self-consciousness of Sherry's work may be a kind of writerly treadmill over a fundamentally nihilistic abyss.

The nuclear heritage that is the core subject matter for Sherry's book is an extreme instance of a situation that calls for disinterested thinking. As Sherry (1991) notes, our nuclear heritage places us, as a species, in proximity to our own death wish: "The pressures of death (as if death were a thing or person), compressing the spiral of life, built as human deaths were replaced by deaths of other creatures and plants, killed by human avoidance until finally humanity could not find anything worthy to assault and blew itself up" (53).

That death wish can be tranferred by deeds of killing others, but Sherry takes that relatively common thought and pushes its logic, wondering whether our recognition of our fasincation with our own lethalness is something that we would, in the name of rationality, wish to control. In exploring the relationship between knowledge and disinterestedness, Habermas (1986) claims "the *only* knowledge that can truly orient action is knowledge that frees itself from mere human interests and is based on Ideas—in other words, knowledge that has taken a theoretical attitude" (301). Sherry's book pushes that ideal of knowledge as disinterested *theoria* to an extreme by testing our theoretical capabilities in an endeavor of species self-knowledge. If we are, as in humanist platitudes, a murderous and barbarous creature (as ample evidence of this century indicates), might we wish to make a "rational" choice based on such a self-analysis?:

> Which poses important questions for Our Nuclear Heritage. Under what circumstances would continuation of the species not be among our highest priorities? If perhaps we were destroying the entire planet or larger frames, would our values allow us to sacrifice ourselves to preserve the lambs? Are there forces subverting our will to do this? Are those forces within us, perhaps the same forces that made us capable? More centrally, how far should we go toward subverting those forces? (55)

Here is where Sherry's thinking, like Melville's, is distinctly less optimistic than Habermas's: for Sherry, disinterestedness is *not* a guaranteed savior. Sherry links our capacity for disinterested thinking to the very forces within us that have made us capable of self-annihilation.

Sherry's own position in *Our Nuclear Heritage* is accurately described in a portion of appendix B:

> Caught between the historian and the idealist, the strategist struggles to win battles without compromising his munitions, his supporters.

> He departs from the canon, oversteps the accords, in search of a victory that has not destroyed the value of his conquests. (234)

Within a culture governed by utility, new writing (including Sherry's *Our Nuclear Heritage*) exists as a disturbing monitory presence. As Sherry observes in his typically self-conscious manner:

> When I use such logic to please the reader, I expect some dissatisfaction because the entire work can be imagined without having to read it. The results appear arbitrary. The high culture, a linguistic one, prefers the illusion of a nonprocedural approach where all written actions are "created" as if freed like birds by poetic spontaneity. Yet looking closer, the self is but an interpreter of stars, of sense and memory, and new writing's value inheres more from a multidimensional presence within the culture than from its use by that culture as the utility language of every day. (248)

Sherry's skepticism and self-questioning assume an ethical dimension, one linked to our capacity for survival understood as an imaginative capacity:

Western thought and its nuclear heritage dominates the emerging world monoculture. If the high culture attempts to develop an alternative agenda to preserve diversity in culture and in the gene pool, it must do so by questioning assumptions of self and thought.

Nothing can be accepted at this level. I have been told that I do not need to question myself so deeply by persons whose questions have pierced deeply. I must respond that we must question our very existence if we are to preserve it at all. We must think of the apocalypse to avoid living it. (246–47)

Sherry's *Our Nuclear Heritage* is a primer for such thinking. It instructs us in a thinking that, while skeptical, playful, and self-conscious, moves toward a new mapping of human knowledge. The (survivalist) hope behind such a mapping is that a much broader legislative body and mind may emerge to think both of apocalypse and its alternatives.

Notes

1. Sherry's (1991) comments here echo my own frustrations as an academic and as an administrator: that we, the disciplined, professionalized, specialized faculty allow and are often complicit with compartmentalization, mistakenly thinking that such atomization provides us with protection and power (by means of a specialized form of knowledge) rather than realizing that it partializes our knowledge and leaves the integration (or more often separation) of our knowledge in the hands of a managerial caste (which then professes to be unable to get us to communicate with one another).

2. Thoreau (1989), 98. For discussions of Thoreau and factuality, see also Stanley Cavell (1981) and Cameron, *Writing Nature* (1989).

3. A book that might profitably be compared to *Our Nuclear Heritage* is Melville's *White-Jacket* (1990), for each is a political tract and neither is merely personal expression. As Melville's "novel" becomes a social and structural study—of working relations on board a man-of-war—rather than a novel of personal development or even narrative development, Sherry's book, published in the New American Poetry Series, is propelled, like Melville's by structural and social issues, by a sociology of knowledge. There is also more than a passing resemblance to Melville's *The Confidence Man*, particularly in Melville's dizzying shifts of perspective, his scathing anti-transcendentalist humor, and his insistence on a book that resists unification or closure or the predominance of *a* perspective. Sherry's *Our Nuclear Heritage*, though, clings to the spars of system more than Melville's light-extinguishing and ultimately bleak novel.

4. A noteworthy accomplishment of a number of contemporary innovative poets (including Sherry) is that poetry has begun to thrive on nonverse traditions. A range of different but accomplished sentence-based books have appeared over the past fifteen years, including Sherry's *Our Nuclear Heritage* and *Popular Fiction*, Ron Silliman's *Paradise, Tjanting,* and *Ketjak,* and Lyn Hejinian's *My Life*. These works—unlike the more mainstream (and more stylistically uniform) vogue of the prose poem in the 1960s and 1970s—exhibit considerable differences and range. Silliman's sentences tend to be more modular, declarative, and propositional; Sherry's sentences often have a nineteenth-century elegance, complexity, and self-critical quality to them; Hejinian's sentences are often highly lyrical, opulent, sensual, at times having a traditionally literary ring to them, as well as at times taking on a Stein-like quality of the sentence-as-object as in Stein's *Tender Buttons.*

5. On unalienated work, see also Silliman (1987c).

6. Sherry's thinking here is one of the best extensions I've read of Raymond Williams's (1977) axiom that "to write in different ways is to live in different ways" (205). The seriousness of that axiom—not merely stated as an outsider experimentalist's self-interested, self-preening wish—lies in considering the axiom as a life-ordering principle that may shake the way one lives. (Cf. the intersection of poetry and living in the work of John Cage, Gary Snyder, Judy Grahn, and others.)

12. Reading and Writing Ron Silliman's *Demo to Ink*

Each sentence a citizen. Each sentence counts, and each retains and enacts its full expressive variety.

Each one teach one. Toward what is such didacticism aimed? Not one target but many, among which one is training in reading cultural artifacts; if you will, a political semiology. "Any number of men will distribute themselves at the urinals so as to permit each a maximum of space."

Poet as indigenous ethnographer, and The Alphabet as (among other things) a massive amassing of observation, a Great Poem of the Bay Area. "These are just the facts." Yes, at times they are: a flat actuality, like once modern and now merely mod modular sofa units where each piece seems interchangeable or like minimalist music or like Dos Passos's camera eye (and thus each a bit dissimilar too). But of equal importance is the interrogation and exposure of assemblage and options therein: "Realism, // so-called, alienates, by virtue / of the shell posed around objects." Not just a description of things, but the coming into being of the text itself as an object of ongoing consideration: "Each letter a wedge in the still space of the page." Thus a little like a sister-singer from Oakland, there, this, that, of, the materiality of each word. And a consideration of the rhythm of embedding: "A short sentence is a rhythmic unit." Often on buses or subways—public forms of conveyance—sentence structures we are familiar with.

"The words combine, forming meaning." We witness it, and we know we are witnessing; therefore, we are not merely witnesses, but participants, collaborators, accessories. Playing a blue-jeaned Wittgenstein, he revels in the endless variety of how sentences come to mean. His books are poems, we are reading poems, we are asked to think about it. "Think here: you are reading a poem // —already this defines you." *Not this*: flip the pages, he reached for her whatever, she responded, castle or condo in the background, it was so real I thought I was really there, I didn't even know I was reading a book. Instead, the integrity of the line and of the sentence: "That each line be created equal is contra-narrative." What might such citizens do? Let's see. Cheetahs never prosper. I learned quickly to love his love of puns and to respect the necessity of their interruption of other more consecutive forms of logic. Who only can lecture should not have children. A love of melopoeia makes a good daddy (enough to sustain the love of twins, of which punning is such a love). What was I about to say? I'll think of it again later. That very word "later."

A slight shifting of letters. Is this book beautifully made? Yes it is. Charles Alexander is known to make books so, and this one has a gorgeous cover, generously clear printing, reasonably thick and somewhat luxurious paper, sufficient white space, and is sold at a fair price. One impression is of the many facts assembled, a huge montage. His is the low bid. There are whole sentences that are principally sounds, that direct attention down to the letter or the syllable. "Details differ, // thus they mean." Is this a typo (bottom of page 152): "(he's maybe 18 years old, thin fuzz of first bear)."? Maybe at 18 he is becoming a bear. Maybe a beard is merely a bear with a *d* added? "I don't write these texts so much as shed them, shells left behind that should you find them years alter should prove no less opaque to you than to me: who was that masked man?" That one, top of page 148, I puzzled over. Years alter or years later. Years do alter. Proofreading, like the compulsion to pop bubblewrap, is habit-forming. The bank swallow kept skimming the lake for gnats unaware that below the tiny bugs was an impressive and beautiful lake. Did the bank swallow later experience regret for having missed the sublimity of the lake? Which altar? A tropical criticism leans toward its source. The ghost of Randall Jarrell and ghosts of New Yorker and Bostonian conservatism howl in harmony: But where is the evaluation in it? Criticism must make judgments (as if attention weren't already one such discrimination). Therefore, is this a good book? Yes it is. Is this his best book? No it is not; he has written many good books and the reading of this one should not replace the reading of those (including the long, ungainly, spectacular and still exciting earlier ones like *Ketjak* and *Tjanting!*). Are you happy sad Randall pacing the shoulder of these pages, turning around a little dumbfounded, staring into the confusing headlights of an oncoming modernism that seems too enthusiastic and energetic for the graceful melancholy of your tender monologues? Maybe you preferred tennis, maybe you played tense. Baseball too plebeian? There's lyricism there. "Willie: the pure products of America never were (what was most beautiful was neither the catch nor the throw, but the long high arc of the ball off Vic Wertz' bat)." And "The next page is another country, the moment a pop fly hovers before dropping back to earth."

The excitement of thinking may be paired with its monotony. The personal lyric is stuck with its predictable epiphany. I guess he does get a little scared of endings, must fumble them a little. Now that my paragraphs have gotten bigger, I can dig into a particular thinking and go on with it. Must the bulk of the developing paragraph obligate me to do so? The politics of writing is not to be located in the writing's alleged content, but in the relationships established between reader and writer. I have taught his writing in classes at the university—but be goddamned good & careful, oh pale academic, oh sinkerball Ramon, the classroom is not the be-all and end-all of poesis, in spite of the implicit cruising in New Criticism, oh cute poem won't you have a date with me. What I found was what I had found: his writing inspires other writing. Is generative. A joint-stock company: squeezing of sentences all around. For nearly twenty years I have been reading Henry David Thoreau's *Journals* (which run to nearly two million words). I am often impressed with the sheer bulk of his activity, am amazed that he would care sufficiently to write and write and write, especially on a project that was evidently for its own sake. I am beginning to have some of the same wonder before The Alphabet, at the steadiness of the writing, the sustained effort, laboring leisurely & enthusiastically. For whom is a tropical criticism written? What is the difference between such tropism and imitation? If he were to say to me, "your writing has an uncanny resemblance to my own," would that be a true compliment, for inhabiting a remarkably similar inspirational space, or a backhanded compliment, for spending so much time in what amounts to little more than superficial imitation? Tropical criticism gives up (as ornamental) expository prose's "natural" argumentative structure, eschews the skeletal subtext of consecutive logic as its "right" foundation. But is it nonetheless really without explanation? If explain also means to spread out, can you tell me the difference between an oil slick and a gentle visible fog? Between dye and dialog? He tells me that his new spray formula is biodegradable: it'll kill the mildew on your vinyl siding restoring a bright colorful appearance to your house without harming azaleas or other shrubs. "The specificity of the avant-garde audience is sociological"—pleased to meet you. Quotation is evaluation; an anthology a gathering of a specific garland of flowers. I feel the joy of writing sentences, different sentences, their expansion and contraction, their movement toward completion (which is not completion per se). Is it the same as his joy in writing sentences? I could call him up. Would that be criticism or friendship? He had become (groan over the years) convinced of the dullness of most criticism, its form (did she say "forum"?) said it all (in advance). "This is a test." A testing out, akin not averse to scientific method—first a hypothesis, then its testing out. A poem may begin with a preestablished (more later about whom and how and so on) designation of its construction. In *demo* (which I at first misprinted as *demon*), Silliman (1992) often constructs sentences with several different directions of proceeding built in, one shading of the sentence being a slight distortion. "Met against metaphor (I want white rooms): the cast is clear." Or more concisely: "Eminent ptomaine." One seeming caution presented, though it is really only a phrase I pick out and recontextualize now because I want it to seem to move in this specific direction, warns against "humor mistaken for humor." What else could humor be? If poetry can be considered as a kind of knowledge, as epistemological inquiry, then Silliman's insistent, at times aggressively juvenile, use of puns had best be kept in mind. Most philosophy is not funny. That error is one way in which philosophical writing, oddly enough, may be characterized as sentimental (in the sense of a prophylactic sequestering in language that eventually becomes, unintentionally, self-mocking). "Terms of enjambment." What goes with what, what might go with what, a testing out, a list, besides, besidedness, and in the equality a playing out of the most critical issues of citizenship (which could not get played out in more didactic, content-centered forms of poetry). "Three women escorting 40 seven year olds onto the bus (taste you can count on) . . . it's 9:00 a.m. and the 'nickel whores' are already out in front of the Town Pump." Why can't critical discourse turn suddenly descriptive? He likes to delete articles; I can't do it because for me it makes sentences sound like they're being spoken by Tonto. If I make my attention sequential, going page by page, what have I rescued myself from? He walked out on the ice, aware of the barely frozen-over pond, and he kept thinking about critical prose's hidden romantic excesses, trapped bubbles that would boom and moan. In the course of his longer writing projects, a self-consciously made visible sense of the work's own emerging, the work's processes and sites of composition, which become other dimensions of an exploration of how to be present or here. Demo(cra)tic thinking. A tropical criticism reflects both the soil it grows in and the light-source that it tends toward. "Elements are gathered (punctuation forms a low wall) — trying to decide before my name is called whether to answer 'present' or 'here.'" Tropical delight. "Form is passion." One premise of *demo* is the refusal of a sentence to be one thing only: "It has been twenty years since the Democratic Party carried a majority of the white vote in a Presidential election (the docents in white coats), my mother says of the cutbacks at Bechtel, 'I'm only one-third nuclear now.'" But what does go with what (and so does *what*, for that matter), and within the unit of the sentence there is some accommodation for difference. Traces not so much of a political correctness (which is *their* corrosive and oppressive agenda) but rather a constantly self-critical, self-inquiring labor of observation and terminology. "Each stanza is a poem each word . . . the tiny body given breadth by the wheelchair (what is found within a wall)." When has a sentence been adequately thought about? By whom (and under what circumstances)? An accumulation of many of them virtually guarantees that a sentimental rhetorically coercive epiphanic lyrical intensity will be avoided. But not always (nor should it be?). We are learning how to read; we are being encouraged to read (see) many things. "Small children on the bus often sit or stand on their seats backwards, ignoring the passing streets in favor of that larger puzzle, the society of the bus." "Tin sun, one broom" — that one stops us, dead in our tracks?, circles under the pop up, it's not the put out he's after but the rapt attention to trajectory, object, floating (throating) sensation. "How write poetry amid such chatter, but *listen to it*." Don't hurry, you have all day (but in fact you don't).

Anyway, you have found a way to proceed — which is the most generous thing about his writing: it transmits the enthusiasm of finding ways to proceed! Squeak of the brakes: first, from up the block; then, closer: What poet does not know the sound of the mailman's truck? Criticism too is labor suited to circumstances. To whom might this be useful, and how? Must a series of questions (forever after) feel like it alludes to *Sunset Debris*? "I wanted each sentence to leave a question in mind — a sense of puzzlement — vague, at first, but capable of being formulated." "To understand is to 'follow.'" "Force" is one of Ron Silliman's oddest compositions, most self-differing of anything of his I know, most discontinuous, jumpy — least sentence-like. Sediments, layers, etymo-archaeology of word and gesture and product. From "The term yoyo dates back only to the 1920s" to "The man on deck gives you a high five" to "In Britain, monarchy is but / a theme park" to "Or / that you would call your clothing concept // Banana Republic, only to sell / out to a chain, and this // The Gap." His writing as a sifting through of fact. "A pyramid of dots (∴∵), international symbol for 'toner out.'" How long will that symbol have meaning? Did it five years ago? Ten? Will toner be used in ten years? Over the time of The Alphabet, many such changes: daypacks, skateboards, spreadsheet, tie-dye, Vietnam Vets' Center, velcro. . . . "That moment in history when mailbox rental shops suddenly multiplied." "Having grown up with a typewriter keyboard, I have a bad attitude toward this device called a mouse." Is superficiality anything other than a failure of attention, an inability to interpret? "Give the cat a tonic." "Built on small square lots right after World War 2, these boxy houses (low ceilings with swirled cement look) were thought to be 'ranch style'—three-speed bike dominates foyer." "The pen streaks across the page, leaving stains of thought." I am writing this (by pen) in my assistant dean's office, believing as I do that poetry is often written and read on stolen time. If someone comes to my door I must put this away in favor of reports, agendas, and memoranda. Or jacaranda, coleus, and amaryllis? Yunte said the pay phone ate up a lot of his quarters as he tried for a few days to reach Lyn. Admittedly, aestheticism (as a poetic style) and New Critical reading methods do have a completely different political meaning in contemporary China than in contemporary America (where such gestures are politically/poetically reactionary and nostalgic). Even so, are the Misty Poets principally careerist, contained within Westernized versions of the poet-in-exile and a romanticized tale of freedom of expression in an allegedly totalitarian state? What does it mean for the leading Chinese poet in exile, living in Denmark and publishing in Sweden, to choose to translate the poems of Seamus Heaney? Get met; it pays. Has the baby been thrown out with the bathwater when "communist" poets, now "free," choose to emulate uncritically the poetic capitalist/commercial mainstream?

Are the allures of publication, prizes, institutionalization, grants, and employment sufficient sirens to lure all sailors? Critical appraisals of poetry have one feature in common: a complete lack of economic candor. What "major" American poet would submit to extensive financial disclosure forms? Is there in such writing—his and this—the potential for a conflict between preconception and the hazards of expression? His work never feels like it's running out of gas. One model of craft depends upon a great amount of rewriting; such writing amounts to readjustment of raw expression to an acceptable form of professionalized behavior. Though it does have aspects of the automatic in it, by virtue of its extensive preconception Ron's writing isn't exactly that either. Since he is committed to revealing the scene of writing, how does that commitment affect what he chooses to present as the particular described instances of composition? As his writing—in virtually *any* particular form of composition—moves toward conclusion, I do not detect evidence of regret. Is it honesty or merely uninteresting self-indulgent triviality (posing as a weightier form of self-consciousness) to note that, midway, I have changed formulas, rejecting a last paragraph of 128 sentences as too much bulk for this essay's (minimal) publication market. When some sentences go on for a long time I get confused as to whether they should conclude with a period or a question mark—especially the ones interrupted by a dash and concluded with a definite statement? Short sentence as counterpunch: Clay decks Liston with straight short sudden left. If a certain percentage of the sentences are his (i.e., directly quoted) and not mine, what is the pivotal percentage at which point this essay ceases to be my own thinking? Was it ever that? By virtue of the extensiveness and directness of Silliman's familial history, especially in *ink*, one is tempted—and by the archness of tone conveyed by "one" I mean "not I"—to call this his most personal writing to date. The way blurb-writing invades all critical prose.

If you first write a surplus of sentences, when you revise you can take out some of the weaker ones. "Next to me on the train a little white-haired man is reading a pamphlet, *Tips on Getting Published*." I spent most of the late afternoon stewing in an unspecified anger: was it because I lost my pen, or the cancelled golf game, or a beautiful spring day seen through an office window, or a rejection letter and its misunderstanding of my use of the journal form, the tedium of a meeting with overtones of a dysfunctional family, or the residue of an odd unresolved dream? "This is about my emotions." Even after six years of groundwork, we hesitate to commodify our men's group experience into weekend workshops. "Men in business suits, especially if overweight, often look like adolescents playing dress-up." I see blue hydrangeas blooming in the backyard, but my memory yields up incomplete information about soil acidity and its relationship to blue versus pink blooms. "A young Latino man watches me intently, distrustfully, as I write."

In his manic phase (on its ten-year schedule), my friend seized the P.A. system in the principal's office and told the whole school he was being held prisoner because he chose to wear a bandanna to teach in. "The headphones and dark glasses give her the 'walled off' look." That action, and the subjunctive iteration that he could kill an assistant principal, have in no way enhanced my friend's prospects of long-term employment in the public school system. Why is this, I wonder, the narrative I close with, this in the face of Ron's healthy, compassionate, and very excellent book?

"As market culture expands in order to create through absorption a single world ideological system, there remain two basic varieties of aesthetic form which continue, however fitfully, to subsist on the outside: pre-market cultural genres, predominantly rural, peripheral even in the context of the Third World, and those market modes which openly contest the primacy of capital, at the one end forms which previously were associated with feudal courts, the historic avant-gardes, and at the other the militant nostalgia of 'folk art.'" "When I'm anxious I monolog."

ENDNOTE that might be read as a PREFACE

All sentences in quotation marks are from Silliman (1992). I have deliberately not included page numbers because I wanted to integrate quoted sentences in ways that made page numbers intrusive. One point of a tropical criticism would be to abolish the distance implicit in more traditional, scholarly manners of quotation.

As for the notion of tropical criticism itself, the idea stems from my conversations and correspondence with Charles Bernstein. Specifically, Bernstein (1987a) articulates some possibilities for a tropical criticism in his verse-essay "Artifice of Absorption":

> The obvious problem is that the poem said in any
> other way is not the poem. This may account for
> why writers revealing their intentions or
> references ("close readings"), just like readers
> inventorying devices, often say so little: why
> a sober attempt to document or describe runs so
> high a risk of falling flat. In contrast, why not
> a criticism intoxicated with its own metaphoricity,
> or tropicality: one in which the limits of
> positive criticism are made more audibly
> artificial; in which the inadequacy of our
> explanatory paradigms is neither ignored

nor regretted but brought into fruitful play.
Imagine, then, oscillating poles,
constructing not some better diadicism, but
congealing into a field of potentialities
that in turn collapses (transforms) into yet other
tropicalities. This would be the criticism of desire:
sowing not reaping.

(1992, 16)

Conclusion

In "Criticism and the Crisis in American Poetry" (Lazer 1996, chapter 1),
I claim that "ours *is* a lively age, an age of strife, controversy, and, in a
very specific sense, crisis. But the writing that would challenge the generational continuity and 'canonized revolution' that [critics such as] Altieri
and Breslin bemoan, has been systematically ignored for a period of ten
years by these very critics, the arbiters of what Bernstein calls 'official verse
culture.'" In *Opposing Poetries*, I attempt to correct such oversights, to
introduce and argue for the value of a broad range of experimental poetries. The work of these poets puts forward a different paradigm of poetic
production and poetic vocation, a paradigm that, unlike the more limited,
craft-oriented models of the mainstream, might allow poetry once again to
become more fully a part of our political, intellectual, and emotional lives.

Over the nine years of critical consideration represented in *Opposing
Poetries*, there have been some significant developments with regard to the
community of poets engaged in experimental poetries. Within the United
States, the reception for innovative poetries, particularly for Language
Writing, has improved moderately. For example, a handful of poets identified as Language poets now occupy positions within academia—Charles
Bernstein, who holds a chair in poetry at SUNY-Buffalo; Susan Howe,
who teaches at SUNY-Buffalo; Barrett Watten, who teaches at Wayne
State; and Bob Perelman, who teaches at the University of Pennsylvania,
are examples of the slight thaw in university hiring practices. Nonetheless,
as Golding (1995) points out, an academic position per se does not address
the more complex issue of institutional location and function. As Golding
notes, "relatively few Language writers make a full-time living in English
departments, and even fewer are employed *as poets*, to teach creative writing" (148). And many of the finest experimental poets (many of whom
have no interest whatsoever in employment within academia) continue in
jobs in the computer industry, independent business consulting, psycho-
therapy, publishing, and other careers that enliven and broaden the base
of discussion and experience within the literary community.

There are, at present, a number of critics who write essays and books on
Language Writing, including Marjorie Perloff, Jerome McGann, George
Hartley, Linda Reinfeld, Peter Quartermain, Charles Altieri, Jed Rasula,
Marnie Parsons, Keith Tuma, Walter Kalaidjian, and Alan Golding. In-
deed, as the case of Nathaniel Mackey illustrates, the activity of a single

poet-scholar can bring about important changes. Mackey's critical writing, gathered together in *Discrepant Engagement: Dissonance, Cross-Culturality, and Experimental Writing* (1993), provides an extensive grounding in Caribbean writings (such as the work of Edward Kamau Brathwaite and Wilson Harris). Mackey's is an astonishingly integrated critical intelligence. His book offers a richly polyvocal context for reading Robert Duncan, Robert Creeley, Amiri Baraka, Charles Olson, Clarence Major, Wilson Harris, and others, while also paying careful attention to the examples of key figures in jazz such as Thelonious Monk and John Coltrane. As in the anthology work of Jerome Rothenberg and Pierre Joris (1995) the result of Mackey's writing—poetry and critical prose—is a powerfully broadened context for reading and understanding poetry.

And many more literary journals (than was the case nine years ago) are willing to publish essays on experimental writing, including Language writing. (For example, Chapter 10 of this volume was published in the *American Poetry Review*.) In the 1990s, a number of new literary magazines and small presses have extended the network of publication and distribution for experimental poetries, though perhaps an equal number of important presses, magazines, and distribution centers have ceased operations.

One of the most exciting developments of the past few years has been the internationalization of the experimental poetry community. Over the past ten years, exchanges between American Language poets and their counterparts have taken place in China, Russia, the former Yugoslavia, New Zealand, England, Italy, Austria, and France. As Marjorie Perloff (1990) has pointed out, the work of American Language poets figures prominently in French anthologies of contemporary American poetry. In China, Sichuan Art and Literature Publishing House published a bilingual collection, *Selected Language Poems*, in 1993 that also included several essays on contemporary innovative American poetries. Zhang Ziqing, a Chinese scholar at Nanjing University who is currently completing a history of twentieth-century American poetry, gives considerable attention to experimental poetries, especially the work of Language poets. Jeff Twitchell, an American scholar who spent a number of years teaching at Nanjing University, is providing an important introduction, by means of essays and translations, to the work of post-Misty Chinese poets such as the Original Poets. For spring 1996, *River City* plans an issue devoted to contemporary Chinese writing, including important critical writing by Yunte Huang, a Chinese scholar-poet who is introducing innovative Chinese poetries to the West as well as completing the first translation of Pound's *Pisan Cantos* into Chinese. The ambitious new year-book/anthology *Exact Change* (no. 1, 1995) presents innovative poetry in a decidedly international context, including work by Susan Howe, Michael Palmer, and Beverly Dahlen along with substantial selections of poetry from China (including the Original Poets), Germany, Canada, Russia, the Caribbean, France, Ireland, and the United Kingdom. In April 1995, Cornell University hosted an international poetry conference that included a reading by Bei Dao, a discussion of the poetry of Che Qianzi, and readings and talks by, among others, Rosmary Waldrop, Pierre Joris, and Rachel Blau DuPlessis. (Indeed, the writings of Waldrop, Joris, and others call into question the very identification of poetry with nationality.) The summer of 1995 featured a poetry festival in Vancouver to celebrate the work of Robin Blaser, a gathering that included many of the poets and critics mentioned throughout *Opposing Poetries*. In Canada, particularly in Toronto, Montreal, and Vancouver, important experimental writing communities exist, and the work of Canadian writers such as Steve McCaffery, bp Nichol, and Nicole Brossard are influential among American experimental writers.

As I revise this Conclusion, I must also acknowledge the way e-mail contributes to the internationalization of exchanges in poetry and poetics. The e-mail–based Poetics discussion group, for example, routinely includes conversations, questions, publication information, and poems from participants in the United Kingdom, New Zealand, Australia, Canada, and the United States. No doubt, though, the most significant accomplishment in the internationalization of innovative poetries is the first volume of the massive, ambitious anthology *Poems for the Millennium: The University of California Book of Modern and Postmodern Poetry*, edited by Jerome Rothenberg and Pierre Joris (1995). This volume, *From Fin-de-Siècle to Negritude*, gathers together (as no previous anthology has) the staggering international scope of twentieth-century innovative poetries, including substantial selections by Mallarmé, Cavafy, Darío, Valéry, Jarry, Max Jacob, Apollinaire, Pessoa, Pound, Cendrars, Duchamp, Marinetti, Khlebnikov, Kruchenykh, Mayakovsky, Kandinsky, Klee, Trakl, Tzara, Ball, Arp, Schwitters, Stein, Stevens, Joyce, Eliot, Sitwell, Mandelstam, Lorca, Breton, Zukofsky, Bunting, Williams, Césaire, Senghor, Ahkmatova, MacDiarmid, Kenji, Brecht, Tolson, Ponge, Hikmet, Hughes, Wen Yiduo, Guillén, Neruda, Shimpei, Ekelöf, Radnóti, Yi Sang, Orpingalik (Netsilik Eskimo), Arunta (Australia), Allama Prabhu (Kanmada, India), Duncan, Baraka, Aborigine Sound Poems, Awotunde Aworinde, Ortiz,

Cantares Mexicanos, Mac Low, Olson, Jabès, Songs from the Society of Mystic Animals, and many others. I present this listing to give only a small indication of the diversity and range of innovative poetries gathered together by Rothenberg and Joris. Eventually, such a compilation has the capacity to alter in fundamental ways the contexts, history, reading, and writing of poetry.

Domestically, the resistance to experimental poetries within the academy, particularly within MFA programs in creative writing, remains intense (though the students entering such programs often have broader reading interests than the faculty who teach them). To the best of my knowledge, in 1995 there is not, for example, a single Language Writer who holds a full-time position in any of the approximately three hundred programs in creative writing in the United States. But there *are* signs of possible changes. Even at the University of Iowa, whose MFA program is often caricatured as the template for the national explosion of such programs, reportedly the current students (Fall 1995) are most interested in the work of Michael Palmer, and many students at Iowa are writing poetry openly influenced by Language Writing and other innovative poetries. Within the Associated Writing Programs itself, as seen in recent issues of its publication the *AWP Newsletter*, there is serious discussion about the inadequacies of current workshop methodologies. Indeed, many poet-professors working *within* the creative writing institutitions are calling for a re-invention of the workshop, the cornerstone of creative writing programs' pedagogy.

But the principal cultural institutions that Charles Bernstein calls "official verse culture"—the interlocking institutions for reviews, awards, accreditation, jobs, and "major" publication—remain, for the most part, nearly as xenophobic as they were nine years ago when I began the series of essays represented in *Opposing Poetries*. The new editions of anthologies of American literature, while greatly improved in the representation of women and African-American writers as well as in the range of multicultural contributions, still do not adequately address the issue of aesthetic diversity. Important early mid-twentieth-century poets, such as Gertrude Stein, William Carlos Williams, and Louis Zukofsky, are often represented with trivial and/or minimal selections (and in the case of Williams often with selections that domesticate and minimalize his accomplishments). More recent poets of significant innovative practices, such as Robert Duncan, George Oppen, Jack Spicer, John Cage, Jackson Mac Low, David Antin, Jerome Rothenberg, Lyn Hejinian, Susan Howe, and Charles Bernstein, are rarely included at all. Similarly, as I argued in "Anthologies,

Poetry, and Postmodernism" (1996, chapter 7), the anthologies' representation of multiculturalism exhibits a pernicious aesthetic narrowness. I am in full agreement with Nathaniel Mackey's (1993) assessment:

> My view is that there has been far too much emphasis on accessibility when it comes to writers from socially marginalized groups. This has resulted in shallow, simplistic readings that belabor the most obvious aspects of the writer's work and situation, readings that go something like this: "So-and-so is a black writer. Black people are victims of racism. So-and-so's writing speaks out against racism." It has yet to be shown that such simplifications have had any positive political effect, if indeed they have had any political effect at all. . . . Failures or refusals to acknowledge complexity among writers from socially marginalized groups, no matter how "well-intentioned," condescend to the work and to the writers and thus, hardly the solution they purport to be, are a part of the problem. (17–18)

In fact, there are a number of contemporary African-American poets—including Nathaniel Mackey, Erica Hunt, Will Alexander, Harryette Mullen, Lorenzo Thomas, Clarence Major, and Ishmael Reed—whose poetry merits inclusion in anthologies truly committed to a range of expression.

Among younger practitioners of innovative poetries—writers who are mainly in their twenties and thirties—the 1993 conference held at SUNY-Buffalo (Writing from the New Coast, 31 March–2 April 1993, subsequently published as a double issue of *O-blek* magazine) demonstrates that there is a great deal of vitality, interest, and productivity within that extended community. At present, it is too early to determine to what extent the work of emerging innovative writers will distinguish itself—by affirmation, modification, and rejection—from the work of now more established Language Writers. The editorial "State of the Art" for the new magazine *apex of the M* (Daly et al. 1994) points toward some of the areas for criticism, skepticism, and questioning as the various writing projects of avant-garde poetries are considered and critiqued by a new generation of practitioners:

> Why, in a society in which communication between human beings is constantly discouraged and threatened, does a participatory valorization of this disintegration become the primary mode of many of the arts?
> We wish to question, but not as "humanists," the rampant formalism

of so much of the art of the past two decades: art that far from challenging, instead mimics and acquiesces to, the methods used for the trans-
mission of information and experience in a media age. The time has
come for us to move beyond an understanding of innovation that operates on what has proven to be a merely ostensible, or predominantly
formal (or is it aesthetic?), level of change. The increasing convention-
ality of "innovation," leading to the socially inept dead-end of autono-
mous forms, remains unscrutinized as an agent of potentially universal
indifference in a world more and more determined in its course of ano-
nymity by the same break-up of language that experimental poetry in
particular glorifies as a mode of resistance. (5–6)

As the editors of *apex of the M* correctly point out, the assumed cor-
relation between formal "innovation" and social or political resistance
is, at best, a slippery assumption. For example, as Language poetry
itself becomes somewhat institutionalized—within and without academia,
through various presses, magazines, reading series, anthologies, and ar-
chives—certain formally "innovative" gestures lose their force and become
the means of a conformist, imitative practice lacking in the oppositional
energies suggested by Charles Bernstein's (1992) definition: "poetry is aversion of conformity" (1). The most superficially obvious habit of avant-
garde poetries—an appearance of fragmentation—itself is questioned by
the editors of *apex of the M* as perhaps merely (passively?) mirroring or
glorifying a contemporary phenomenon. The editors are also correct to
point out that avant-garde poetries also carry with them an at times hidden assumption of "progress": "We might point out here the possibility of
a disturbing parallel between the rhetoric of innovation as proclaimed by
the avant-garde, beginning at least with the Futurists and the Vorticists,
and the actual innovations that have continuously maimed and expropri-
ated the world's spiritual and natural resources in the name of, and in
capitulation to the myth of, modern progress" (7).

As poets such as Bernstein, Silliman, Sherry, Hejinian, and Howe have
done in establishing a critical relationship to earlier modernisms, the
poets/editors of *apex of the M*, the writers present at the Writing from the
New Coast conference, and other younger writers, will, of course, establish their own critical relationship to their predecessors in innovation. As
the editors of *apex of the M* (Daly et al. 1994) make clear, one possible contrastive basis for such a poetic inheritance may focus on the place of the
sacred in poetry:

We would also want to open in the pages of this journal the question as to whether there can be a purely secular form of alterity, of whether the relationship with the other can exist independently of an acknowledgement of the sacred. Of course in utilizing the word sacred, or the word spirit, we run the risk of being misunderstood. Emily Dickinson defined "spirit" as "the Conscious Ear." Much of the writing that interests us and that we are attempting to publish seems to be at least partially formed through this "Conscious Ear." It should go without saying that we invariably and without hesitation separate our use of the words sacred and spirit from conventional religious systems. (6)

As I have argued in several chapters in *Opposing Poetries*, there are a great number of formally innovative poets for whom the issues of spirit and the lyrical fall *within* their poetic practice, even while that spirituality and lyricism may be practiced in an ambivalent or self-questioning manner. Clearly, the work of poets such as Susan Howe, Rachel Blau DuPlessis, bp Nichol, Nathaniel Mackey, Lyn Hejinian, and Charles Bernstein engage such issues, as does the work of earlier poets such as Robert Duncan, H.D., and George Oppen.

One particular caution and criticism that I would level at the Language Writing community is that many of its finest writers have become increasingly careerist and settled in their activities. There are virtually no magazines that provide a sustained public forum for arguments and interchange among these writers. Many of the best Language Writers—who in the 1970s and 1980s engaged in very exciting, provocative critical writing—have gradually retreated from such activity. Too many of these writers now tend their own poetic careers, and the earlier more exciting levels of disturbance, annoyance, and innovation are waning. What is missing is a public venue for critical exchange and appraisal—a need that is only partially met by on-line discussions. Such an absence is felt all the more acutely at a time when many innovative poets may, in fact, be producing their best and/or most ambitious work. Admittedly, I do have some reasons to doubt my assertion of a diminishing critical exchange. Specifically, I am thinking of the many provocative critical books recently published or forthcoming shortly: Mackey (1993), Byrd (1994), Howe (1993), Damon (1993), Taggart (1994), Scalapino (1994), Golding (1995), Rasula (1995), and books forthcoming from Bob Perelman and Bruce Andrews. Also, the (electronic, on-line) Poetics discussions group, which now includes participants from New Zealand, Australia, the United Kingdom, Taiwan, and Canada as well as a wide range of U.S. participants, holds open the prospect for more decentralized, intelligent conversation about poetry and its cultural contexts.

Dana Gioia (1993) argues that "there still exists a huge audience for poetry in America, old and new, but it is now so segmented and atomized, that it shares almost no common ground" (13). For Gioia, such a situation of decentralized activity causes some anxiety: "Since there is no center to literary life, a critic in New York or San Francisco now has as much trouble understanding changes in poetry as does a reader in Fargo or Tuscaloosa" (13). Personally, I prefer Charles Bernstein's (1992) more celebratory mode: "There is of course no state of American poetry, but states, moods, agitations, dissipations, renunciations, depressions, acquiescences, elations, angers, ecstasies; no music to our verse but vastly incompatible musics; no single sentiment but clashes of sentience: the magnificent cacophony of different bodies making different sounds" (1). While Bernstein (1992) acknowledges "the sharper ideological disagreements that lacerate our communal field of action" (1), he proposes an affirmation of difference in poetry:

> What I hear, then, in the poetries of this New American fin de siècle is an implicit refusal of unity that is the result of our prodigious and magnanimous outpouring of words. In saying this, I register my own particular passion . . . for poetry that insists on running its own course, finding its own measures, charting worlds otherwise hidden or denied or, perhaps best of all, never before existing. (1)

As I have argued in *Opposing Poetries*, the writing of a literary history that hopes for a somewhat accurate mapping of the present verges on the impossible. Gioia and Bernstein posit a credible multiplicity, though the tenor of their responses to that condition remains quite different. Rasula (1995) maps out four zones in today's poetry world:

> (1) The Associated Writing Programs, consisting of some three hundred institutionalized venues of creative writing instruction; (2) the New Formalism, with a small but visible number of adherents, whose goals are supported by a combination of small presses, large trade publishers, and a few highbrow quarterlies; (3) language poetry, with a well established alternative press network, and a considerable critical reputation; and (4) various coalitions of interest-oriented or community-based poets (which obviously renders this fourth zone more heterogeneous and fluid than the others). (440)

One might argue for the existence or emergence of other zones by giving greater emphasis to oral poetries, poetry slams, and multimedia/electronically based poetries that no longer take up exclusive residence in a print culture. To consider such a proliferation of sites, approaches, assumptions, and practices, readers, professors, and critics of poetry will need to devise new modes of questioning and pedagogy. To date, one of the most productive lines of questioning—an approach that does not negate or domesticate the vast differences within today's poetry world—is that raised by Maria Damon in *The Dark End of the Street* (1993) and in subsequent essays and addresses when she begins her consideration of a text with a seemingly simple question: What is the cultural work being done by this poem/poet? Such a question avoids the claustrophobia of myopic theme-based readings. Mores positively, Damon's approach *assumes* the complex cultural and material location of poetry as essential to the acts of reading and interpretation.

What may be needed today is not so much a multicultural pedagogy as a polyvocal pedagogy. Jed Rasula (1995) argues that "the polyphonic ambition to 'do the police in different voices' (as Eliot's *Waste Land* was originally titled) needs to be retained not only as validating a national poetry as composed of different social groups, but also as the agent of complexity within individual voices—a co-inherence of 'divergent cultural knowledges,' and an 'ethics of antiphony' " (287–88). In a similar vein, Nathaniel Mackey (1993), quoting the Martinican writer Edouard Glissant, argues, "In opposition to a universalizing and reductive humanism, we must develop a theory of particular opacities" (261). For Mackey, at present, "we need more than content analyses based on assumptions of representationality. The dislocating tilt of artistic othering, especially as practiced by African-American artists, deserves a great deal more attention than it has been given" (284). As Mackey and Baraka indicate, the work of jazz artists, especially John Coltrane and Thelonious Monk, may provide analogies and paths toward a polyvocal norm. For example, Monk's right-wrong notes, his humor, and his articulate odd silences and syncopations, if applied to metrical considerations in poetry, point up the inherent triviality and reductiveness of traditional binary (stressed-unstressed) prosody.

But to return to Rasula's (1995) mapping of four zones in today's poetry world, these zones point, inevitably, to narratives of literary history and to an earlier divergence:

Tracing the lineage of these groups or zones is tricky, although going back thirty years the four easily resolve into two: formalism and open-form poetry. These two, in turn, are resolved into a split or fractious One inasmuch as they represent a dispute over the legacy of early twentieth-century modernism. The formalist-academic school can be depicted as a triumph of New Critical appropriation of the modernist tradition for a so-called postmodernist neoformalism. The underground (in Allen's 1960 gathering) arose partly with indifference to, and partly in dispute of, academic custodial claims to modernism. A key distinction is that the school of civility sought closure in relation to the modernist provocation, whereas the "New American" antitypes proclaimed modernism as an ongoing unfinished project. (440–41)

But on this issue—the closed or open-ended nature of modernism—the current evidence is overwhelmingly in favor of a continually arriving generative wave of modernism(s) in American poetry. One can point to the many reissuings of work by Gertrude Stein (including facsimile editions of *Tender Buttons* and *The Making of Americans*, republication of *Stanzas in Meditation*, *Geography and Plays*, and *Everybody's Autobiography*, and the publication of *The Stein Reader*) and Stein's importance to Ron Silliman (and his *New Sentence* [1987b]) and Lyn Hejinian (and her *Two Stein Talks* [1986] and *My Life* [1987]); reinterpretations of the Harlem Renaissance with new emphasis on Alain Locke's 1925 anthology *The New Negro* (with its attention to the visual and musical arts as well as poetry, fiction, and intellectual prose) and Jean Toomer's (1988) multigenre work *Cane*; rediscovery and republication of work by Laura Riding, H.D., and Louis Zukofsky; sustained attention to William Carlos Williams's writing of the 1920s (especially *Spring and All* [in W. C. Williams 1986] in its full mixed-genre form); as well as the monumental first volume of Jerome Rothenberg and Pierre Joris's (1995) global anthology *Poems for the Millennium* which should, once and for all, discredit as exclusionary, ill-read, and over simplified the outmoded but perhaps still prevailing academic fixation on a narrow high modernism as an adequate representation of "modernism" generally.

Whereas most poetry to emerge from the institutional enclaves of programs in creative writing exhibit the workshop's twin allergies—to critical theory and to the modernist critique of meaning and representation—Language Writing, as Rasula (1995) notes, represents an extension and reinvigoration of modernist practice:

What distinguished language poetry from the outset was its emphasis on articulating a poetics: that is, preserving and extending the sense of poetics as social engagement as well as methodological provocation. Language poetry specifically laid claim to the vanguard impulse within modernism that had been effaced by New Critical recuperations, and consistently ignored by the AWP; and it was aided in this quest by the concurrent rise of critical theory in academia. (Language poetry can be thought of as the specific attempt to rethink New American poetics in light of continental theory—structuralism, semiotics, Frankfurt school ideology critique, and discourse theory.) (442)

An irony (which I point out [Lazer 1996, chapter 1] and which Rasula himself notes) is that instead of critical theory paving the way for the reading of innovative poetries in academia, the rise of theory coincides with the virtual inaudibility of experimental contemporary poetries.

But to address only the dynamics of poetry versus theory in the academic curriculum is to miss a more fundamental change in writing itself. Rasula (1995) offers the following version of writing's changing nature in the late twentieth century:

> The printed page is no longer the sole medium of writing: electrical pulsations on a monitor dissolve print fixity into print fluidity, which is an oxymoron. Ever since Hesiod's encounter with the Muses, the poet has been conceived of as the Muses' medium, the raw material instrument through which the poem is transmitted. The poet is also a "control," in the mediumistic sense (at a seance the control is the person transmitting spirit voices), a proxy for phantoms. There is a final, more contemporary sense of control, which Norbert Wiener derived from the Greek word for steersman: cybernetics. So, in the founding myth of poetic inspiration, Hesiod—putting his voice at the disposal of the Muses—converts poetry into cybernetics. As a theory of control in systems behavior, cybernetics has always been positioned at the prosthetic interface, that juncture at which the tool may become an extension of the person, or the person an extension of the tool. (45–46)

Clearly, Rasula is correct: the printed page is no longer the sole medium of writing. Even so, there are a number of different ways to conceptualize this transitional era. As Myron Tuman (1992) argues, "For now many of us are straddling these two worlds, drawing strength from each—but for how much longer?" (138). Tuman has in mind the worlds of print and on-line literacy. Thinking in a similarly configured sense of our era, Richard Lanham (1993) concludes, "It is only when we compare print to its pixeled analogue that we realize how talismanic the physical book and journal have become" (20).

Lanham and Tuman each cite George Steiner's already retrospective regret for the marginalization of "traditional" reading:

> In "The End of Bookishness," George Steiner remarks on the historical connection between books and monasteries: "I would not be surprised if that which lies ahead for classical modes of reading resembles the monasticism from which those modes sprung. I sometimes dream of houses of reading—a Hebrew phrase—in which those passionate to learn how to read well would find the necessary guidance, silence, and complicity of disciplined companionship." (Lanham 1993, 27)

I think of Steiner's houses of reading as the museum of intensive reading: *a kind of attentiveness in reading wed to a specific historical era of textuality and professionalized reading.* Lanham states rather neutrally, "Writing created one breed of seriousness; electronic text is now creating another" (85).

Considerations of a newly emergent on-line literacy, though, especially when written by those of us straddling two eras and who were raised in a worship of the book, tend to take on a moral (and moralistic) tone. Tuman (1992), though, points out the inevitability of new modes of literacy:

> We seem to have little idea of just how dynamic (hyperactive?) the computer screen is likely to become once the hardware and software are in place to support real-time video and the wizardry of multimedia. Richard Kearney cites a relevant and troubling, albeit undocumented, statistic: "that since the arrival of multi-channel press-button TV in the US, less than 50 per cent of American children under the age of 15 have ever watched a single programme from start to finish" (1988, p. 1). Some might be tempted to find hope in such numbers, given the dreadful programming on TV, yet "zapping," as anyone with such a device must realize, has far more to do with pacing than with judgment, more to do, that is, with our exploiting the hypertextual capability of a new online technology in order to assemble a more pleasing (more postmodern?) procession of images. A new cultural landscape, one grounded in computer technology, will affect all of us, professors and students alike. All of us, and not just hyperactive adolescents, will zap. (69)

For Tuman, an expert in the teaching of composition, the issue of changing structures of attention is of immediate pedagogical concern:

> Here then is the central question before us as educators and as citizens. What, if anything, are we in danger of losing—or conversely, what might we gain—when students in large numbers and eventually people throughout society begin "writing," not just by linking items in a database or conversing online, but by integrating words with pictures, moving as well as still, and sounds? Here, at one level, the initial answer is obvious, if seemingly circular. It depends on one's attitude about the tradition of print literacy. (117)

As I argue in Chapter 11 of this volume (in my reading of James Sherry's *Our Nuclear Heritage*) poetry, and particularly innovative poetries, might play a significant (though neither predominant nor grandiose) role in an understanding of thinking itself. Similarly, if we are witnessing, via digitalization, the gradual emergence of new modes of human attention, innovative poetries may play an important role in conceptualizing, embodying, and exploring those changes. While many print-culture fundamentalists decry the emergent on-line literacy as a decline, a failure, and a falling off of more cherished modes of concentration, readers and writers steeped in the many-faceted experimentalisms of twentieth-century poetry may be uniquely positioned to argue for a continuity of attention structures. (In that fine malapropism of Yogi Berra, for many innovative poets, the attention stuctures engendered by digitalization may seem like "déjà vu all over again.")

Within the many communities of contemporary experimental poetries, digitalization is already effecting significant changes. From the many electronic journals, hypertext, multimedia, CD-ROM, and conventional CD productions of the last five years to the development of a multifaceted Electronic Poetry Center at SUNY-Buffalo, the nature of reading, writing, and publication *are* undergoing a dramatic change. Indeed, one can legitimately begin to wonder about the necessity and efficacy of the traditional hard-copy publication of poetry, particularly the book-projects whose current press runs are often no more than 500 to 750 copies. Indeed, the motives for such book publication come into question, and the ideological and institutional links of modes of publication to professional strictures become more apparent with the increasing access to the radically decentralized modes of electronic publication and distribution. Of course, to further complicate such a narrative, which can sound like a "march of progress" story told in the book world, at the same time that electronic publication is developing a significant market presence, so too are many innovative practitioners of the book arts creating new book formats in partnership with experimental poetries. Indeed, a study of book arts, from Mallarmé to the present, could lead one to the argument that nearly all present forms of hypertext have already been accomplished (in concept and in print) in the much neglected areas of experimental poetry and innovative book arts.

As Rasula's (1995) history from Hesiod to cybernetics indicates, the pressures applied by digitalization to the book are also retrospective in nature. In this Conclusion, looking beyond the concerns addressed thus far in *Opposing Poetries*, I am arguing that we, the readers and writers of innovative poetries, participate actively in theorizing this current era of pressure and change in modes of writing, reading, publishing, and distributing. This era—perhaps a cusp—asks us to reassess, both proleptically and retrospectively, the uses and cultures of the word (and thus, by implication, of the book). My specific bias is to consider (and promote) what part *poetry* might play in thinking through these related issues.

From my perspective, the most intriguing element of the simultaneously forward-and-backward-looking pressure of digitalization is the recurring consideration of the complex intersection in poetry of the oral and the written. Jack Foley (1993) astutely gathers together the work of Eric A. Havelock and Walter Ong, each of whom have written on the implications of a much earlier shift from an oral culture to a print culture:

> *The figure of the heroic poet listening to "an inner music" is a mythologizing of the act of reading.* What has reading to do with poetry? What happens when, as Eric A. Havelock puts it, "the muse learns to write"? The Homeric poet's blindness is an indication that he has nothing at all to do with writing. There was no Braille in Homer's day. At its beginnings, poetry is rooted in physical presence and in sounds, and, whatever the labyrinthine complexities of its history—and they are many—it always maintains some sort of connection to its purely oral past. (Foley 1993, 72)

Interestingly enough, Foley's own "essay" quoted above, "Words & Books; Poetry & Writing," is in fact also a script for a two-voice performance. An audiotape version of the essay, then, differs from the written version. Thus much of Foley's writing, including *Adrift* and *Gershwin* (1991), are "published" in written *and* audio formats, existing self-consciously and productively at the intersection of oral and written traditions. It is the era of contestation, coincident with the rise of philosophy and the turf warfare between poets and philosophers that Plato expresses, that Ong and Havelock explore as they theorize the complexities (and interesting loopings back) as oral cultures enter an era of writing. Our present moment seems to me to be the third note in that chord: oral culture; written culture; online culture. In locating his own work at the intersection of the oral and the written, Foley's project bears an important relationship to a range of similarly situated work by Jerome Rothenberg, David Antin, bp Nichol, Steve McCaffery, Jake Berry, Michael McClure, John Taggart, Johanna Drucker, Jed Rasula, and others who explore this particular intersection of values. Indeed, one could argue that the conflict between the oral and the written, made explicit by Robert Grenier's 1971 (written) pronouncement, "I HATE SPEECH," is a productive tension within a broad range of contemporary experimental poetries (including language poetry).

As Foley (1993) argues,

> Yet this is by no means the end of the story. Writing is itself at this moment in a state of crisis. For the first time in its history, it finds itself *in competition* with other modes of expression. Our children, we complain, don't read enough. Listening is declining. *For many years writing was the only way of preserving human speech*, but this is no longer the case. In his book, *The Muse Learns to Write*, Eric A. Havelock reflects upon the new interest in orality which has characterized much scholarship in the past 25 to 30 years. Why, he asks, "should . . . works produced simultaneously in three different countries have all involved themselves in the role of human language in human culture? Why, in particular, this focus on the spoken language in contrast to the written?" His answer is: "We had all been listening to the radio. . . ." The electronic media have already changed the conditions of writing, though the exact nature of that change is not yet clear. . . . What are we likely to experience next? We don't know, but we have an intense sense that it is likely to be *different*. (74–75)

Taken collectively, the writing I have been making reference to in this Conclusion should convince us of the intricate complexity of forces, issues, and institutions at play (and at work) in contemporary manifestations of poetry. Even in (or perhaps because of) its murky, infinitely varied practice, contemporary poetry might be understood as a laboratory or crucible or polymorphous display terminal where key forces are being tested out in a transitional era of language-practice.

As David Antin (1972) argued, residence in the artistic present is not an easy or natural activity. I would argue that such an active investigation of present poetic practice ought to be an expectation of *all* professors of literature (just as a knowledge of past literatures is a reasonable expectation of professors and writers whose activity focuses on present literary production). The current hierarchy of prestige and value in academia—a single-authored book counts most; substantial scholarly articles in refereed scholarly journals count next most; reviews count barely at all—mitigates against an environment in which serious public debate, appraisal, and interest in contemporary poetry (at least in academia) would be possible. The state of poetry reviewing (particularly beyond the communities of innovative poetries) is dismal.

It is my fear that poetry itself—especially in its aesthetic diversity—is disappearing from the contemporary curriculum. What we lose when poetry and poetic thinking disappear from our culture is a kind of intellectual diversity, a disappearance that bears an ominous off-rhymed relationship to similar disappearances of biodiversity from our ecosystem. Perhaps the diminished importance of poetry in the curriculum stems, in part, from the accurate critiques launched in the early and mid-1980s of the mainstream poetic product—critiques (recounted in Lazer 1996, chapter 1) of the dullness and lack of ambition in the work of many of the most touted poets of the day. Perhaps also the allure of critical theory in the 1970s, 1980s, and the present decade contributed too to that diminished importance, convincing many of the best students of literature that critical theory was where they might find the most engaging (and playful and challenging) cultural critiques.

But, as I have been arguing throughout *Opposing Poetries*, contemporary poetry too has an important role to play in the intellectual, cultural, and political debates of the present moment. As James Sherry (1991) argues, we do not have to make delusory grandiose claims for poetry's comprehensiveness and greatness. Instead, the present moment—of specialization and compartmentalization of knowledge—calls rather for a more democratic and participatory expectation for practitioners of poetic knowledge. If poetry's mode of inquiry is to become again a part of serious social and cultural thinking, then poets too must actively reconceive of the place of their mode of knowledge within a broad sociology of knowledge.

As I have demonstrated in *Opposing Poetries*, the poets and the writing already exist for a renewed (and renewing) participation of poetry within our cultural, intellectual, and emotional lives. A first step would be for the range of these innovative poetries to be read, considered, and discussed by an equally broad range of readers.

Works Cited

Adorno, Theodor. 1974. "Lyric Poetry and Society." *Telos* 20:56–71.

———. 1984. *Aesthetic Theory*. New York: Routledge and Kegan Paul.

Allen, Donald. 1960. *The New American Poetry*. New York: Grove.

Altieri, Charles. 1984. *Self and Sensibility in Contemporary American Poetry*. Cambridge: Cambridge University Press.

Andrews, Bruce. 1987a. *Give Em Enough Rope*. Los Angeles: Sun & Moon Press.

———. 1987b. Interview with Marjorie Perloff.

———. 1988. *Getting Ready to Have Been Frightened*. New York: Roof Press.

———. 1989. "Total Equals What: Poetics and Praxis." *Revista Canaria de Estudios Ingleses*. 18 April:53–65.

———. 1990. "Poetry as Explanation, Poetry as Praxis." In *The Politics of Poetic Form: Poetry and Public Policy*, edited by Charles Bernstein. New York: Roof Press.

———. 1991. "Paradise and Method." Transcript of talk delivered at Saint Mark's Church, New York City, 7 April.

Andrews, Bruce, and Charles Bernstein, eds. 1984. *The L=A=N=G=U=A=G=E Book*. Carbondale: Southern Illinois University Press.

Antin, David. 1972. "Modernism and Postmodernism: Approaching the Present in American Poetry." *Boundary 2*, vol. 1, no. 1:98–133.

———. 1974. "Some Questions about Modernism." *Occident* 8 (spring): 7–38.

———. 1976. *Talking at the Boundaries*. New York: New Directions.

———. 1984. *Tuning*. New York: New Directions.

———. 1991. *Selected Poems: 1963–1973*. Los Angeles: Sun & Moon Press.

———. 1993. *What It Means to be Avant-Garde*. New York: New Directions.

Ashbery, John. 1976. *Self-Portrait in a Convex Mirror: Poems*. New York: Penguin Press.

Barthes, Roland. 1975. *The Pleasure of the Text*. New York: Hill and Wang.

———. 1977. *Roland Barthes by Roland Barthes*. New York: Hill and Wang.

———. 1986. *The Rustle of Language*. New York: Hill and Wang.

Bernstein, Charles. 1980. *Controlling Interests*. New York: Roof Books.

———. 1983. *Resistance*. Windsor, Vt.: Awede Press.

———. 1986. *Content's Dream: Essays, 1975–1984*. Los Angeles: Sun & Moon Press.

———. 1987a. *Artifice of Absorption*. Philadelphia: Singing Horse Press/Paper Air. Reprinted in his *A Poetics*. Cambridge: Harvard University Press, 1992.

———. 1987b. *The Sophist*. Los Angeles: Sun & Moon Press.

———. 1992. *A Poetics*. Cambridge: Harvard University Press.

———. 1994. *Dark City*. Los Angeles: Sun & Moon Press.

Burke, Kenneth. 1973. *The Philosophy of Literary Form: Studies in Symbolic Action.* 3d ed. Berkeley and Los Angeles: University of California Press.

Byrd, Don. 1994. *The Poetics of the Common Knowledge.* Albany: State University of New York Press.

Cage, John. 1983. *X: Writings '79–'82.* Middletown: Wesleyan University Press.

———. 1993. *Composition in Retrospect.* Cambridge: Exact Change.

Cameron, Sharon. 1989. *Writing Nature: Henry David Thoreau's Journal.* Chicago: University of Chicago Press.

Cavell, Stanley. 1981. *The Senses of Walden.* San Francisco, Calif.: North Point Press.

Coward, Rosalind, and John Ellis. 1977. *Language and Materialism: Developments in Semiology and the Theory of the Subject.* London: Routledge and Kegan Paul.

Daly, Lew, Alan Gilbert, Kristin Prevallet, and Pam Rehm, eds. 1994. "State of the Art." *apex of the M* 1:5–7.

Damon, Maria. 1993. *At the Dark End of the Street: Margins in American Poetry Vanguards.* Minneapolis: University of Minnesota Press.

Darragh, Tina. 1989. *Striking Resemblance.* Providence, R.I.: Burning Deck.

Deleuze, Gilles, and Felix Guattari. 1983. *Anti-Oedipus: Capitalism and Schizophrenia.* With a Preface by Michel Foucault. Minneapolis: University of Minnesota Press.

Dews, Peter, ed. 1986. *Autonomy and Solidarity: Interviews with Jürgen Habermas.* London: Verso.

Du Plessis, Rachel Blau. 1985a. "For the Etruscans." In *The New Feminist Criticism: Essays on Women, Literature, and Theory,* edited by Elaine Showalter. New York: Pantheon. Reprinted in her *The Pink Guitar: Writing as Feminist Practice.* New York: Routledge, 1990.

———. 1985b. *Writing Beyond the Ending: Narrative Strategies of Twentieth-Century Women Writers.* Bloomington: Indiana University Press.

———. 1986a. "An Essay on Beverly Dahlen's *A Reading.*" *Ironwood* 27:159–69. Reprinted in her *Pink Guitar: Writing as Feminist Practice.* New York: Routledge.

———. 1986b. *H. D.: The Career of That Struggle.* Sussex, Great Britain: Harvester.

———. 1987a. "Draft #3: Of." *Sulfur* 20:23–27.

———. 1987b. *Tabula Rosa.* Elmwood, Conn.: Potes & Poets Press.

———. 1987c. " 'Whowe': An Essay on Work by Susan Howe." *Sulfur* 20:157–65. Reprinted in her *Pink Guitar: Writing as Feminist Practice.* New York: Routledge.

———. 1988a. "Draft #6: Midrush." *Temblor* 7:50–55.

———. 1988b. "18 Jan 1988: a letter among letters." *Sulfur* 22:188–93.

———. 1990. *The Pink Guitar: Writing as Feminist Practice.* New York: Routledge.

Eshleman, Clayton. 1985. "Response to Mary Kinzie." *Sulfur* 13:153–57.

Foley, Jack. 1991. *Gershwin*. San Francisco: Norton Coker Press.

———. 1993. Adrift. Berkeley, Calif.: Pantograph.

Foster, Edward. 1990. "An Interview with Susan Howe." *Talisman* 4:14–38.

Foucault, Michel. 1983. Preface to *Anti-Oedipus: Capitalism and Schizophrenia*, by Gilles Deleuze and Felix Guattari. Minneapolis: University of Minnesota Press.

Fox, Howard. 1987. "Avant-Garde in the '80s." *Art and Design* 3, nos. 7–8:28–32.

Gioia, Dana. 1992. *Can Poetry Matter? Essays on Poetry and American Culture*. Saint Paul, Minn.: Graywolf.

———. 1993. "Notes Toward a New Bohemia." *Poetry Flash* 248:7, 13, 14.

Golding, Alan. 1995. *From Outlaw to Classic: Canons in American Poetry*. Madison: University of Wisconsin Press.

Grenier, Robert. 1971. "On Speech." *This* 1 (unpaginated). Repr. 1986, in *In the American Tree*, edited by Ron Silliman, 496–97. Orono, Maine: National Poetry Foundation.

Habermas, Jürgen. 1986. *Knowledge and Human Interests*. Translated by Jeremy Shapiro. Cambridge: Polity Press.

Havelock, Eric Alfred. 1986. *The Muse Learns to Write: Reflections on Orality and Literacy from Antiquity to the Present*. New Haven: Yale University Press.

Heidegger, Martin. 1971. *Poetry, Language, Thought*. New York: Harper and Row.

Hejinian, Lyn. 1986. "Two Stein Talks: 'Language and Realism' and 'Grammar and Landscapes.'" *Temblor* 3:128–33; 134–39.

———. 1987. *My Life*. Los Angeles: Sun & Moon Press.

———. 1992. *The Cell*. Sun & Moon Classic Series 21. Los Angeles: Sun & Moon Press.

———. 1994. *The Cold of Poetry*. Los Angeles: Sun & Moon Press.

Hoover, Paul, ed. 1994. *Postmodern American Poetry: A Norton Anthology*. New York: Norton.

Howe, Susan. 1989. *A Bibliography of the King's Book: Or, Eikon Basilke*. Providence, R.I.: Paradigm Reprinted in *The Nonconformist's Memorial Poems*. New York: New Directions, 1993.

———. 1990a. *The Europe of Trusts*. Los Angeles: Sun & Moon Press.

———. 1990b. *Singularities*. Middletown: Wesleyan University Press.

———. 1993. *The Birth-mark: Unsettling the Wilderness in American Literary History*. Hanover, N.H.: Wesleyan University Press, published by University Press of New England.

Jabès, Edmond. 1976. *The Book of Questions*. Translated by Rosmarie Waldrop. Middletown: Wesleyan University Press.

Jameson, Fredric. 1984. "Postmodernism, or The Cultural Logic of Late Capitalism." *New Left Review* 146 (1984): 53–92.

Jay, Gregory S. 1987–88. "Values and Deconstruction: Derrida, Saussure, Marx." *Cultural Critique*: 153–96.

Kearney, Richard. 1988. *The Wake of Imagination: Ideas of Creativity in Western Culture*. London: Hutchinson.

Kenner, Hugh. 1975. *A Homemade World: The American Modernist Writers*. New York: Knopf.

———. 1987. Comments made during television documentary *Voices and Visions: William Carlos Williams*. PBS; produced by the New York Center for Visual History.

Kostelanetz, Richard. 1993. *Dictionary of the Avant-Gardes*. Pennington, N.J.: A Cappella Books.

Kristeva, Julia. 1984. *Revolution in Poetic Language*. Translated by Leon S. Roudiez. New York: Columbia University Press.

Lanham, Richard. 1993. *The Electronic Word: Democracy, Technology, and the Arts*. Chicago: University of Chicago Press.

Lauter, Paul, ed. 1994. *The Heath Anthology of American Literature*. 2d ed. 2 vols. Lexington, Mass.: D. C. Heath. (1st ed., 1990)

Lazer, Hank. 1992. *Doublespace: Poems, 1971–1989*. New York: Segue.

———. 1996. *Issues and Institutions*. Vol. 1 of *Opposing Poetries*. Evanston: Northwestern University Press.

Lehman, David. 1991. *Signs of the Times: Deconstruction and the Fall of Paul de Man*. New York: Poseidon.

Locke, Alain LeRoy, ed. 1925. *The New Negro: An Interpretation*. New York: A. and C. Boni.

Mackey, Nathaniel. 1993. *Discrepant Engagement: Dissonance, Cross-Culturality, and Experimental Writing*. Cambridge: Cambridge University Press.

Marcuse, Herbert. 1978. *The Aesthetic Dimension: Toward a Critique of Marxist Aesthetics*. Boston: Beacon.

Marx, Karl. 1964. *The Economic and Philosophic Manuscripts of 1844*. New York: International Publishers.

Meese, Elizabeth. 1986. *Crossing the Double-Cross: The Practice of Feminist Criticism*. Chapel Hill: University of North Carolina Press.

Melville, Herman. 1969. "Bartleby the Scrivener: A Story of Wall-Street." In *Great Short Works of Herman Melville*. New York: Harper.

———. 1990. *White-Jacket: Or, The World in a Man-of-War*. Oxford: Oxford University Press.

Merwin, W. S. 1963. *The Moving Target*. New York: Atheneum.

Messerli, Douglas, ed. 1983. Special Manifesto issue. *Washington Review* 9, no. 2.

———. 1984. *River to Rivet: A Poetic Trilogy*. Washington, D.C.: Sun & Moon Press. Contains texts of *Some Distance* (1982; New York: Segue); *Dinner on the Lawn* (1982; College Park: University of Maryland Press); and *River to Rivet: A Manifesto* (1984).

———. 1994. *From the Other Side of the Century: A New American Poetry, 1960–1990*. Los Angeles: Sun & Moon Press.

Nash, Susan Smith. 1994. "Beyond the Language Movement: A Manifesto of Aesthetics in a Time of Communication, Plague, and a New World Order." *Taproot* 4 (spring): 3–4.

Nelson, Cary. 1989. *Repression and Recovery: Modern American Poetry and the Politics of Cultural Memory, 1910–1945*. Madison: University of Wisconsin Press.

Oakeshott, Michael Joseph. 1962. "The Voice of Poetry in the Conversation of Mankind." In his *Rationalism in Politics and Other Essays*. New York: Basic Books.

Olson, Charles. 1947. *Call Me Ishmael*. Repr. 1967, San Francisco: City Lights.

Perelman, Bob. 1984. *To the Reader*. Berkeley, Calif.: Tuumba Press.

Perloff, Marjorie. 1985. *The Dance of the Intellect: Studies in the Poetry of the Pound Tradition*. New York: Cambridge University Press.

———. 1988. "Interview with Douglas Messerli." *Aerial* [Douglas Messerli issue] 4:29–49.

———. 1990. "*Traduit de l'américaine*: French Representations of the 'New American Poetry.'" In her *Poetic License: Essays on Modernist and Postmodernist Lyric*. Evanston: Northwestern University Press.

———. 1991–92. "Talk Writing." *American Book Review* 13, no. 5:8, 24, 25, 30, 31.

Pinsky, Robert. 1976. *The Situation of Poetry: Contemporary Poetry and Its Traditions*. Princeton: Princeton University Press.

Rasula, Jed. 1995. *The American Poetry Wax Museum: Reality Effects, 1940–1990*. Urbana, Ill.: National Council of Teachers of English.

Retallack, Joan. 1985. *Circumstantial Evidence*. Washington, D.C.: S.O.S. Books.

———. 1993. *Errata suite*. Washington, D.C.: Edge Books.

Rorty, Richard. 1979. *Philosophy and the Mirror of Nature*. Princeton: Princeton University Press.

Ross, Joe. 1988. "Something That's Where." *Aerial* [Douglas Messerli issue] 4:60–64.

Rothenberg, Jerome, and Pierre Joris, eds. 1995. *From Fin-de-Siècle to Negritude*. Vol. 1 of *Poems for the Millenium: The University of California Book of Modern and Postmodern Poetry*. Berkeley and Los Angeles: University of California Press.

Scalapino, Leslie. 1994. *Objects in the Terrifying Longing Taking Place*. New York: Roof Books.

Sherman, Paul. 1986. *In Search of the Primitive: Rereading David Antin, Jerome Rothenberg, and Gary Snyder*. Baton Rouge: Louisiana State University Press.

Sherry, James. 1985. *Popular Fiction*. New York: Roof Books.

———. 1991. *Our Nuclear Heritage*. Los Angeles: Sun & Moon Press.

———. 1992. Letter to Hank Lazer, 16 June.

Silliman, Ron. 1978. *Ketjak*. San Francisco: This.

———. 1985. *Paradise*. Providence, R.I.: Burning Deck.

———. 1981. *Tjanting*. Great Barrington, Mass.: The Figures.

———. 1987a. *Lit*. Elmwood, Conn.: Potes & Poets Press.

———. 1987b. *The New Sentence*. New York: Roof Books.

———. 1987c. "Of Theory, To Practice." In *The New Sentence*. New York: Roof Books.

———. 1992. *Demo to Ink: Being Six Parts of the Alphabet*. Tucson, Ariz.: Chax Press.

Simpson, Louis Aston Marantz. 1963. *At the End of the Open Road: Poems*. Middletown, Conn.: Wesleyan University Press.

———. 1975. *Three on the Tower: The Lives and Works of Ezra Pound, T. S. Eliot, and William Carlos Williams*. New York: Morrow.

———. 1981. *A Company of Poets*. Ann Arbor: University of Michigan Press.

———. 1986. *The Character of the Poet*. Ann Arbor: University of Michigan Press.

———. 1988. "The Poet's Theme." *Hudson Review* 4:93–141.

Smith, Rod. 1988. "Thinking about Talking about Messerli." *Aerial* [Douglas Messerli issue] 4:65–69.

Stein, Gertrude. 1962. *Selected Writings of Gertrude Stein*. Edited and with an Introduction and Notes by Carl Van Vechten, and with an essay on Gertrude Stein by F. W. Dupee. New York: Random House, Modern Library.

———. 1972. "Composition as Explanation" (1926). In her *Selected Writings*. New York: Vintage Books.

Stevens, Wallace. 1947/1954. *Collected Poems*. New York: Knopf. Repr. 1982.

Taggart, John. 1944. *Songs of Degrees: Essays on Contemporary Poetry and Poetics*. With a Foreword by Marjorie Perloff. Tuscaloosa: University of Alabama Press.

Thoreau, Henry David. 1989. *Walden*. Princeton: Princeton University Press.

Toomer, Jean. 1988. *Cane: An Authoritative Text, Backgrounds, Criticism*. Edited by Darwin T. Turner. New York: Norton. (Originally published 1923, New York: Boni and Liveright)

Tuman, Myron. 1992. *Word Perfect: Literacy in the Computer Age*. Pittsburgh: University of Pittsburgh Press.

Vendler, Helen. 1981. "Understanding Ashbery." *New Yorker*, 16 March. Reprinted in her *The Music of What Happens: Poems, Poets, Critics*. Cambridge: Harvard University Press, 1988.

———. 1988. *The Music of What Happens: Poems, Poets, Critics*. Cambridge: Harvard University Press.

Volosinov, V. N. 1986. *Marxism and the Philosophy of Language*. Translated by Ladislav Matejka and I. R. Titunik. Cambridge: Harvard University Press.

Weinberger, Eliot. 1988. "A Final Response." *Sulfur* 22:199–202.

Williams, Raymond. 1977. *Marxism and Literature*. New York: Oxford University Press.

Williams, William Carlos. 1925. *In The American Grain*. New York: A. and C. Boni.

———. 1970. *Imaginations*. Edited and with introductions by Webster Schott. New York: New Directions.

———. 1974. *The Embodiment of Knowledge*. Edited and with an Introduction by Ron Loewinsohn. New York: New Directions.

———. 1986. *The Collected Poems of William Carlos Williams*. Vol. 1, *1909–1939*, edited by A. Walton Litz and Christopher MacGowan. New York: New Directions.

Wright, James Arlington. 1963. *The Branch Will Not Break: Poems*. Middletown, Conn.: Wesleyan University Press.

Index

Adorno, Theodor, 85, 87–88, 119
Alexander, Charles, 169
Alexander, Will, 181
Allen, Donald
  The New American Poetry, 7
Almack, Edward, 62
Altieri, Charles, 55, 177
Anderson, Laurie, 108
Andrews, Bruce, 2, 6, 77–94, 142, 160
  "Confidence Trick," 89–90, 92
  "Getting Ready to Have Been
    Frightened," 86
  "Plex," 83–84, 86
  "Praxis," 78–79
  "Swaps Ego," 79–80
Antin, David, 3, 29, 73, 95–109, 132,
    136, 146, 192
  The Black Plague, 105–7
  "Code of flag behavior," 104–5
  definitions, 102
  "a list of delusions of the insane /
    what they are afraid of," 104–5
  "Modernism and Postmodernism:
    Approaching the Present in
    American Poetry," 107
  "scenario for a beginning medita-
    tion," 108
  Selected Poems, 95–109
  "who are my friends," 104–5
Armantrout, Rae, 63
Arp, Jean, 98
Ashbery, John, 13, 42, 65, 79, 81,
    123–24, 136, 137, 143
  "Hop o' My Thumb," 79
Atherton, Hope, 66

Bacon, Francis, 96, 97
Baraka, Amiri, 185

Barthes, Roland, 3, 68, 110–15, 118, 119,
    122
Bataille, Georges, 46
Blake, William, 108, 158
Bernstein, Charles, 2, 3–4, 6–15, 18,
    20, 25–27, 40, 54, 75, 77, 81, 96, 97,
    123–46, 147, 175–76, 177, 182, 184
  "The Academy in Peril: William
    Carlos Williams Meets the
    MLA," 25
  "Amblyopia," 14
  Artifice of Absorption, 11–12
  Content's Dream, 126, 133, 145
  Dark City, 123–46
  "Dark City," 142–46
  "Debris of Shock/ Shock of Debris,"
    139–40
  "Emotions of Normal People,"
    137–39
  "Heart in My Eye," 140–41
  "From Lines of Swinburne," 13
  "The Lives of the Toll Takers,"
    129–30
  "Locks Without Doors," 134
  The Sophist, 11–15
  "Standing Target," 137–39
  "Surface Reflectance," 13
  "The Value of Depression," 14
  "The Voyage of Life," 12–13
Blaser, Robin, 179
Bloom, Harold, 28, 68
Brathwaite, Edward Kamau, 178
Breitweiser, Mitch, 67
Breslin, James E. B., 177
Brossard, Nicole, 179
Bruce, Lenny, 130
Burke, Carolyn, 37
Burke, Kenneth, 109

Byrd, Don, 183

Cage, John, 3, 23, 65, 70, 71, 72, 88, 96, 97, 100, 104, 107, 108, 126, 129, 134, 149
Cavell, Stanley, 11
Cendrars, Blaise, 101
Coltrane, John, 178, 185
Coolidge, Clark, 6, 125
Coward, Rosalind, and John Ellis, 83, 84, 86

Dahlen, Beverly, 46, 53, 54, 58, 179
Damon, Maria, 183, 185
Dao, Bei, 179
Darragh, Tina, 65
Deleuze, Gilles, and Felix Guattari, 54, 77, 78, 79–81
Democritus, 149
Derrida, Jacques, 16, 17, 19, 67, 68, 97, 108
Descartes, René, 96, 97
Dews, Peter, 150
Dickinson, Emily, 56, 62, 71–72, 76, 140, 183
Dos Passos, John, 168
Duchamp, Marcel, 3, 100, 104
Duncan, Robert, 63, 65
DuPlessis, Rachel Blau, 2, 30, 34–59, 66
    "Crowbar," 35, 40–41
    "Drafts," 35, 55, 56–59
    "An Essay on Beverly Dahlen's *A Reading*," 53
    "For the Etruscans," 36, 39, 56
    HOW(ever), 35, 39
    "Megaliths," 42
    "Praxilla's Silliness," 39
    Tabula Rosa, 34–59
    "Writing," 35, 36, 37, 42–58
Dylan, Bob, 130

Edwards, Jonathan, 62
Eliot, T. S., 23, 25, 66, 81, 96, 130, 134, 142, 185
Emerson, Ralph Waldo, 57, 72, 74, 157
Eshleman, Clayton, 54, 68

Foley, Jack, 190–91
Foucault, Michel, 78, 97, 139, 140
Fox, Howard, 122
Fraser, Kathleen, 58
Freud, Sigmund, 31, 65
Frost, Robert, 50, 75, 95, 97, 118, 143, 146

Gioia, Dana, 126, 184
Glissant, Edouard, 185
Goethe, Johann, 85
Golding, Alan, 177, 183
Greenblatt, Stephen, 67
Grenier, Robert, 6, 191

Habermas, Jürgen, 4, 149–52, 161, 162, 163, 164
Harris, Wilson, 178
Harryman, Carla, 33, 67
Havelock, Eric, 190, 191
Hawking, Stephen, 158, 162
Hawthorne, Nathaniel, 147, 155, 156
H. D., 35, 37, 40, 186
Heaney, Seamus, 173
Heidegger, Martin, 31, 61, 88
Hejinian, Lyn, 2, 29–33, 46, 47, 52, 58, 63, 77, 81, 125, 186
    My Life, 29–33
Hoover, Paul
    Postmodern American Poetry, 128, 132
Howard, Richard, 66
Howe, Susan, 2, 58, 60–69, 72, 77, 81, 142, 183
    Articulation of Sound Forms in Time, 60–63, 66–69

A Bibliography of the King's Book: Or,
   Eikon Basilike, 60, 62
   Pythagorean Silence, 60, 63
Huang, Yunte, 178
Hunt, Erica, 181

Ignatow, David, 2, 23
Ives, Charles, 137

Jabès, Edmond, 37
Jacobus, Mary, 36
Jahlen, Myra, 35
Jameson, Fredric, 85
Jarrell, Randall, 169
Jay, Gregory, 55
Johnson, Lyndon, 104
Joyce, James, 96

Kandinsky, Wassily, 71, 98
Kenner, Hugh, 103, 108
Kierkegaard, Søren, 14
Klawans, Stuart, 16–18, 19
Kostelanetz, Richard, 125, 130, 134
Kristeva, Julia, 2, 36, 39, 49, 58, 59, 68,
   84

Lanham, Richard, 188
Lauter, Paul
   Heath Anthology of American Litera-
      ture, 2d ed., 128, 132
Lehman, David, 67, 68
Levertov, Denise, 2, 23
Levine, Philip, 136
Locke, Alain, 186
Lowell, Robert, 46, 95, 96
Lyotard, Jean-François, 97, 150

McCaffery, Steve, 179
Mackey, Nathaniel, 177–78, 181, 183,
   185
Mac Low, Jackson, 82, 88, 100, 149

Major, Clarence, 178
Mallarmé, Stéphane, 68, 74, 85, 160
Marcuse, Herbert, 83, 89, 90, 91, 92
Marx, Groucho, 130
Marx, Karl, 92
Mason, Jackie, 130
Matthiessen, F. O., 62, 66
Meese, Elizabeth, 35–36, 37–38, 39
Melville, Herman, 68, 147–50, 155–57,
   165
   Moby-Dick, 156–57
Merwin, W. S., 50, 100
Messerli, Douglas, 3, 110–22
   "Aller Et Retour," 115–17
   "On Edge," 115–17
   Maxims from My Mother's Milk/
      Hymns to Him: A Dialogue,
      110–22
   "En Route (Narcissus)," 120–22
   Washington Review, Manifesto
      Edition, 114
Metzger, Deena, 36
Miller, Perry, 62, 66
Monk, Thelonious, 178, 185
Mullen, Harryette, 181
Murry, J. B., 65

Nash, Susan Smith, 132
Nelson, Cary, 77, 90, 93–94, 96
Nichol, bp, 179
Nielsen, A.L., 70
Nietszche, Friedrich, 150

Oakeshott, Michael, 109
Olson, Charles, 65, 67
Ong, Walter, 190, 191
Oppen, George, 40, 41

Palmer, Michael, 6, 179, 180
Pascal, Blaise, 75
Paul, Sherman, 102, 107

Perelman, Bob, 85
Perloff, Marjorie, 32, 72, 96, 101, 102, 178
Plato, 97, 101, 109
Poe, Edgar Allan, 147, 155
  Eureka, 155
  "Man of the Crowd," 148
Pound, Ezra, 20, 23, 25, 66, 81, 96, 134, 142, 158

Qianzi, Che, 179

Racine, Jean, 96
Ransom, John Crowe, 96
Rasula, Jed, 183, 184–87, 190
Rauschenberg, Robert, 3, 100, 104
Reed, Ishmael, 181
Retallack, Joan, 2, 70–76
  Errata suite, 70–76
Riding, Laura, 7, 186
Rilke, Rainer Maria, 57
Rogin, Michael Paul, 67
Rorty, Richard, 95, 101, 109
Ross, Joe, 115, 117
Rothenberg, Jerome, 101, 108
Rothenberg, Jerome, and Pierre Joris, 178, 179–80, 186
Rowlandson, Mary, 66

Scalapino, Leslie, 183
Shelley, Percy Bysshe, 132, 152, 162
Sher, Gail, 58
Sherry, James, 4, 147–67, 192
  Our Nuclear Heritage, 147–67
Silliman, Ron, 2, 4, 6–15, 18, 20, 25, 26, 27, 29, 36, 41, 45, 77, 81, 92, 96, 125, 162, 168–76, 186
  Demo to Ink, 168–76
  Lit, 8–10
  "The New Sentence," 8

Simpson, Louis, 2, 20–28, 100, 136
  "To Celebrate Williams," 24–25
  Three on the Tower, 23
Smith, Dave, 46
Smith, Rod, 112
Socrates, 95
Stein, Gertrude, 15, 17, 18, 30, 32, 33, 49, 51, 53, 65, 72, 75, 76, 81, 90, 96, 100, 108, 122, 125, 128, 132, 142, 152, 180, 186
Steiner, George, 73, 188
Stevens, Wallace, 71, 74–75, 96, 117–18
Swinburne, Charles, 134

Taggart, John, 183
Tate, Allen, 96
Thomas, Dylan, 97
Thomas, Lorenzo, 181
Thoreau, Henry David, 8, 61, 71, 100, 132, 135, 154, 159, 170
Toomer, Jean, 186
Tuman, Myron, 73, 187–89
Turner, Ted, 90
Twitchell, Jeff, 178

Vendler, Helen, 68, 79, 123–24, 125
Volosinov, V. N., 82, 85, 86, 87, 88, 91

Waldrop, Rosmary, 179
Watten, Barrett, 6
Weinberger, Eliot, 39
Weiner, Hannah, 65
Williams, Raymond, 84, 85
Williams, William Carlos, 2, 17, 19–28, 32, 65, 67, 96, 103, 108, 121, 126, 128, 180, 186
  "To Elsie," 25
  The Embodiment of Knowledge, 26
  Kora in Hell: Improvisations, 21–22, 24
  Paterson, 23

"The Red Wheelbarrow," 21–22, 25
Spring and All, 20–22, 25, 27
Wittgenstein, Ludwig, 102, 105, 108,
   145, 169
Wright, James, 100
Wordsworth, William, 103

Yeats, Willam Butler, 97

Ziqing, Zhang, 178
Zukofsky, Louis, 180, 186